Guilt and Defense

GUILT AND DEFENSE

On the Legacies of National Socialism

in Postwar Germany

THEODOR W. ADORNO

Translated, Edited, and with an Introduction by

JEFFREY K. OLICK

ANDREW J. PERRIN

HARVARD UNIVERSITY PRESS

Cambridge, Massachusetts

London, England

2010

Library of Congress Cataloging-in-Publication Data

Adorno, Theodor W., 1903–1969.
[Schuld und abwehr. English.]
Guilt and defense : on the legacies of national socialism in postwar Germany /
Theodor W. Adorno, translated, edited, and with an introduction by Jeffrey K. Olick
and Andrew J. Perrin.
p.   cm.
Includes bibliographical references and index.
ISBN 978-0-674-03603-1 (alk. paper)
1. National socialism—Germany—Public opinion.   2. Denazification—Germany—
Public opinion.   3. Postwar reconstruction—Germany—History.   4. Public opinion—
Germany.   5. Germany—Politics and government—1945–1990.   6. Germany—
History—1945–1990.   7. Institut für Sozialforschung (Frankfurt am Main, Germany)
I. Olick, Jeffrey K., 1964–   II. Perrin, Andrew J., 1971–   III. Title.
DD256.6.A35 2010
943.086—dc22   2009052859

Contents

PART THREE: The Debate with Hofstätter

PART FOUR: Working Through the Past

Preface and Acknowledgments

T HIS BOOK has a complicated history and a long pedigree of interlocu-
tors and commentators. It began with Jeffrey Olick's investigation of
Adorno's provocative comment on "the house of the hangman" and, sepa-
rately, with Andrew Perrin's translation of Adorno's 1964 lecture on public
opinion. A common history in Braulio Muñoz's seminars at Swarthmore
College on critical modern social theory, and annual Swarthmore alumni
dinners at the American Sociological Association conferences, provided
the intellectual and institutional infrastructure for our collaboration.

This book has benefited from the interest and help of numerous people
who have commented on the ideas and process of its translation and publication. First and foremost, we thank Kai-Uwe Loeser, without whose
early work on the nuts and bolts of the translation our task would have
been much more difficult. The project benefited as well from critical discussions at the Cultural and Political Sociology Workshop at the University of
North Carolina, Chapel Hill; the Sociology Colloquium at Columbia
University; the conference "Interactionist Approaches to Collective Memory"
at Northwestern University; the Institute for Advanced Studies in Culture
at the University of Virginia; the Institute for Arts and Humanities at the
University of North Carolina, Chapel Hill; and the graduate seminar in
European social theory in the Sociology Department at the University of
Virginia. We thank the many family, friends, and colleagues with whom we

have discussed the project both in general and in detail, and whom we have often queried about translation issues, including Asher Biemann, Craig Calhoun, Gaby Finder, Gregg Flaxman, Jeff Grossman, Volker Heins, David Jenemann, Daniel Levy, John McGowan, Dirk Moses, Jeff Spinner-Halev, Christiane Sembritzki, John Torpey, Chad Wellmon, Bettina Winckler, and Heino and Susanne Winckler. In addition, we heartily thank Michael Aronson at Harvard University Press for his enthusiastic support, as well as Hilary Jacqmin for her diligence and patience.

Special thanks are due to Natassia Rodriguez, James Knable, and Tara Tober for research assistance and to J. Craig Jenkins for archival materials. Funding was provided by the National Endowment for the Humanities, collaborative grant number RZ-50623-06, and by a Faculty Fellowship to Andrew Perrin in the fall of 2007 at the Institute for Arts and Humanities at the University of North Carolina, Chapel Hill, as well as by research funds to Jeffrey Olick by the Dean of the College of Arts and Sciences at the University of Virginia. Permission to publish the English translation of *Schuld und Abwehr,* the major text in this book, was graciously granted by *Europäische Verlagsanstalt* of Hamburg. We are grateful to Columbia University Press for permission to include Henry W. Pickford's outstanding translation of Adorno's "The Meaning of Working Through The Past," and call attention to Pickford's excellent commentary on that text in his book, *Critical Models: Interventions and Catchwords* (Columbia University Press, 1998). We are also grateful to Manuel Querin at Suhrkamp Verlag for friendly assistance.

Throughout this work, as through everything else, we were each sustained by our extraordinary partners, Bettina Winckler and Eliana Perrin.

Our decision to divide our project into two volumes might seem strange at first; it is certainly not where we began. Beyond the issue of length that would have been involved in reproducing all relevant passages from the 1955 *Group Experiment* in one volume (the German original ran to more than 550 pages) and the limits that would have placed on our ability to include other materials, however, good substantive reasons became clearer as we worked on the main text and surrounding materials.

Most important, while we hope this work will receive the widest possible audience, the different themes will likely be of interest to different constituencies. In this first volume, we frame the material in intellectual-historical and political contexts, as well as in terms of Adorno's overall intellectual engagement with empirical research and German politics. Conjoining Adorno's essay "Guilt and Defense" with his much better known essay "The Meaning of Working Through the Past," and presenting the debate with Peter Hofstätter as the forgotten thread connecting them, not only adds to our understanding of the latter essay, but makes clear why the former is so much more important than its place in scholarly memory to this point indicates. Our introductory essay to this volume therefore provides a broad overview of the significance of this work in Adorno's oeuvre and places Adorno's work within its social and political context.

In the companion volume, our focus is more methodological and theoretical than historical; there we present materials of enduring relevance for contemporary understandings of public opinion. Just as we have recapitulated the methodological and theoretical matters here to frame "Guilt and Defense," in our introduction to the companion volume, *Group Experiment: The Frankfurt School on Public Opinion* (Harvard University Press, forthcoming), we reconstruct the work's lineages with an eye to the present state of work in the field and to the conceptual contributions to be found in that lineage. Inevitably, pieces in one book refer to materials only presented in the other, which we nevertheless hope will be a stimulus to curiosity rather than a hindrance to understanding (a selection here and there—for instance the "Colburn Letter"—appears in both); each volume is relevant, but not necessary, to the comprehension of the other.

Note on Translation

THE DIFFICULTIES of translating Adorno are by now infamous. Many of those difficulties, of course, stem from the allusive, dialectical, and sometimes intentionally obscure qualities of Adorno's prose style as well as from the philosophical and aesthetic complexity of his ideas. This work, however, in comparison to works like *The Dialectic of Enlightenment, Minima Moralia,* or *Negative Dialectics,* to mention just three of the most notorious examples, does not present the same sort of challenges to the translator, or at least not as many of this sort, though to be sure they do occasionally arise here as well, particularly in the response to Hofstätter. This is not to say, however, that the work does not present unique challenges of its own. To a great extent, these stem from the fact that the work includes long excerpts from discussion transcripts. Spoken language does not look like written language on the page. Speakers start and stop, do not always speak in full sentences, misuse words, fail to achieve subject-verb agreement, and are incoherent in a multitude of other ways. Moreover, they often do so in regional and class dialects that sometimes tempt the translator to Faulknerian renderings (though we resisted this temptation to the same extent as or perhaps slightly more than the original text did). And finally, given the nature of the subject matter—its emotionally laden qualities as well as its susceptibility to extreme and irresponsible rhetoric—the speakers often utter a great deal of substantive nonsense. So the challenge is how much coherence to insert into the translation that did not in fact exist in the original. One tends to sputter in different places in a German sentence than in an English one, and such sentences break down in essentially untranslatable ways. We have thus done our best to reconstruct just enough to make it as clear in the translation as it was in the original, which means that some utterances do in fact remain incoherent or incomprehensible. This is because they were.

An additional problem that stems from the presentation of spoken discourse is that words that are ordinary in one language are not necessarily so in another. A good example here is *Vorwurf,* which is most accurately translated as "reproach." But a poorly educated speaker in English would not colloquially say the "The Americans reproached us for . . ." Occasionally, then, for the sake of substantive accuracy over stylistic faith, we have left the more accurate translation, even when it produces a more stilted or formal-sounding sentence in English than existed in the German. Other words, in contrast, have a very specific translation but can take on a variety of different shadings. An example here is *Schuld,* which is directly translated as "guilt." But *Schuld* can also mean "fault" or even "crime," especially when an article is attached in German—that is, *die Schuld* or *eine Schuld*—which does not work as well in English. Here we have pursued the inflection we thought fit the sense best on a case-by-case basis. Finally, perhaps the most significant term in the study, *Abwehr,* is challenging as well, because it can mean "defense"—as in "defense mechanism"—but can also mean "defensiveness." Indeed, it would have been reasonable to title the study in English "Guilt and Defensiveness," which might have been more faithful to the original sense. But the rare references to this study in English-speaking scholarly literature have consistently employed the rendering "Guilt and Defense," and we have chosen not to buck this trend.

We HAVE included Adorno's notes to his work throughout (as chapter endnotes), and we have occasionally provided footnotes of our own where clarification is needed. In addition, we have provided brief clarifications set off by square brackets within the text.

The original publication of *"Schuld und Abwehr"* includes, within the text, cictation of the transcript and page number of each excerpt from the transcripts of the group discussions. These citations have been deleted throughout. They may be found in Pollock (1955). Our reasoning here was that anyone interested in locating the relevant passages in the original transcripts would work from the original German text. Moreover, Adorno consistently identifies the composition of the sessions from which each excerpt is drawn, e.g. "From a session with Bavarian dignitaries . . ." or "As in the discussion with fashion school students already cited . . ." These descriptors should enable careful readers to determine when passages separated by many pages are in fact from the same transcripts as easily, if not more easily, than including the original transcript numbers and pages.

The Original Publications

Theodor W. Adorno. *"Schuld und Abwehr."* chapter 5 of *Gruppenexperiment: Ein Studienbericht,* edited by Friedrich Pollock. *Frankfurter Beiträge zur Soziologie,* vol. 2. Frankfurt: Europäische Verlagsanstalt, 1955. Pp. 278–428.

Peter R. Hofstätter. "Zum Gruppenexperiment von Friedrich Pollock: Eine Kritische Würdigung." *Kölner Zeitschrift für Soziologie und Sozialpsychologie* 9 (1957): 97–104.

Theodor W. Adorno. "Replik zu Peter R. Hofstätter's Kritik des Gruppenexperiments." *Kölner Zeitschrift für Soziologie und Sozialpsychologie* 9 (1957): 105–117.

Theodor W. Adorno. "Was bedeutet: Aufarbeitung der Vergangenheit." Radio Lecture, Hessicher Rundfunk, February 7, 1960. In Theodor Adorno, *Critical Models: Interventions and Catchwords.* translated by Henry W. Pickford. New York: Columbia University Press, 1998. Pp. 89–103.

Part One

INTRODUCTION

Guilt and Defense:
Theodor Adorno and the
Legacies of National Socialism
in German Society

JEFFREY K. OLICK

ANDREW J. PERRIN

*For the sake of reconciliation, authentic works must blot out
every trace of reconciliation in memory.*

—Adorno, *Aesthetic Theory*

IN THIS book we present four texts, three of which have never before
been either translated or republished. They include, first and foremost,
"Schuld und Abwehr" (Guilt and Defense), a long essay by the great
German (and half-Jewish) intellectual polymath—musicologist, sociologist, philosopher, literary theorist, and essayist—Theodor W. Adorno. This
essay was published in 1955 as part of a larger work, *Gruppenexperiment*
(Group Experiment), edited by Friedrich Pollock. *Gruppenexperiment* includes both an elaborate theoretical and methodological discussion of the
concept of public opinion and the results, both quantitative and qualitative, of the first major study conducted by members of the so-called
Frankfurt School after their return from American exile.[1] The study, conducted mostly in 1950–51, was a massive investigation into legacies of
National Socialist ideology among a large and diverse, if not quite representative, sample of postwar West Germans. Adorno's essay, *"Schuld und
Abwehr"* (Guilt and Defense), forms the bulk of the study's qualitative
analysis section and constitutes a stand-alone contribution.[2] We present
Group Experiment's more general discussion of the theory and methodology of public opinion in a separate volume, to be published shortly after

this one, though we also summarize that material here in order to explain the context of *"Schuld und Abwehr."*

Following the 1955 publication of *Gruppenexperiment,* its authors, Adorno in particular, were strongly criticized by the psychologist Peter Hofstätter in the *Kölner Zeitschrift für Soziologie und Sozialpsychologie (Cologne Journal of Sociology and Social Psychology).* This critique was published along with Adorno's rather angry but nonetheless profound response. We include here both Hofstätter's review and Adorno's response because the exchange makes clear what was at stake, not only for German society but also for the analysis of repressed legacies of difficult history more generally. None of these three pieces—"Guilt and Defense," Hofstätter's review, or Adorno's response—is well known, even to enthusiastic readers of Adorno and critical theory; in what follows, we seek to explain why that might be the case and what is missed by ignoring these key works.

In the first place, we show how ignorance of these texts makes it quite difficult to understand one of Adorno's best known and most widely read political writings, the essay "Was bedeutet: Aufarbeitung der Vergangenheit" (The Meaning of Working Through the Past), which we reprint here as well—for the first time in its proper context. Our goal in doing so, however, is not simply to contextualize a famous essay. More important, Adorno's eager involvement in this large-scale empirical research project (one of several in which he was involved over his career) paints a more complex picture of his attitudes toward empirical research than is commonly assumed—namely, the mistaken belief that he simply disdained it. Moreover, we seek to show what is uniquely informative about this entire thread—from the *Gruppenexperiment* to "Aufarbeitung"—in the work of this well-studied but nevertheless still elusive icon of twentieth-century thought, and what is of enduring value in the insights this thread produced.

Given the widespread contemporary interest in such related topics as memory, trauma, transition, and reconciliation following violent conflicts, Adorno's analysis has lessons that transcend its immediate context. Our story begins, however, by showing how tied up Adorno's interventions were with his moment—though that story is perhaps best told from its end: the complex historical situation of "Aufarbeitug," Adorno's culminating essay on working through the past.

I. Between Two Epochs

After his return to Germany in 1949, Adorno was significantly occupied, even beyond *Group Experiment,* with questions surrounding the proper education for democracy, particularly where democracy had failed so radically, and with the role of remembering the past in such an effort. As he puts it in "Guilt and Defense," he began from the premise that "during the twelve years of totalitarian information, propaganda, and education the indoctrination went so deep that it could not simply be erased by a (military) defeat" (p. 138 below). In this regard, he was at odds with the dominant view after 1949, when the Federal Republic of Germany was founded.

To be sure, the idea of "reeducating" Germany had been debated at length among exiled German intellectuals and others during and immediately following the war (Olick 2005). Many intellectuals, and some Allied politicians and military planners, saw "reeducation" as necessary, given the extent of what had occurred in the Nazi years, and how deeply entrenched they believed the attitudes that supported it had been in the population. Nevertheless, many others saw such measures as unnecessary once there had been successful "regime decapitation"—through the elimination of the Nazi leadership and the purging of German society by means of the process of "denazification." In fact, denazification was widely considered a failure, partly as a result of the muddled ambitions and inherent arrogance of the idea of reeducating an entire nation, and partly due to the unavoidable administrative difficulties of such a massive undertaking, which involved examining the pasts of millions of individual Germans. Nonetheless, among postwar German political elites, the question of Nazi legacies was seen as having been mostly solved institutionally: now that Germany had democratic institutions and was dealing with necessary issues of restitution and reparation, it could look forward to closing the books on the Nazi past. By the early 1950s, by the same token, with the desire to integrate West Germany into the Western Cold War alliance, it was certainly expedient for the Western occupation authorities as well to believe that Germany's authoritarian tendencies were a thing of the past. The main message of West German political rhetoric throughout the 1950s, under its venerable leader, Chancellor Konrad Adenauer, was thus that West Germany was now a solid democracy and a reliable partner for the West.

Adorno first presented "Aufarbeitung" at a conference of educators organized by the German Coordinating Council of the Societies for Christian-Jewish Cooperation in Wiesbaden on November 6–7, 1959. His apparent goal was to outline what he believed a proper education for democracy in post-war Germany would involve and why it was necessary, even—indeed especially—ten years into the life of the new state.[3] When the Council subsequently published documents from the conference, including Adorno's "Aufarbeitung," it justified the effort in terms of "the realization that in all parts of our country, a growing number of teachers are concentrating more and more attention on the search for vivid depictions of the recent German past and for fundamental, practical guidance concerning effective programming of the relevant instruction" (Stahl 1961: 87). It was Adorno's purpose both there and elsewhere, and that of the conference's conveners, to provide such "practical guidance." The need for it quickly became all the more clear when, in the following months, a large wave of anti-Semitic vandalism occurred, beginning with the December 25, 1959, desecration of the Cologne synagogue, which was followed by more than 680 incidents across both West and East Germany (with further incidents occurring elsewhere). Adorno's "Aufarbeitung" was thus particularly timely, though in complex ways—because of its multiple afterlives and even more because of its complicated genesis.

For the entire first decade of West German history, left-wing and other commentators had criticized what they saw as the "restorative character" of Chancellor Konrad Adenauer's government and of West German society more generally, in which the vigor for economic recovery seemed to push aside, indeed compensate for, any concerns about the national past.[4] The chancellor's response to the events of the Christmas season thus provided little reassurance to those critics, Adorno included.

In a radio and television address on January 16, 1960 (Schwarz 1975: 409f), to be sure, Adenauer repudiated the events, calling them "a shame and a crime." He went on, however, to characterize them as "almost exclusively boorishness." The perpetrators, he argued, were stupid adolescents rather than serious political extremists, and he called for the following response: "If you catch a hoodlum anywhere, punish him on the spot and give him a sound thrashing. That is the punishment that he has earned." In response to diplomatic objections from Israel and others, as well as to a large demonstration that took place in Berlin on January 8, 1960, Adenauer sought to calm what he saw as overblown anxieties. To Jews in Germany he made this promise: "You can be fully at ease. This state stands behind you with all its power; I give you my word." The real danger that Adenauer perceived, however, seemed to be the negative repercussions for Germany's reputation, and he warned that outrage against the perpetrators was turning into "a wave of hate against the Germans in general." Given the record, he asserted, this was unjust: "To our opponents abroad and to doubters abroad, the unanimity of the entire German people in the condemnation of anti-Semitism and of National Socialism has shown itself in the most complete and strongest way imaginable. The German people has shown that these thoughts and tendencies have no foundation in it." Repeating a well-established defense against accusations of a collective guilt, he claimed that "the majority of the German people in the time of

National Socialism served National Socialism only under the hardest force of dictatorship. In no way was every German a National Socialist." Fairness demanded, Adenauer implied, that "one should have gradually recognized that abroad as well." In the final analysis, however, he simply reasserted that "in the German people National Socialism, dictatorship has no roots, and the few incorrigibles who are still around will have no success. I guarantee it."

Against this background, it is thus perhaps even more clear than when reading Adorno outside of this context what was so important about his famous essay: in it, Adorno repudiated the entire basic myth of the Federal Republic, which as Adenauer's statements illustrated, asserted a complete rupture—a so-called caesura—between the Nazi period and the new democratic West Germany. In contrast, Adorno charged, "the past that one would like to evade is still very much alive. National Socialism lives on, and even today we still do not know whether it is merely the ghost of what was so monstrous that it lingers on after its own death, or whether it has not yet died at all." Against the founding justification of the West's antitotalitarian demonology—in which Soviet Communism was the true sequel to Nazi fascism—Adorno most famously asserted: "I consider the survival of National Socialism *within* democracy to be potentially more menacing than the survival of fascist tendencies *against* democracy" (p. 214 below). This statement was clearly not, as some have interpreted it, one of a general preference for Marxism over liberalism (it was nothing of the sort) but a direct critique of West Germany's failure to live up to its own promise, coupled with an explication of that failure's source—the un-worked-through Nazi past.

The political timeliness of Adorno's "Aufarbeitung" was thus all the more clear when he presented it for a second time, three weeks after Adenauer's apologia, over the *Hessischer Rundfunk* (Hesse State Radio) on February 7, 1960. Although he had originally formulated his argument before the wave of vandalism, the timeliness of his diagnosis was fully apparent when he argued that "the readiness today to deny or minimize what happened" was a defense against "unconscious guilt" and that "there is much that is neurotic in the relation to the past: defensive postures where one is not attacked, intense affects where they are hardly warranted by the situation, and absence of affect in face of the gravest matters" (p. 214 below). While not explicitly directed at Adenauer, since Adorno had first written "Aufarbeitung" before the attacks and Adenauer's response to them, Adorno's assessment could not help but be read as an indictment. As he commented in 1962 (Adorno 1998: 307), since he had first presented "Aufarbeitung" "before the filthy wave of anti-Semitism lent it a sad topicality," this was a case in which "sociological theory to a certain extent had preceded empirical reality and been confirmed by it." As we will see, this was something of an understatement, given the older history of Adorno's position—prior to even the education conference of the previous month—in which he had long theorized the possibility of such residual fascist attitudes. Moreover, as we will also see, Adorno had more concrete reasons for his position than his formulation in his 1962 comments implied; they were in fact based not just on theory but on a great deal of empirical analysis—including that of *Group Experiment*.

THE relationship of Adorno's statement to its epoch is even more complex than this brief account indicates. For instance, the occasion of his first delivery of "Aufarbeitung," despite subsequent events, shows that his position— that the German response to the Nazi past was profoundly inadequate and threatened to undermine the possibility of West German democracy— was in many ways already becoming more widely accepted, at least in some political and intellectual circles. The Societies for Christian-Jewish Cooperation, which had sponsored the education conference, were well established by 1959 (Foschepoth 1993), and as their statement quoted earlier indicates, there was a growing interest among at least some educators in ways to present the past to a new generation of students who had not lived through it, at least not at an age of political awareness.

Many changes in German attitudes toward the past were indeed under way at the time, instigated not only by the generational changes taking place but by a series of past-related events as well. In 1956–57, a stage version of the *Diary of Anne Frank* played throughout Germany (followed by the Hollywood film in 1959), resonating in powerful ways among ordinary Germans (though to be sure Adorno evaluated that resonance critically as well in his essay). In 1958, criticism that the West German government had not adequately pursued prosecution of remaining Nazi criminals resulted in the establishment of a center in Ludwigsburg (the *Ludwigsburger Zentralstelle*) for the prosecution of National Socialist crimes, which led to a series of notorious trials in Frankfurt in 1963–66. In 1957–58, there was growing opposition in Germany to the deployment of nuclear weapons on West German soil in which a past-inspired pacifism played a significant role. In 1959, following poor electoral performance, the Social Democratic Party, at its party congress in Bad Godesberg, abandoned its oppositional Marxist stance—which had been based on its belief that it was the rightful heir to power since it alone had opposed the Nazis—and declared that it now strove for a more mainstream role. In 1961, the capture and Jerusalem trial of Adolf Eichmann in galvanized public attention, though to be sure not always in a philo-Semitic direction.

In 1961 as well, the Berlin Wall was erected, which for many called into question the entire history of Adenauer's foreign policy.

Thus, when Adorno delivered the presentation yet a third time—to the Socialist German Student Association (SDS) in Berlin on May 24, 1962—his position was poised to become emblematic of a new era, despite the setbacks of 1959–60. In fact, Adorno's essay—and in particular his comment about fascism within democracy—was taken as something of a rallying cry for a more profound caesura. Moreover, the distinction he drew between "mastering the past" *(Vergangenheitsbewältigung),* which he saw as the expression of a desire to forget it, and the Freudian-inflected "working through the past" *(Aufarbeitung der Vergangenheit)* that he instead called for became a central trope of a new left-wing and student movement's accusations against the prior generation, which they saw as culpable for failing to acknowledge its crimes and thus for allowing fascist tendencies to persist, and which explained its failure to achieve "real" democracy. Adorno's "Aufarbeitung," or at least the slogans drawn from it (not least his additional sarcastic comment that "in the house of the hangman one should not speak of the noose"), became part of this new left-wing movement's rhetorical repertoire and something of a shibboleth for its supposedly new and finally correct acknowledgment of German responsibility for the past and hence preparedness for democracy.

BEYOND the essay's three German lives between 1959 and 1962, and the subsequent appropriation of its language as slogans, "Was bedeutet: Aufarbeitung der Vergangenheit" has lived on, even outside the domestic German context. It was first translated and republished (under the title "What does 'Digesting the Past' Mean?") in *Education for Democracy in West Germany: Achievements—Shortcomings—Prospects* (Stahl 1961), published in 1961 under the auspices of the *Atlantik-Brücke* (Atlantic Bridge), an association founded in 1952 for the advancement of German-American understanding (modeled on the U.S. Council on Foreign Relations), thus an enterprise aimed at a highly influential audience. This book's preface said its goal was to give "a comprehensive and objective picture of the efforts being made in the German Federal Republic to educate the German people for democracy," in the face of what it saw as misrepresentations of West Germany from the Communist East: "Through this book," wrote the association's leaders, Arnold Bergstraesser and Walter Stahl, "we would like not only to inform our American friends of the achievements and the shortcomings of democracy in Germany but also to enable them to see the different aspects of the entire German picture in proper proportion" (Stahl 1961: v). How exactly Adorno's "Aufarbeitung," given its highly critical diagnosis, would contribute to that balanced view is not entirely clear in retrospect, though Stahl discusses Adorno's essay in his introduction as a necessary part of educating people to understand their own motives and as evidence of the will to gain such understanding.

Adorno's "Aufarbeitung" appeared again in English some twenty-five years later in a collection of essays and materials published after the so-called Bitburg affair of 1985 (Hartman 1986), when U.S. president Ronald Reagan, over vociferous objections not only from Jewish groups but from a majority of the U.S. Senate as well, participated in a reconciliation cere-mony at the military cemetery at Bitburg as part of a fortieth-anniversary commemoration of May 8, 1945, the end of the second World War.[5] The problem was that forty-nine former members of the Waffen-SS were also buried at Bitburg, and critics charged that Chancellor Helmut Kohl had wanted the ceremony not only as a quid pro quo for agreeing to deploy American mid-range nuclear missiles on West German soil but also as part of his alleged more general neoconservative program to displace the Nazi period as the centerpiece of German memory (Habermas 1989). For critics, Bitburg stood for the discreditable effort to relativize the crimes of the Nazis and to equate victims and perpetrators, all part of an effort to repress the moral, political, and civilizational import of the Holocaust and the uniqueness of Germany's responsibility for it. In this context, the renowned literary critic Geoffrey Hartman (1986) credited Adorno with having antic-ipated by twenty-five years the problem of relativization raised by Bitburg, as well as having provided a durable vocabulary for thinking through the ethics and politics of memory. Given its fame, Adorno's "Aufarbeitung" was a logical choice for a volume on Bitburg. Indeed, for the same reasons, this essay, particularly its outline of a genuine "working through," has also been discussed in contemporary treatments of "transitional justice" and the poli-tics of memory—yet further disconnected from its original context. (Another famous statement, the philosopher Karl Jaspers's 1946 essay *The Question of German Guilt*, whose fate we will mention again, has experienced a similarly decontextualized afterlife in the transitional justice literature.)

In recent years, finally, Adorno's "Aufarbeitung" has been reprinted in col-lections of his work, in both the 1998 *Critical Models: Interventions and Catchwords* (Adorno 1998) and the 2003 collection of his works on anti-Semitism, the Holocaust, and memory, *Can One Live after Auschwitz? A Philosophical Reader* (Adorno 2003). In these collections, "Aufarbeitung" is placed within the context of his overall oeuvre, but its historical and po-litical—to say nothing of social-scientific—context is relatively lacking.

THE foregoing production and reception history of Adorno's provocative essay raises at least three problems. First, as the essay has rarely been presented with the kind of context we have just outlined, it has been vulnerable to exactly the kind of misuse that so much of Adorno's critical theory is directed against: namely, reification. This seems most apparent in the Bitburg collection (Hartman 1986), which transplants a historically situated intervention into a distant later context. Second, the "Aufarbeitung" itself includes significant references—for instance to a "scholarly dispute" about the "house of the hangman" and to "group experiments in the Institute for Social Research"—that are surely obscure to all but those most expert in the history of the Frankfurt School.[6] Even many who are relatively knowledgeable about Adorno are not well versed in the more social-scientific aspects of his work, which is much neglected even in the secondary literature on him (Perrin and Jarkko 2005). Until now, the *Group Experiment*—to which, again, "Aufarbeitung" can be seen as a coda—has never been available in English[7] and remains relatively unknown even in German, to say nothing of the subsequent debate with Hofstätter to which Adorno refers, and in which he first makes his accusation about "the house of the hangman."

The second problem is connected directly to a third: about the inadequacy of the story told thus far, namely the implication that Adorno's 1959 (or 1960) presentation of "Aufarbeitung," in the context of the anti-Semitism wave, was the beginning of the essay's life or that the 1962 version of it was directed mainly at the new generation, which took it as something of a foundational statement. In truth, the 1959–62 presentations are better understood as the culmination or summation of a long process, and the subsequent uses of the essay more as its afterlives. For "Aufarbeitung" was in many ways a conclusion to nearly a decade of work on the legacies of National Socialism and their role in the development of West German democracy. Again, the story of that work is surprisingly absent from the reputation of Adorno and the Frankfurt School, and even from a great deal of the scholarship about them, which is more interested in Adorno as a philosopher of the Enlightenment's contradictions and as an aesthetic critic. It is this absence we seek to remedy here.

II. *The Authoritarian Personality* and Other Sources

As Adorno and many others have noted, the experience of exile feels removed from the continuity of time, and can produce something of a "Rip van Winkle" effect. "The years of the fascist dictatorship," Adorno wrote in an aphorism from 1954 (quoted in Müller-Doohm 2005: 330), "do not fit into the continuity of [the émigré's] life. . . . If he returns, he will have aged and yet remained as young as he was at the time of his banishment. . . . He imagines that he can pick up where he left off." The problem with this formulation is that while it captures well the subjective discontinuities of the exile's experience, it can lead us too readily to neglect the objective continuities. For indeed, despite the many turns, surprises, and ruptures to be found in any intellectual biography and all the more so in Adorno's, there are certain consistencies that run through Adorno's work like a red ribbon, without which his responses to the vicissitudes and exigencies of his changing contexts are inexplicable. The origins of "Aufarbeitung" are indeed to be found not only in *Group Experiment* but at least as far back as 1950, in *The Authoritarian Personality* (Adorno et al. 1950), in his diagnosis of National Socialism as an expression of narcissism (Adorno 1978), and even in his research for Paul Lazarsfeld on radio music (Jenemann 2007).

As already noted, like most German exiles, Adorno was profoundly concerned during and at the end of the war with what should be done about Germany. As always, however, he embraced the dialectical tensions in his own view, though interestingly projecting them from himself onto the situation. As he wrote in 1944, in *Minima Moralia* (Adorno 1974: 56), "To question what is to be done with defeated Germany, I could only say two things in reply. Firstly: at no price, on no conditions, would I wish to be an executioner or to supply legitimations for executioners. Secondly: I would not wish, least of all with legal machinery, to stay the hand of anyone who was avenging past misdeeds. This is a thoroughly unsatisfactory, contradictory answer. . . . But perhaps the fault lies in the question and not only in me."

The last sentence of this passage is particularly interesting, as it fits well with Adorno's more general assessment of the problems of an individualizing psychological approach, or at least an approach that associates the distinction between psychology and sociology with that between subjectivity and objectivity. This issue ran through all of Adorno's work, and was indeed of crucial significance in the later *Group Experiment,* where it might have seemed as if he was employing a reductively psychological explanatory strategy, given his psychoanalytic vocabulary there. As he later described the goals of his work on *The Authoritarian Personality* in "Scientific Experiences of a European Scholar in America" (Adorno 1998: 230), however, "to be sure, in contrast to a certain economic orthodoxy, we were not dismissive of psychology, but acknowledged its proper place in our outline as an explanatory aspect." Nevertheless, he claimed, "we followed what I believed to be the plausible idea that in the present society the objective institutions and developmental tendencies have attained such an overwhelming power over the individual that people . . . are becoming, and evidently in increasing measure, functionaries of the predominant tendencies operating over their heads. Less and less depends on their own particular conscious and unconscious being, their inner life." The work on the "authoritarian personality," then, was clearly influenced by psychoanalytic methods and concepts, as was that on the *Group Experiment*, but was wary of the tendency toward individualization and an overemphasis on subjectivity, which Adorno's approach saw as inappropriate given contemporary social conditions.

Indeed, since the dispute between the Institute's director, Max Horkheimer, and the psychoanalyst Erich Fromm in the late 1930s (Jay 1985), the core members of the Institute for Social Research (Horkheimer, Adorno, Leo Löwenthal, and Friedrich Pollock) were concerned that the goal of psychoanalysis was to accommodate the patient to a social context that was objectively dissonant, and that it thus expressed a reactionary impulse.[8] In contrast, Adorno emphasized that his approach was concerned with objective conditions rather than subjective states. *The Authoritarian Personality*, he later claimed, therefore advanced the insight that, as Müller-Doohm (2005: 299) puts it, "the threat to democratic societies arises not just from the attitude and behavior of a relatively small minority of declared fascists, but from the syndrome of an unexpressed, potential fascism that comes from the hidden layer of the personality." This hidden layer was the result of the authoritarian character structure, which—according to an older line of research from before the Frankfurters emigrated *(Studies in Authority and the Family)*—was related to family structure; this potential was held to be objective. "Psychological dispositions," Adorno wrote in "Freudian theory and the Pattern of Fascist Propaganda" (1978: 135), "do not actually cause fascism; rather, fascism defines a psychological area which can be successfully exploited by the forces which promote it for entirely non-psychological reasons of self-interest." "Fascism," he continued, "is [thus] not a psychological issue."[9] This was despite his emphasis on it as an expression of narcissism; the point was that this narcissism inhered, like his own question about revenge, in the objective situation rather than in subjective experience.[10]

Like psychological studies, Adorno wrote (1998: 235), *The Authoritarian Personality* had aimed "to determine present opinions and dispositions." More important, however, they were "interested in the fascist potential." This comes from outside the individual, from sociological conditions. This view is perfectly consonant with the one that underlay Adorno's contributions to *Group Experiment*. As he put it in a memo to assistants on the project (Wiggershaus 1994: 439–40), "our study is more concerned with intellectual supply than with intellectual demand. . . . The central interest of the study is therefore not directed towards the subjective at all, but rather to those elements of consciousness which are objectively predetermined and prescribed and disseminated socially; it is directed, precisely, toward the objective spirit, the German ideology." This matches as well the approach he had already advanced in 1944 in *The Psychological Technique of Martin Luther Thomas' Radio Addresses* (Adorno 2000), a content analysis Adorno carried out in collaboration with Löwenthal of speeches by an American fascist agitator. After outlining a small repertoire of Thomas's psychological techniques of persuasion, which Adorno saw as similar in form to those of Hitler, Adorno concluded this pilot study with an explanation of how and why this propaganda works: "it simply takes people for what they are: genuine children of today's standardized mass culture who have been robbed to a great extent of their autonomy and spontaneity" (Adorno 1978: 134). (There is indeed a strong similarity between the expository procedures Adorno employed in his analysis of Thomas's propaganda and those he employed in the later "Guilt and Defense.")

Interestingly, Adorno's emphasis on the objectivity of character structures behind the subjectivity of individual psychology is also connected to the view he developed in a seemingly more distant context: the study of radio music that he embarked on in 1938–1941 as part of—though largely at odds with—Paul Lazarsfeld's Princeton Radio Research Project (Jenemann 2007). In contrast to Lazarsfeld (1969), who approached music as a market researcher seeking to measure the success or failure of a product, Adorno characterized his approach to radio music as that of a musician. The question of whether respondents liked or disliked a particular piece, for Adorno, completely neglected the objective qualities of the music. These objective qualities included not just the musical content but the effects of the medium and the social context.

For Adorno, a radio broadcast or a recording destroyed the living qualities of the musical experience. First, the intervention of the electronic medium for him destroyed the sound. Second, the inability of the listener to respond destroyed the social relationship of audience and performer: the very question of a reified "response" ignored the way radio music had become a socially produced "second nature" in the first place; the very question of liking or disliking music that had become what Adorno called a "utility"—something in the background used for purposes other rather than an aesthetic experience in and of itself—was in his view nearly entirely beside the point. Indeed, treating the listener as a consumer and as a respondent missed the ways such research, and entertainment produced to receive high marks in such research, constructed the listener as a passive vessel with no need to think for himself.[11] Taste, requiring cultivation, is not the same as preference, merely requiring reaction. The emphasis here on objective rather than subjective qualities was thus consistent with the emphasis on objective potential for fascism in ideology rather than merely in or as a result of subjective dispositions. In addition, as we will see, there is a strong connection between Adorno's characterization of the passive listener and his later characterization in *Group Experiment* of the isolated survey respondent whose "opinion" the survey elicits.

WHEN Adorno first returned to Germany in 1949, he thus did so not only with the experience of the exile's "damaged life," as he put it in the subtitle to *Minima Moralia*, but with a wealth of experience that was simultaneously steeped in the procedures and approaches of American-style empirical research yet fundamentally critical of it. Nevertheless, Adorno's position on empirical research has been frequently misunderstood. One view implies that he was forced during his exile to accommodate, however unsuccessfully, to empiricism, which he abandoned as quickly as circumstances allowed him. This view, however, cannot account for the vigor with which he engaged in his empirical work: not only the Princeton radio project (where, despite his disagreements with Lazarsfeld, he was quite productive) but also *The Authoritarian Personality* (about which he wrote enthusiastically), his study of Martin Luther Thomas, a study of the *Los Angeles Times* horoscope pages that he conducted on a return trip to California in 1951 *(The Stars Down to Earth),* and work in postwar Germany, where he was for many years closely engaged with the Institute's studies of German political attitudes and other topics (alongside abstract works of philosophy like *Negative Dialectics* and *The Jargon of Authenticity*). A second view is that Adorno ran hot and cold on empiricism, both intellectually and in reaction to exigencies, finally repudiating it altogether in the late 1950s and 1960s in the context of the so-called positivist dispute.

Neither of these views adequately appreciates the dialectical tension Adorno maintained, with fair consistency, from his first years in America on the Princeton project to his last lectures on sociology in 1968. Indeed, he returned to Germany very much with the intention of putting what he had learned in the United States to positive use in the reconstruction of his native land (Müller-Doohm 2005; Wiggershaus 1995). He had long intended to extend his work on the authoritarian personality into post-war Germany. However, after having asked, along with Horkheimer in the 1944 *Dialectic of Enlightenment*, "why mankind, instead of entering into a truly human condition, is sinking into a new kind of barbarism" (Horkheimer and Adorno 1972: xi), the question following the Nazi defeat was how to go on living after Auschwitz.[12] Given the widespread characterization of Adorno as the ultimate German mandarin, however, he did not turn entirely in expected directions. Indeed, he repudiated the solutions that were emerging in the immediate postwar years, like those of Friedrich Meinecke (1950) or Alfred Weber (1947), which sought a return to the German virtues to be found in the intellectual and aesthetic tradition. Most famously, Meinecke had called for the formation of "Goethe Societies," which would present and discuss the great works of the German Enlightenment; Weber had put his faith in a reinvigorated *Bildung,* a nineteenth-century notion of individual fulfillment through education. As Peter Hohendahl (1995: 51) has pointed out, Adorno was too critical to embrace *Bildung,* despite what one might expect to be his affinity for it. *Bildung,* Adorno implied, was inappropriate to an age that did not in fact allow much room for an autonomous individual who could seek fulfillment through *experience (Erfahrung),* if it had ever been what its advocates had claimed for it. In German, moreover, the term for experience—*Erfahrung*—is as freighted as *Bildung,* and Walter Benjamin (1969: 84) had already described its demise when he wrote in his essay "The Storyteller," following the First World War, that "never has experience [*Erfahrung*] been contradicted more thoroughly than strategic experience by tactical warfare, economic experience by inflation, bodily experience by mechanical warfare, moral experience by those in power," an account Adorno echoed.

For Adorno, *Bildung* was, in the last analysis, the result of a tradition that had produced Auschwitz: "The aureole of culture, the principle that the mind is absolute," he wrote years later in his philosophical magnum opus, *Negative Dialectics* (Adorno 1973a: 367), "was the same which tirelessly violated what it was pretending to express. After Auschwitz," he concluded, "there is no word tinged from on high, not even a theological one, that has any right unless it underwent a transformation." The restoration of *Bildung* could thus not help but be complicit in maintaining the system that had brought about its negation. As he had put it when he was still in America, in *Minima Moralia* (Adorno 1974: 55), "the idea that after this war life will continue 'normally,' or even that culture might be 'rebuilt'—as if rebuilding of culture were not already its negation—is idiotic. Millions of Jews have been murdered," he continued sarcastically, "and this is to be seen as an interlude and not the catastrophe itself." Here Adorno was referring to the most common use of the term "catastrophe," by which was meant the destruction of *Germany* and *German* culture, not that of the Jews.[13] (This insight would return in his 1957 riposte to Hofstätter's attack on the *Group Experiment.*)

III. In the House of the Hangman

Neither Horkheimer nor Adorno could be certain what they would find when they returned to Germany. To be sure, Germany was by 1949 one of the most surveyed populations in history. Beginning with the march of British and American troops into German territory in the spring of 1945, the Psychological Warfare Division of the U.S. army, later OMGUS (Office of the Military Governor, U.S.) and after 1949 the high commissioner of Germany (HICOG), conducted nearly daily polls and other studies aimed at gauging Germans' attitudes and culture (Merritt 1995; Merritt and Merritt 1970, 1980; Stern 1992). However, the impact of those studies both in general and on the Frankfurt scholars in particular is difficult to assess. A great deal of the wartime social-scientific scholarship on Germany was conducted by or in collaboration with (often Jewish) German émigrés, including associates of the Institute for Social Research like Herbert Marcuse, Löwenthal, and Franz Neumann, who produced a large number of reports and handbooks for the U.S. government. These creative scholars had a significant effect on the staffs of the government research enterprises with whom they were involved as teachers, trainers, and intellectual inspirations, and much of the subsequent research work in Germany during the occupation was strongly influenced by their theories and insights (Stern 1992: 111–114). Nevertheless, the evidence is strong that their work did not have all that much influence on the actual course of the occupation, which was an affair run largely by the military establishment, which was more likely to be concerned with Communism than anti-Semitism (though there is evidence that the problem of anti-Semitism was so large that it could not be ignored, particularly on several occasions when violence broke out [Bergmann 1997]).

As a legacy for future work, several problems from the complex situation of postwar Germany did emerge in the careful work that went into the OMGUS reports between 1945 and 1949. For instance, as Stern (1992: 110) documents, an April 1946 OMGUS report addressed the inadequacy of surveys for developing accurate measures of people's attitudes and intentions because, as the report stated, survey responses "often are reproductions of the standard phrases of editorials in current German newspapers. . . . The whole attitude gives the impression of an attempt at justification rather than honest analysis." This was increasingly the case over time as Germans learned what was expected of them on such surveys and mimicked official political discourse. A second, not unrelated problem was the inadequacy of the procedures for measuring latent, rather than just manifest, anti-Semitism (124), an issue the Frankfurt scholars had already theorized about in the context of their work on *The Authoritarian*

Personality. While it is unlikely that these reports ever had any concrete effects on occupation policy (or on *Group Experiment*), they did raise concerns in the War Department. Nevertheless, the response was largely one of resignation (126).

Horkheimer first visited postwar Germany in May 1948, by which time the geopolitical concerns of the emerging Cold War had already pushed aside most remnants of a punitive stance toward Germany; an end to denazification and a new wave of amnesties had accompanied an emerging concern for consolidating a new political system for the Western zones alone. Whatever concerns the OMGUS reports might have raised, the zest for "reeducation," as already noted, was largely dissipated. While Horkheimer was invited back to explore the possibility of taking up a "restitution chair" at the university in Frankfurt (which he did) to make up for the position he had lost in 1933, it was clear neither to him nor to the entrenched leadership of the university what exactly his role would be. As he wrote to his wife after meeting with the university leadership for the first time, "they are not yet sure whether to see me as a relatively influential visitor from America or as the brother of their victims—to think of whom means having a memory. They will have to plump for the latter" (Wiggershaus 1995: 398). Horkheimer himself was not sure which he was—the role of Jewish identity in his life was transformed through the contemplation of National Socialism—though he threw himself eagerly into the intellectual refounding of the Federal Republic through his early important role at the university in Frankfurt and through his reconstruction of the Institute for Social Research (Albrecht et al. 1999).

Making arrangements not only for his own academic future but for the future of the Institute as well, whose reconstruction was principally funded by the U.S. government under the auspices of John J. McCloy's HICOG (Jäger 2004: 254; Schwartz 1991), Horkheimer emphasized the role the Institute could play in reconstruction and in the culture of the new West German democracy (Albrecht et al. 1999; Wiggershaus 1995: 432). In his words, the Institute's work would combine an "extension of the German tradition of social philosophy and the humanities" with the "most advanced empirical research methods of modern American sociology" (Wiggershaus 1995: 432). Even if that was not exactly how Adorno would have put it, it was not entirely at odds with his hopes (which Horkheimer clearly shared) to extend the investigation they had done for *The Authoritarian Personality* into *German* character, which had always been a not-so-hidden goal of that and related studies. As Adorno put it in his 1951 lecture "On the Current Status of Empirical Social Research," given at a German public opinion conference (450), "the remnant of German humanistic sociology urgently requires the use of empirical methods as a corrective measure." On the other hand, "the true significance of empirical methods lies in the critical motivation they contain."

A great deal, therefore, rested on the Institute's first project, through which the Frankfurters sought to demonstrate the value of what they had learned in America but understood through their uniquely German perspectives in an area sure to generate discomfort for Germans and the occupation authorities alike: the continuing residues of National Socialism in the German population. Work by German intellectuals who had returned to live there and who sought a prominent role in German public and intellectual life was sure to have a greater effect, and hence carried greater risks, than the work done by the minor research agencies of the occupation authority, which produced reports largely for a distant ministerial midlevel. Certainly there were real risks to working in America, particularly as McCarthyism had already begun; in contrast Germany provided political security for the critical theorists. But the intellectual and reputational risks there seemed to the Frankfurt scholars all that much greater.

IV. *Group Experiment* and the Concept of Public Opinion

While Horkheimer, Adorno, and their Frankfurt colleague Friedrich Pollock were clear about what they had learned in America, and Horkheimer wanted the Institute's work to serve as a conduit between two different worlds of intellectual sensibility, the starting point for the project was nevertheless vintage critical theory. While steeped in the language of public opinion research, the Frankfurters still harbored the suspicion that such research was, like the consumer society it served, atomistic and thus supportive of a reified status quo:

> The progress of a science that is able to develop methods with the help of which it can register and under some circumstances predict the truly subtle reactions, opinions, and wishes of people is undeniable. It is also an indisputable gain that one can check political and economic decisions against the reactions of the governed. Nevertheless, one should also not fail to recognize that the convergence of social-scientific methods toward those of the natural sciences is itself the child of a society that reifies people. The democratic potential of the new methods is thus not unquestionable, as is so gladly assumed particularly in Germany after the suppression of public opinion by the Hitler

regime. It is not incidental that modern "opinion research" grew out of market and consumer research. It [opinion research] implicitly identifies man under the rubric of consumer. As a result, the diverse tendencies to social control and manipulation that can be observed to derive from modern empirical sociology in the realm of consumer analysis or "human relations" are not merely incidental to the method itself [echoes of Adorno's radio research]. While they [opinion researchers] are led by the principle of the equality of people and allow no privilege in evaluating the attitudes of individual subjects, they nevertheless treat these subjects as they are constituted by the dominant economic and social relations, without examining this constitution itself. The difficulty becomes obvious when the point is to convey with representative surveys what opinions and meanings people have toward questions of general public interest—in other words as soon as one wants to deal with the problem of so-called public opinion with the techniques of empirical social research. (Pollock 1955: 18)*

Despite this, the research design for the project, while highly experimental, was articulated in terms of a friendly corrective to the procedures of modern American empirical research. The methodological introduction (which appears in the companion volume to this one) was filled with references to the latest American research techniques, including those used in studies by Hadley Cantril, Leonard Doob, Walter Lippmann, Lazarsfeld, Harold Lasswell, Bernard Berelson, Morris Janowitz, and Kurt Lewin, along with Freudian and critical theory perspectives.[14] The main goal of combining these two worlds (Freudian and Critical Theory and American social science) was to penetrate beyond what the researchers saw as the surface of public opinion. As Franz Böhm put it in his preface to *Group Experiment* (Pollock 1955: xi), the study set out from the sense that there was a difference between manifest "public opinion" and latent "nonpublic opinion," namely between "the sum of opinions we wish people believed we had as our real opinion" versus "the sum of opinion that we truly have." Böhm referred to "the so-called public opinion, which expresses itself in elections, referenda, public speeches, groups, parliamentary discussions [and] political assemblies" and argued that these could be misleading. They were "only formal expressions we use when we are wearing our Sunday clothes," behind which runs a different discourse "like a second currency." The point of the Frankfurters' method was to evoke this second currency. This distinction between public and nonpublic opinion is clearly

*With the exception of *Gruppenexperiment*'s preface by Franz Böhm and the essay "Guilt and Defense" by Adorno, much of *Gruppenexperiment*'s writing is either a collective product or difficult to ascribe to a single author. Unless indicated, all translations are our own.

analogous to that drawn between manifest and latent personality in *The Authoritarian Personality.**

The inspirational image behind the study, as expressed by Horkheimer, was that of a railway compartment in which discussants would feel less inhibited than usual to express unsanctioned views. The problem was how to get people to express their opinions openly in a research setting. More important was the idea of a *conversation* that lay at the heart of the railway image; for this reason, the Frankfurters preferred the term "group discussion" to the more common "group interview." "It has long since become routine," they argued (Pollock 1955: 30–31), "to apply depth psychology in interviews and to use projective tests, detailed case studies and other techniques to correct and supplement the usual questionnaire methods. The group technique used by our Institute . . . differs from all of these undertakings principally in that it is not satisfied with adding corrections at a later stage, but already begins at an early stage, while opinions are being ascertained *in statu nascendi.*" Indeed, this goal of capturing opinion in the process of becoming is connected to the Frankfurters' reformulation of the very concept of opinion itself, an issue we take up elsewhere.

As noted, the methodological argument began by historicizing the conditions for opinion formation:

> The assumption of the existence of an opinion of every individual is questionable. That everyone possesses his own opinion is a cliché of the Modern. In earlier social epochs, the spiritual cosmos was, on the one hand, much too strongly constructed and strictly controlled for everyone to be able to have or to have been able to develop a private opinion about everything—the expression itself [private opinion] is specifically liberal—; on the other hand, the information and communications possibilities were too limited for the overwhelming majority of people to have been in the situation to have an opinion about everything imaginable. Today, when in the large industrial states information about nearly everything is widespread, the mass of informational material has grown to such an extent with the complexity of all social relations that it is even difficult for the expert himself to form an opinion about everything in his own most narrow field. . . . Insofar as opinion research proceeds from the assumption that one has to have an opinion about everything, it succumbs to the danger of misleading people in its interviews to statements about which they have no real conviction, which are not even their opinions. Exactly this contradiction between the demand for an opinion and the inability to have an opinion seduces numerous individuals to accept stereotypes

---

*We include the full text of Böhm's preface in our companion volume, *Group Experiment: The Frankfurt School on Public Opinion in Postwar Germany* (Harvard University Press; forthcoming).

that derive from their vain efforts to opine while according the prestige of participation (Pollock 1955: 18)

In contrast, the Frankfurt scholars' approach strove to move beyond the putative monistic assumptions of contemporary opinion research to a more profoundly social view: "Exactly the effect of an immeasurably grown potential for communication nevertheless no longer allows grasping the individual as a monad whose opinion crystallizes and persists simultaneously in isolation and in empty space" (Pollock 1955: 21). As a result, "realistic opinion research" had to approach as nearly as possible the actual conditions in which opinions came about. Opinions are highly variable, are limited to a narrow range of issues, and form in the process of group dynamics (indeed, the researchers favorably cited the work of Robert Bales on group dynamics.) The charge of *Group Experiment* to opinion research was thus that "it must free itself from the prejudice that opinion as the property of the individual is both in its majority stable and that its transformations are secondary" (21). The generalizable hypotheses they stated at the beginning thus included the following: "The opinions and attitudes of people to the themes that claim general or public interest and can therefore constitute the materials of public opinion do not arise and operate in isolation but in continuous interrelation between the individual and the society that affects him mediately and immediately. They are often not particularly fixed, but represent a vague and diffuse potential. They frequently become clear to the individual only during debate with other people" (32).

Moreover, opinions "change relative to the mood and situation in which the individuals find themselves and the most diverse tendencies can variously step into the foreground of consciousness" (32).[15]

The ontological principle behind these statements was that "the concept of public opinion presumes a social organization or group whose members have to have more or less shared experiences." As a result of this principle,

> here it will be endeavored to differentiate the concept of public opinion by attending to the structure of the opinion-shaping group. In the process, the consciousness arises that public opinion does not represent a simple sum of individual opinions, but contains an overarching collective moment. One can speak of public opinion only where there is something like a uniform group structure sui generis (Pollock 1955: 21).

Once again, objectivity comes before denuded subjectivity. Given this understanding of public opinion, the purpose of the research, as already stated, was to identify "the objective spirit—the German ideology" that was expressed through the articulations of the participants in the discussions. As Adorno wrote later in more general reflections on the contributions of empirical research in postwar Germany, "the task of empirical social research in Germany is to clarify strictly and without any transfiguration the objective nature of what is socially the case, an objective reality that is largely hidden from individuals and even the collective consciousness" (quoted in Müller-Doohm 2005: 337).

So HOW did they actually proceed, and what did they find? The researchers sought situations that would mimic "natural" settings as much as possible, allowing observation of opinion as a discursive process in which contrary views played out against one another and in which positions changed constantly. They began by testing versions of a fictional letter (the "Colburn Letter," reprinted here) by a fictional sergeant in the U.S. army to a newspaper back home conveying a negative assessment of German national character, particularly highlighting Germans' unwillingness to acknowledge what they had done during the Third Reich. Researchers, who led the discussions, presented this fictional letter to 137 separate groups of Germans and interpreted 121 of the resulting discussions for their study. The purpose of the letter was to *provoke* the so-called nonpublic opinion. While Horkheimer's initial hope was for random groups, pilot studies found that such heterogeneous contexts were not conducive to participation, so they revised the method to work through relatively homogeneous groupings in familiar settings.

The research consisted of quantitative analysis of both the participants and their responses and of follow-up interviews with individuals, as well as qualitative analysis of the "opinions" and the group dynamics that formed them. The results were challenging. More than 60 percent of participants did not actually speak in the group discussions, which would later open the opportunity for critics to charge that the research report misrepresented the results. Qualitative analysis, which came in the form of Adorno's essay "Guilt and Defense," was based on and illustrated with a narrow subset of the responses.

In his contributions to the final report, Adorno argued powerfully that the social conditions for manipulative mass psychology and the potential for totalitarian allegiance persisted in Germany. These conditions were the result of what he charged was a "collective narcissism," which manifested itself in the virtuosic deployment of defense mechanisms corresponding "to the extent of unconscious guilt one has to suppress"—the statement he would repeat so publicly in "Aufarbeitung." In "Guilt and Defense," he fleshed out the extent of the syndrome. As if anticipating Adenauer's 1960 response to the wave of anti-Semitic vandalism, Adorno characterized the psychodynamic as follows: "It seems to be a law of present-day social psychology that what one has practiced oneself is always what makes one most resentful. The unconscious motives for this, closely related to the projection mechanism, need not be discussed here; suffice it to say that, as soon as one has condemned false generalization, it is easy to distance oneself from National Socialism, and that once this has been accomplished without too much cost it is easy to put oneself in the right and to make yesterday's persecutor today's victim" (p. 104 below). Indeed, this argument was already present in *Minima Moralia* of 1945, where he had written that "the obviousness of disaster becomes an asset to its apologists: what everyone knows, no one needs to say—and under cover of silence is allowed to proceed" (1974: 233). Adorno was thus merely reprising earlier theories, redeemed by empirical study, when he stated in 1959–62 that he was more concerned with the persistence of fascist tendencies within German democracy than against it. The foregoing makes clear why.

V. Reception and Response

As already indicated, Horkheimer in particular was quite concerned with the project's explosive potential. There were indeed fine lines to be observed between being critical of German sensibilities and appearing vengeful, being friendly to the Americans and appearing to be their agents, and being critical of the government and having no influence. In the 1930s, the Institute had been a left-wing, principally Marxist enterprise; Horkheimer was thus concerned—both because of the changes in his worldview as well as his fine-tuned sensitivity to the political situation—that the Institute now appear more mainstream.[16] More specifically, he was anxious to prove the intellectual vitality of the methods the Institute was purveying, wanting to establish its scientific stature by showing what the Frankfurters were capable of, particularly with an eye toward their future role (Claussen 2008: 263; Wiggershaus 1995: 450).

Beyond these issues, the Frankfurt scholars knew how poorly the critical efforts of others had been received by postwar German intellectuals. In 1945, the psychoanalyst Carl Jung had formulated a thesis of German collective guilt in an interview with a Swiss newspaper and later in a widely publicized essay (Jung 1989; Olick 2005). His accusations were vigorously attacked by numerous German commentators, most prominently Erich Kästner, a world-famous children's book author who after 1945 had become feuilleton editor of the American-sponsored *Neue Zeitung*. Jung argued that the "collective guilt" of the Germans was "for psychologists a fact, and it will be one of the most important tasks of therapy to bring the Germans to recognize this guilt" (Jung 1989: 52–53); Kästner's withering response was that "it sounded as if the important man had swallowed the trumpet of final judgment" (Kästner 1998: 520). In 1946, the psychologist Alexander Mitscherlich (Mitscherlich and Mielke 1949) had written a report, "Science without Humanity," analyzing the worldviews and self-justifications of doctors tried at Nuremberg. His Heidelberg colleagues roundly condemned him for *Nestbeschmutzung* (soiling one's own nest).[17]

Among many other cases, the Frankfurt scholars were also surely mindful of the example of Jaspers, who had delivered a series of lectures, "The Question of German Guilt," in Heidelberg in 1945–46.[18] The book version of those lectures (Jaspers 2000) has remained an enduring reference for decades, and it received a resurgence of attention particularly after 1989 in the context of debates over so-called transitional justice (Kritz 1995) as well as in disputes about the Nazi past of philosopher Martin Heidegger, at whom at least some of Jaspers's argument was directed.[19] For many commentators since the 1980s, Jaspers's argument about the need to acknowledge responsibility for the past has been taken as a founding moral document of the Federal Republic's political culture. Indeed, in the context of the "historians' dispute" of 1985–86 (Maier 1988), Adorno's protégé Jürgen Habermas (1989) identified Jaspers as the embodiment of the responsible political culture that was under attack by neoconservatives, who wanted to underwrite a less damaged national identity by decentering memory of the Nazis. Jaspers himself, however, was so disappointed with his argument's reception (or lack thereof) in postwar Germany that he gave that disappointment as the reason he and his wife finally left for Switzerland in 1948 (Jaspers 1967: 164; Olick 2005). For Jaspers, a "state and a people that did to the Jews what never should have been allowed to happen and did not grasp this after the catastrophe and did not draw the consequences had lost every claim" (1967: 164). Jaspers remained a controversial figure— something Horkheimer was not willing to be—until his death in 1969, particularly because of his opposition to nuclear weapons and generally critical stance toward the Federal Republic.

Horkheimer, Adorno, and Pollock were also well aware of methodological criticisms *The Authoritarian Personality* had garnered, though the most important of these did not appear until 1953 (Wiggershaus 1995: 465), after the *Group Experiment* research was conducted but before the bulk of the writing was finished.[20] Two responses to *The Authoritarian Personality* in particular concerned Adorno and Horkheimer a great deal. First, the British-American sociologist Edward Shils (1954) charged that their concern with right-wing authoritarianism to the exclusion of left-wing versions had skewed the results of the study and indicated naïveté in regard to the Soviet Union. This was one reason the authors moved from their famous "F-Scale" (*F* for fascism) to a more generalized A-scale (*A* for authoritarianism).

A second criticism was a more direct challenge to Adorno's overall theoretical approach, namely the charge that the argument was circular because it hypothesized a phenomenon—fascist potential—and then designed research to prove its existence (Christie and Jahoda 1954; see also Martin 2001). This criticism went to the heart of Adorno's worldview—his firm belief in the distinction between objectivity and subjectivity and in the goal of theoretically informed scholarship to reveal hidden objectivities. As he thus put it rather defensively in his 1969 memoir "Scientific Experiences of a European Scholar in America" (1998: 235), "If *The Authoritarian Personality* made a contribution, then it is not to be found in the absolute conclusiveness of its positive insights, let alone in its measurements, but above all in its conception of the problem, which is marked by an essential interest in society and is related to a theory that had not previously been translated into quantitative investigations of this kind." For Adorno, it was important to recognize that there was always a tension in empirical research "between the reliability and the profundity of its findings," and as always he aimed at the latter. Again, his entire approach was motivated by his belief, stated in the introduction to *The Authoritarian Personality,* "that the political, economic, and social convictions of an individual often form a broad and coherent pattern, as if bound together by a 'mentality' or 'spirit'" (Adorno et al. 1950: 1).

Even more than in the collaborative California study *(The Authoritarian Personality),* a very large number of scholars—including such later prominent figures as Habermas, Ralf Dahrendorf, Ludwig von Friedeburg, and Helmuth Plessner—were involved on and off in the work on *Group Experiment.* It is interesting to note in this context that many of the younger researchers at the Institute had what might be seen as compromised backgrounds (Plessner 1991); in line with their goals for reeducation, the Institute's leaders had sought to cast their net rather widely. They engaged as well with prominent senior figures in the German sociological establishment, like René König and Helmuth Schelsky. König was a friendly but distant associate; Schelsky rejected overtures and kept his distance, and was indeed rather hostile to the Institute's aims.[21]

Slippage, complexity, and irreconcilable differences were inevitable given the diversity of perspectives, as were insecurities about the methodological soundness of the project; several of the participants, for instance Dahrendorf (2002), complained about what they saw as the chaotic unfolding of the research, among other aspects. The 1955 book is thus filled with caveats and emphasizes again and again the provisional character of the work. The book itself includes a heavy and dry scholarly apparatus and is obviously not meant for popular consumption. Wary of the work's possible impact and cognizant of the risks it posed, because of both its content and its complexity, Horkheimer chose to keep his distance. He was not named as a contributor or even as a responsible party, as he had been on *The Authoritarian Personality*. Nonetheless, to lend the 1955 publication whatever added legitimacy he could, he commissioned the prominent legal scholar and politician Franz Böhm, who had not been associated with the study or with the Institute, to write the preface. All this was insurance against rejection.

Adorno was nevertheless quite disappointed when König, who was editor of the *Cologne Journal of Sociology and Social Psychology,* informed him of the rather polemical review the journal was going to publish by Hofstätter (though König tried to mitigate this blow by publishing a very positive review of *The Authoritarian Personality* in the same year). Putatively defending the "positivist-atomistic" method, which the Frankfurt approach criticized, Hofstätter disputed their interpretation of their own data. He argued, for instance, that if one reinterpreted the data to take into account the large numbers of participants who had remained silent, among other things, one had to conclude that the data did not convincingly demonstrate more than a 15 percent proportion of participants who voiced undemocratic attitudes. Because this proportion did not differ significantly from that to be found in other countries, Hofstätter argued, one also had to conclude that there was no significant "legacy of fascist ideology" in German attitudes.

On that basis, Hofstätter went on to charge that the critical interpretive methods the Frankfurters employed in their analysis were nothing more than self-fulfilling accusations: in contrast to the old idea of "in vino veritas" (in wine truth), he described the Frankfurters' premise as an unfair "in ira veritas" (in anger truth), claiming that the statements elicited through their method indicated nothing other than that people can be goaded into saying just about anything. He thus characterized their analysis as "nothing but an accusation, that is to say a summons for genuine psychic contrition" (p. 195 below). But for him, he said, "there is simply no individual feeling that could satisfactorily correspond to constantly considering the annihilation of a million people." As a result, he argued, these "accusations" were "misplaced or pointless" and did nothing but express "the indignation of the sociological analyst." The Frankfurt researchers, with their implied condemnation of postwar German political culture, were simply asking too much!

According to Stefan Müller-Doohm's biography of Adorno (2005: 384), Adorno took this review very hard, arguing in a January 1957 letter to Franz Böhm that Hofstätter's response was endemic of a wider pattern: "the regressive tendency of the social sciences in Germany." Adorno alleged that a "tacit agreement" existed among the social-scientific establishment, represented by individuals like Hofstätter and Schelsky, among others, to use "so-called factual research" as "a pretext not to recognize or to talk about the things that hurt." He argued that the review expressed "a renewed wish to take science in hand [i.e., co-opt it] once again under the pretext of greater scientific precision." In Müller-Doohm's reading (see also Albrecht 1999: 183), this was the real beginning of what would later become known as the "positivist dispute," in which Adorno, Habermas, and others debated with leading representatives of the philosophy of science in the 1960s, and which is often (although mistakenly) taken as Adorno's final abandonment of all hope for empiricism of any sort.

When König invited Adorno to respond in the same issue in which the review was to be published, Adorno thus did so with a tone of righteous indignation. He began by addressing in thorough and careful detail each of Hofstätter's methodological charges, arguing that Hofstätter ignored all of the qualifications and subtlety they had been so careful to include in the study. But for Adorno, what was most important was his belief that Hofstätter's charges stemmed not from the limits on this kind of scientific inquiry but from what Adorno charged was a defensive unwillingness to acknowledge the reality of German nonpublic opinion, a reality Adorno believed the study had demonstrated overwhelmingly, if not with total scientific irrefutability in all the details. For example, whereas Hofstätter interpreted the large proportion of respondents who remained silent while others articulated undemocratic views as evidence of their disagreement, Adorno argued that there was as little reason to assume they disagreed as to assume that they agreed. "The method," Adorno wrote, "is declared to be useless so that the existence of the phenomenon that emerges can be denied" (p. 208 below).[22]

For Adorno, this and other refusals in Hofstätter's critique manifested precisely the kind of "collective narcissism" the study claimed to have uncovered. Adorno thus sarcastically lectured Hofstätter: "Hofstätter considers 'There is simply no individual feeling that could satisfactorily correspond to constantly considering the annihilation of a million people.' It is [however] the victims of Auschwitz who had to take its horrors upon themselves, not those who, to their own disgrace and that of their nation, prefer not to admit it" (p. 208 below). Quoting Hofstätter's language, Adorno continued: "The 'question of guilt' was 'laden with despair' for the victims, not for the survivors, and it takes some doing to have blurred this distinction with the existential category of despair, which is not without reason a popular one." In a characteristic rhetorical move for him, Adorno then took a common expression to be found as far back as Cervantes—"In the house of the hanged, one should not mention the noose"—and made a subtle play on words to illustrate his point: "But in the house of the *hangman* one should not mention the noose; one might be suspected of harboring resentment" (p. 208 below) (emphasis added).

Hofstätter's, of course, was not the only immediate reaction to *Group Experiment*.[23] A number of others raised similar objections that the study overinterpreted the proportion of nonrespondents largely as an indicator of antidemocratic potential. Others, moreover, questioned whether the structure of latent opinions was really as deep as Adorno's analysis indicated, though this critique could in fact lead to greater rather than less concern for the future of German democracy, since one would presumably *prefer* that such attitudes be latent. A number of the reviews, however, were quite positive, praising the study's methodological innovations. In fact, as Alex Demirovic (1999: 367) has pointed out, it had the most practical consequences of all the Institute's work. The Institute in fact saw its methods as potentially useful for screening candidates for public service on the basis of their genuine openness to democratic attitudes. During the course of the research and writing, the Institute was thus party to discussions with the office of Theodor Blank, which was in charge of constructing a West German military. Officials in Blank's bureau were quite interested in the ways the Frankfurters' study addressed attitudes toward remilitarization, resistance to which the Frankfurters had interpreted as a lack of support for the new democracy. Indeed, Hofstätter's critique took issue precisely with this interpretation (as, incidentally, had König).

VI. Assessment

It is now clearer what Adorno was referring to in his 1959–62 speeches on working through the past. It is also possible to evaluate better whether he had good reason to do so. Moreover, the foregoing history also makes clear what was so *politically* important about his 1959–62 statements, which clearly went much deeper than a reaction to Adenauer's inadequate response to anti-Semitism.

It is also worth noting that in addition to the interventions of Jung, Mitscherlich, Jaspers, and others already noted, Adorno and his colleagues were certainly far from the first to address the topic of German guilt with a psychological or psychoanalytic vocabulary. For instance, in the spring of

1944, the Joint Committee on Postwar Planning, which was supported by U.S. professional associations like the American Neurological Association, the American Psychiatric Association, and the National Committee for Mental Hygiene, held a series of meetings in New York whose purpose was to bring to bear the resources of "the scientific disciplines which specialize in the study of human behavior and how it manifests itself under different conditions" on the question of planning for postwar Germany. The organizing principle of their work was the so-called psycho-cultural approach, which asserted that while political and economic dimensions were important, "the basic foundations of all social problems are how people feel, think, and act" (Brickner 1945: 381). The project's leader, moreover, a psychiatrist named Richard M. Brickner, had published in 1943 a widely noted book, *Is Germany Incurable?* Apparently Eleanor Roosevelt found it very impressive (Gerhardt 2002; Olick 2005) and Adorno referred to it in "Guilt and Defense". Brickner's thesis—which he developed under the tutelage in cultural matters of renowned anthropologist Margaret Mead— argued that Germany possessed a "paranoid" culture characterized by "megalomania," "the need to dominate," a "persecution complex," and "retrospective falsification" (Brickner 1943: 37). In this light, Adorno's psychoanalytic approach was clearly not as uncommon—or as extreme in its condemnation—as those who resisted it implied.

Moreover, the kinds of substantive assertions about German culture that Adorno and his colleagues were making, whether based on systematic research or not, were not uncommon (including the lay methodological belief that truth emerges from the model of the railway compartment encounter). As Böhm put it in his preface to *Group Experiment,* some of the nonpublic opinion "could be heard shouted from every rooftop"—an assertion much criticized by Hofstätter. In the 1950 "Report from Germany" published in the American Jewish magazine *Commentary,* for instance, émigré philosopher Hannah Arendt (who had little admiration for Adorno) described the self-absorbed and defensive reaction she received when she revealed to Germans she encountered, for instance in a train compartment, that she was a German Jew: "This is usually followed by a little embarrassed pause; and then comes—not a personal question, such as 'Where did you go after you left Germany?'; no sign of sympathy, such as 'What happened to your family?'—but a deluge of stories about how Germans have suffered (true enough, of course, but beside the point); and if the object of this little experiment happens to be educated and intelligent, he will proceed to draw up a balance sheet between German suffering and the suffering of others" (Arendt 1950: 345). Another important set of observations, in many ways in dialogue with Adornian thought, came in "Resentments," a famous

1966 essay by the writer and Auschwitz survivor Jean Améry.[24] Améry was certainly reacting to the 1959 anti-Semitism wave and perhaps following Adorno as well, when he wrote that "it was not at all necessary [for the development of his resentment] that in German towns Jewish cemeteries and monuments for resistance fighters be desecrated. Conversations like the one I had in 1958 with a South German businessman over breakfast in the hotel were enough. Not without first politely inquiring whether I was an Israelite, the man tried to convince me that there was no longer any race hatred in his country. The German people bear no grudge against the Jewish people, he said" (Amery 1986: 67). Interestingly, the resentment trope has had a number of different afterlives. In the classical formulation, one does not speak of the noose in the house of the *hanged*. In Adorno's 1957 pun, one does not speak of the noose in the house of the *hangman* for fear that one might be *suspected* of *harboring* resentment, which was surely Améry's issue. In various commentaries, however, the phrase went through yet another permutation, sometimes being repeated as "one might be suspected of *stirring up* resentment" (Claussen 1986). The difference, of course, is in who is being resentful, the victims or the Germans. Indeed, the reaction of Améry's businessman points out the possibility, predictable from Adorno's 1955 application of projection theory, that it is the Germans *themselves* who become resentful when one demands "too much" in the way of acknowledgment of the past. This German resentment is captured by the bitter joke that the Germans will never forgive the Jews for Auschwitz, or in reactions such as West German Chancellor Helmut Schmidt's statement at the end of a 1981 trip to Saudi Arabia, during which he had negotiated the sale of West German tanks to this sworn enemy of Israel, that "German foreign policy may no longer be held hostage to Auschwitz" (Moses 2007: 26).

One last piece of this story remains, and it is one that has been nearly completely absent from even the most precise scholarly accounts of the study and from the literature on Adorno and the Frankfurt School. There is, of course, a fine line between legitimate intellectual history and inappropriate ad hominem critique that serious scholars approach only with the greatest trepidation. But what is so interesting in the story of *Group Experiment* and the Adorno-Hofstätter debate is the silence on the issue of Hofstätter's subsequent role in West German public discourse. Indeed, Adorno is virtually the only one who ever seems to have alluded to Hofstätter's questionable past, an allusion that certainly violated all taboos. For instance, Hohendahl (1995: 264–265) identifies Hofstätter as follows: "Peter R. Hofstätter (1913–) retired from the University of Hamburg in 1979.[25] He served in the army throughout the war, first as a psychologist and then in combat. From 1949 to 1956 he lived in the United States, where he held positions at the Massachusetts Institute of Technology and Catholic University in Washington DC; American social psychology had a strong and lasting influence on his work. In 1960 he joined the faculty at Hamburg, where he served as director of the university's Institute for Psychology." Wiggershaus (1995: 476) adds that "Hofstätter was born in Vienna. . . . From 1937 to 1943 he had been an army psychologist, first in the Austrian and then in the German army." In his notes on Adorno's "Aufarbeitung," Henry Pickford (Adorno 1998: 337–338), like many others who mention Hofstätter, simply refers to him as "the respected, conservative psychologist."

There is, however, significant evidence that Hofstätter was no mere bystander, or garden variety "conservative," but an active apologist for National Socialism.[26] In 1941, for instance, Hofstätter published articles on "German custom" ("deutsches Brauchtum") and the pastoral function of National Socialism that perhaps did not reach the level of racial incitement but were nevertheless quite problematic in retrospect (Bergmann 1997: 285). This history came out in the context of a scandal surrounding the June 1963 publication of two articles by Hofstätter in the liberal weekly *Die Zeit*. In those articles ("Mastered Past?" on June 14, and "What Do You Expect from the School Subject Contemporary History?" on June 21), Hofstätter took highly critical positions on the prosecution of Nazi criminals that was taking place in the Frankfurt Auschwitz trials begun that year, as well as on the role of the Nazi past in school curricula—the very issue Adorno had addressed in his speeches of 1959–62.

In the first place, Hofstätter rejected the legal prosecution of war criminals as a misdirected effort based on the illegitimate requirement that Germany "master" its past, which was morally dubious in light of the contemporary possibility of mass destruction; Germany needed to be looking forward rather than back. He thus called for an act of state that "surely does not hide the guilt of the perpetrators, but renounces punishment." In his evaluation of school curricula, moreover, he charged that the requirement that schools address the traumatic memory of the Nazi past was reminiscent of totalitarianism, perhaps not in its content, but in the fact that the effort was dictated from on high; this was, he argued, no lesson in democracy.

Unsurprisingly, Hofstätter's interventions aroused a tremendous response from the newspaper's readers, despite the care with which the editors had distanced themselves from Hofstätter even as they gave him a forum in their pages. Subsequently, Hofstätter was invited to participate in a discussion sponsored by the Liberal Students Association of Germany. At that event, he escalated the conflict when he characterized the mass murder of the Jews as an act of war because Hitler had declared war on the Jews, just as, he claimed, the Jews had declared war on the Germans. In a subsequent letter to the *National-Zeitung*, a radical right-wing publication, Hofstätter repeated the legend of Chaim Weizman's 1939 statement at the World Zionist Congress that if war came, Jews would fight against Hitler, an old saw of the radical right wing. He did subsequently express regret for this statement, but it is a hard cat to put back in the bag.

The emergence of these extreme positions has no bearing on whether Hofstätter's critique of Adorno was factually or methodologically correct. Discreditable figures sometimes make valid arguments, and sympathetic figures sometimes make discreditable arguments. But given the highly personal tone of the attack Hofstätter made, as well as the diagnostic approach Adorno took in his work on such attitudes, it is certainly curious that discussion of this scandal has been, as far as we can tell, completely absent from discussions of the 1957 debate. It is surely not entirely irrelevant.

Indeed, in light of this, while Müller-Doohm (2005) and others claim that the 1957 dispute can be seen as the beginning of the "positivist dispute" of the 1960s over the role of empiricism in social research, it was indeed more than this. It is clear, in light of the foregoing, that the Adorno-Hofstätter debate was a harbinger of the historians' debate of the mid- to late 1980s as well. And so, despite our earlier reticence about Adorno's relevance in the context of Bitburg, it seems as if "Aufarbeitung" works there serendipitously, though only deeply implicitly, as an echo of earlier, forgotten moments—the first time as tragedy, the second time as farce.

It should be noted as well, and by way of summing up, that evaluation of both *Group Experiment* and indeed Adorno's work more generally has often served as a litmus test in ongoing debates about the proper role of memory in German national identity. Given the fame of other works—like those of Jaspers, the Mitscherlichs, and, in the wake of the historians' dispute, the popular book by the journalist Ralf Giordano (1987) accusing Germany of a "second guilt," which refers to the Talmudic injunction that the failure to expiate a crime is itself a crime—it is indeed surprising how seldom one sees a reference to the 1955 *Group Experiment*. This is to be explained partly by the fact that its political import—or at least the import of Adorno's "Guilt and Defense" chapter—is captured more concisely by his "Aufarbeitung." The study's weaknesses and cumbersome presentation are also factors—though one can hardly give textual difficulty as an explanation for avoiding any particular piece by Adorno!

In part, this relative lacuna in scholarly memory is also a function of *Group Experiment*'s moment: whereas "Aufarbeitung" fits the portrait of the emerging consensus of the 1960s, the existence of such arguments in the Adenauer era is less easily fit within epochal profiles. Of course, a great deal of contemporary historical scholarship on the immediate postwar period and the 1950s has focused our attention recently on the widespread sense of victimhood in Germany during those years (see especially Moeller 2001). Given that interest, we hope that Adorno's "Guilt and Defense" will be useful for contemporary scholars of German society, reinforcing as it does much of what that line of scholarship is uncovering; it should, moreover, be an important part of the stories historians tell about that period, because it was indeed a significant event in the reconstruction of German intellectual life, as well as social science.

Indeed, that is yet another reason *Group Experiment* is not well known: the lion's share of interest in Adorno and the Frankfurt School has to do with their work not as social scientists but as literary and cultural critics, as philosophers and social theorists. Part of our hope for this publication (in conjunction with its companion volume on *Group Experiment*'s methodological and theoretical arguments), then, is a corrective to an approach that would downplay their role in the history of the social sciences, both in Germany and more generally. We hope as well that Adorno's insights will contribute to contemporary analyses of memory and strategies of avoidance, issues taken up in important contemporary works like Stanley Cohen's (2001) *States of Denial,* among many others.

Beyond these explanations, we believe, at least part of *Group Experiment*'s absence from scholarly memory is tied up with a persistent resistance to recognizing the syndrome it identifies. There are older examples, like Armin Mohler's (1991) characterization, in the title of his well-known book, of the demand for *Vergangenheitsbewältigung* as a "nose ring" *(Der Nasenring),* implying that the demand for repentance is a handle that has been used by competitors and critics to restrict Germany's national self-fulfillment. We also already saw Helmut Schmidt's comment about German foreign policy being held hostage.

A more recent and directly relevant example of this resistance is the so-called political biography of Adorno published in 2003 (and in English in 2004) by Lorenz Jäger, an editor at the center-right *Frankfurter Allgemeine Zeitung.* Jäger seems at pains to paint Adorno as a sort of confused Marxist, defined by his early associations with Sigfried Krackauer (whom Jäger quotes as saying he was attracted to Adorno because "on a non-physical level I'm homosexual") and Communist Bertolt Brecht. Behind *The Authoritarian Personality,* Jäger contends, lay the desire to find a "scientific means of saying something about the normatively desirable and the pathological in politics." The result was that "in future, [*sic*], people were not only to be simply reactionary but were also to have mental problems. The result was a kind of twentieth-century Inquisition" (Jäger 2004: 143). Regarding *Group Experiment*, Jäger (160) admits that "no one can deny that in the material included in 'Guilt and Defence,' [*sic*] Jews and 'displaced persons' of the post-war period are sometimes described with a degree of prejudice and hostility that is positively frightening." Nevertheless, he argues, "no less clear is the interpreter's carefree tendency to subsume under the suspicion of anti-Semitism remarks that do not belong there." The explanation, Jäger implies, stems from the institutional sponsorship of the study in part through the American occupation authorities: "Anyone reading the study will see that its findings are entirely consonant with the interests of its sponsors." In particular, he argues, "it seemed obvious to the researchers involved in the project that criticism of the Allies was synonymous with nostalgia for National Socialism" (154). One could easily respond, however, that respondents often did in fact use their criticism of the occupation as a screen for unresolved commitments to discredited nationalist positions (Olick 2005): one could not defend the Nazis, but one could attack the occupation. But to see *Group Experiment* as serving the interests of the occupation authorities, in a time when they were seeking to rebuild the army and rehabilitate German society, is clearly wrong. What is surprising is how consistent this misreading is with Hofstätter's.[27]

Despite the successes of *Vergangenheitsbewältigung* in the 1960s and 1970s, and the apparent victory of the liberals in the historians' dispute of the mid-1980s (in effect declared by Federal Republic president Richard von Weizsäcker in his 1985 speech that warned West Germans of their responsibilities to memory), one could indeed argue that a thread of reaction has remained persistent (Moses 2007). The problem with historian Ernst Nolte's (1986) provocation in the historians' dispute that Germany suffers unduly under a "past that will not pass away" was mostly a matter of its shrillness and relative prematurity. Since 1989, aggressive relativization of the German past has given way to the much more successful strategy of ritualization (Olick 2003), which makes clear the value of the statement by Adorno (1997: 306) that serves as the epigraph to this chapter: "For the sake of reconciliation, authentic works must blot out every trace of reconciliation in memory." That was surely the case with Adorno's "Aufarbeitung," and his refusal to tolerate what he saw as the outright lies, more subtle misdirections, and more complex projections of his reacquired German surroundings. Whether he applied that refusal consistently or not, whether it was free of contradiction and slippage or not, is surely an important datum for theory and empirical research.

References

Adorno, Theodor W. *Can One Live after Auschwitz? A Philosophical Reader.* Edited by Rolf Tiedemann. Translated by Rodney Livingstone. Stanford: Stanford University Press, 2003.

————. *The Psychological Technique of Martin Luther Thomas' Radio Addresses.* Stanford: Stanford University Press, 2000.

————. *Introduction to Sociology.* Translated by Edmund Jephcott. Cambridge: Polity, 1999.

————. *Critical Models: Interventions and Catchwords.* Translated by Henry W. Pickford. New York: Columbia University Press, 1998.

————. *Aesthetic Theory.* Translated by Robert Hullot-Kentor. Minneapolis: University of Minnesota Press, 1997.

————. *The Stars Down to Earth.* London: Routledge, 1994.

————. "Freudian Theory and the Pattern of Fascist Propaganda." In *The Essential Frankfurt School Reader,* edited by Andrew Arato and Eike Gebhardt. Oxford: Blackwell, 1978, 118–127.

————. *Minima Moralia: Reflections from a Damaged Life.* Translated by Edmund Jephcott. New York: Continuum, 1974.

————. *Negative Dialectics.* Translated by E. B. Ashton. New York: Continuum, 1973a.

————. *The Jargon of Authenticity.* Translated by Knut Tarnowski and Frederic Will. London: Routledge, 1973b.

————. "Cultural Criticism and Society." In *Prisms.* Translated by Samuel and Shierry Weber. Cambridge, Mass.: MIT Press, 1981, 17–34.

Adorno, Theodor W., Else Frenkel-Brunswik, Daniel J. Levinson, and R. Nevitt Sanford. *The Authoritarian Personality.* New York: Harper, 1950.

Adorno, Theodor W., et al. *Der Positivismusstreit in der deutschen Soziologie.* Frankfurt: Luchterhand, 1972.

Albrecht, Clemens, et al. *Die intellektuelle Gründung der Bundesrepublik: Eine Wirkungsgeschichte der Frankfurter Schule.* Frankfurt: Campus, 1999.

Améry, Jean. *At the Mind's Limits.* Translated by Sidney and Stella P. Rosenfeld. New York: Schocken, 1986.

Arendt, Hannah. "The Aftermath of Nazi Rule: Report from Germany." *Commentary* 10 (1950): 342–353.

Benjamin, Walter. "The Storyteller: Reflections on the Works of Nikolai Leskov." In *Illuminations,* edited by Hannah Arendt and translated by Harry Zohn. New York: Schocken, 1969, 83–110.

Bergmann, Werner. *Antisemitismus in Öffentlichen Konflikten: Kollektives Lernen in der politischen Kultur der Bundesrepublik 1949–1989.* Frankfurt: Campus, 1997.

Bogart, Leo. "The Pollster and the Nazis." *Commentary* 92:2 (1991): 47–50.

Brickner, Richard M. "Germany after the War—Roundtable 1945." *American Journal of Orthopsychiatry* 11 (1945): 381–441.

————. *Is Germany Incurable?* Philadelphia: Lippincott, 1943.

Christie, Richard, and Marie Jahoda. *Studies in the Scope and Method of "The Authoritarian Personality."* Glencoe, Ill.: Free Press, 1954.

Claussen, Detlev. *Theodor W. Adorno: One Last Genius.* Translated by Rodney Livingstone. Cambridge, Mass.: Harvard University Press, 2008.

———. "In the House of the Hangman." In *Germans and Jews since the Holocaust: The Changing Situation in West Germany,* edited by Anson Rabinbach and Jack Zipes. New York: Holmes and Maier, 1986, 50–64.

Cohen, Stanley. *States of Denial: Knowing about Atrocities and Suffering.* Cambridge: Polity, 2001.

Connerton, Paul, ed. *Critical Sociology: Selected Readings.* New York: Penguin, 1976.

Dahrendorf, Ralf. *Über Grenzen: Lebenserinnerungen.* Munich: C. H. Beck, 2002.

Demirovic, Alex. *Der nonkonformistische Intellektuelle: Die Entwicklung der kritischen Theorie zur Frankfurter Schule.* Frankfurt: Suhrkamp, 1999.

Dirks, Walter. "Der restaurative Charakter der Epoche." *Frankfurter Hefte* 9 (1950): 942–955.

Foschepoth, Josef. *Im Schatten der Vergangenheit: Die Anfänge der Gesellschaften für Christlich-Jüdische Zusammenarbeit.* Göttingen: Vandenhoeck und Ruprecht, 1993.

Gerhardt, Ute. *Talcott Parsons: An Intellectual Biography.* Cambridge: Cambridge University Press, 2002.

Giordano, Ralph. *Die zweite Schuld oder von der Last ein Deutscher zu sein.* Munich: Knauer, 1987.

Habermas, Jürgen. *The New Conservatism: Cultural Criticism and the Historians' Dispute.* Translated by Shierry Weber Nicholsen. Cambridge, Mass.: MIT Press, 1989.

Hartman, Geoffrey, ed. *Bitburg in Moral and Political Perspective.* Bloomington: Indiana University Press, 1986.

Herbst, Susan. *Reading Public Opinion: How Political Actors View the Democratic Process.* Chicago: University of Chicago Press, 1998.

Herz, John. "The Fiasco of Denazification in Germany." *Political Science Quarterly* 63 (1948): 569–595.

Hohendahl, Peter Uwe. *Prismatic Thought: Theodor W. Adorno.* Lincoln: University of Nebraska Press, 1995.

Horkheimer, Max, and Theodor Adorno. *Dialectic of Enlightenment* (1944). Translated by John Cumming. New York: Continuum, 1972.

Jäger, Lorenz. *Adorno: A Political Biography.* Translated by Stewart Spencer. New Haven: Yale University Press, 2004.

Jaspers, Karl. *The Question of German Guilt.* Translated by E. B. Ashton. New York: Fordham University Press, 2000.

———. *Schiksal und Wille: Autobiographische Schriften.* Munich: Piper, 1967.

Jay, Martin. "The Frankfurt School's Critique of Marxist Humanism." In *Permanent Exiles: Essays on the Intellectual Migration from Germany to America.* New York: Columbia University Press, 1985, 14–27.

Jenemann, David. *Adorno in America.* Minneapolis: University of Minnesota Press, 2007.

Jung, Carl G. *The Psychology of Nazism: Essays on Contemporary Events.* Translated by R. F. C. Hull. Princeton: Princeton University Press, 1989.

Kästner, Erich. *Splitter und Balken: Publizistik.* Munich: Carl Hanser, 1998.

Kohler, Lotte, ed. *Hannah Arendt–Karl Jaspers: Correspondence 1926–1969.* New York: Harcourt Brace, 1992.

König, René. *Soziologie in Deutschland: Begründer/Veränder/Verfecther.* Munich: Carl Hanser, 1987.

Kritz, Neil J., ed. *Transitional Justice: How Emerging Democracies Reckon with Former Regimes.* Washington, D.C.: United States Institute of Peace, 1995.

Lazarsfeld, Paul. "An Episode in the History of Social Research: A Memoir." In *The European Migration,* edited by Donald Fleming and Bernard Bailyn. Cambridge, Mass.: Harvard University Press, 1969, 270–337.

Maier, Charles S. *The Unmasterable Past: History, Holocaust, and German National Identity.* Cambridge, Mass.: Harvard University Press, 1988.

Martin, John Levi. "*The Authoritarian Personality* 50 Years Later: What Questions Are There for Political Psychology?" in *Political Psychology* 22:1 (2001): 1–26.

Meinecke, Friedrich. *The German Catastrophe: Reflections and Recollections.* Translated by Sidney Fay. Boston: Beacon, 1950.

Merritt, Anna J., and Richard L. Merritt, eds. *Public Opinion in Semisovereign Germany: The HICOG Surveys, 1949–1955.* Urbana: University of Illinois Press, 1980.

———. *Public Opinion in Occupied Germany: The OMGUS Surveys, 1945–1949.* Urbana: University of Illinois Press, 1970.

Merritt, Richard L. *Democracy Imposed: U.S. Occupation Policy and the German Public, 1945–1949.* New Haven: Yale University Press, 1995.

Mills, C. Wright. *The Politics of Truth: Selected Writings of C. Wright Mills.* Edited by John H. Summers. New York: Oxford University Press, 2008.

Mitscherlich, Alexander, and Fred Mielke. *Doctors of Infamy: The Story of the Nazi Medical Crimes.* New York: H. Schuman, 1949.

Mitscherlich, Alexander, and Margarete Mitscherlich. *The Inability to Mourn: Principles of Collective Behavior.* Translated by Beverly R. Placzek. New York: Grove, 1975.

Moeller, Robert G. *War Stories: The Search for a Usable Past in the Federal Republic of Germany.* Berkeley: University of California Press, 2001.

Mohler, Armin. *Der Nasenring: Die Vergangenheitsbewältigung vor und nach dem Fall der Mauer.* Munich: Langen Müller, 1991.

Moses, Dirk. *German Intellectuals and the Nazi Past.* Cambridge: Cambridge University Press, 2007.

Müller-Doohm, Stefan. *Adorno: A Biography.* Translated by Rodney Livingstone. Cambridge: Polity, 2005.

Noelle-Neumann, Elisabeth. *The Spiral of Silence: Public Opinion—Our Social Skin.* Chicago: University of Chicago Press, 1984.

Nolte, Ernst. "Die Vergangenheit, die nicht vergehen will." *Frankfurter Allgemeine Zeitung,* June 6, 1986.

Olick, Jeffrey K. *In the House of the Hangman: The Agonies of German Defeat, 1943–1949.* Chicago: University of Chicago Press, 2005.

———. "What Does It Mean to Normalize the Past? Official Memory in German Politics since 1989." In *States of Memory: Continuities, Conflicts, and*

Transformations in National Retrospection. Durham, N.C.: Duke University Press, 2003, 259–288.

Perrin, Andrew J., and Lars Jarkko. Translators' introduction to Theodor W. Adorno, "Opinion Research and Publicness." *Sociological Theory* 23:1 (March 2005): 116–123.

Plessner, Monika. "Miteinander Reden heißt miteinander träumen: Gruppenstudie mit Horkheimer." *Frankfurter Allgemeine Zeitung,* September 28, 1991.

Pollock, Friedrich. "Empirical Research into Public Opinion." In *Critical Sociology: Selected Readings,* edited by Paul Connerton. New York: Penguin, 1976, 24–49.

———, ed. *Gruppenexperiment: Ein Studienbericht.* Frankfurt: Europäische Verlagsanstalt, 1955.

Schwartz, Thomas. *America's Germany: John J. McCloy and the Federal Republic of Germany.* Cambridge, Mass.: Harvard University Press, 1991.

Schwarz, Hans-Peter, ed. *Konrad Adenauer: Reden 1917–1967.* Stuttgart: Deutsche Verlags-Anstalt, 1975.

Shils, Edward A. "Authoritarianism: 'Right' and 'Left.'" in *Studies in the Scope and Method of "The Authoritarian Personality,"* edited by Richard Christie and Marie Jahoda. Glencoe, Ill.: Free Press, 1954, 24–49.

Stahl, Walter, ed. *Education for Democracy in West Germany: Achievements— Shortcomings—Prospects.* New York: Praeger, 1961.

Stern, Frank. *The Whitewashing of the Yellow Badge: Antisemitism and Philosemitism in Postwar Germany.* Translated by William Templer. Oxford: Pergamon Press, 1992.

Weber, Alfred. *Farewell to European History or The Conquest of Nihilism.* Translated by R. F. C. Hull. London: Kegan Paul, 1947.

Wiggershaus, Rolf. *The Frankfurt School: Its History, Theories, and Political Significance.* Translated by Michael Robertson. Cambridge, Mass.: MIT Press, 1995.

Notes

1. The term "Frankfurt School," which refers to the approaches of those associated with the Institute for Social Research in Frankfurt (and, during the Second World War, in American exile), did not come into general use until the mid-1950s.

2. While Adorno contributed much to the rest of the volume (and others contributed to his essay), this is the only portion of *Gruppenexperiment* fully attributable to him.

3. A related piece was his 1966 radio lecture and essay "Education after Auschwitz" (Adorno 2003).

4. Perhaps the most famous statement of this argument was an essay by Walter Dirks (1950) on "the restorative character of the epoch." Dirks, a Catholic writer and editor of the *Frankfurter Hefte,* one of the most influential journals of the postwar period, was heavily involved in founding the Christian Democratic Union, which he hoped would fuse Christianity with socialism; Adenauer's rather different

intentions for the party clearly prevailed. Between 1953 and 1956, Dirks was a close associate of Adorno at the reconstructed Institute for Social Research in Frankfurt, where he was coeditor of the series Frankfurter Beiträge zur Soziologie (Frankfurt contributions to sociology), in which *Gruppenexperiment* was published.

5. The volume's editor, literary critic Geoffrey Hartman, was mistaken when he claimed it was being published there for the first time in English.

6. In his edition of *Critical Models,* editor Henry Pickford does provide extensive footnotes explaining this and other references. These are, nevertheless, clues rather than the complete dossier.

7. A minor exception is the essay "Empirical Research into Public Opinion," an English version of pp. 15–32 of *Gruppenexperiment,* which was published by Pollock in a critical theory reader (Connerton 1976).

8. As Adorno wrote in *Minima Moralia* (Adorno 1974: 58), "If such a thing as a psycho-analysis of today's prototypical culture were possible; if the absolute predominance of the economy did not beggar all attempts at explaining conditions by the psychic life of their victims; and if the psychoanalysts had not long since sworn allegiance to those conditions—such an investigation would needs show the sickness proper to the time to consist precisely in normality."

9. In contrast, Peter Hohendahl (1995: 52) maintains that "Adorno in particular, while stressing the importance of social and economic elements, remained committed to a psychological approach to the analysis of National Socialism and anti-Semitism." While this may seem at odds with the argument we are presenting, the crux of the issue is in exactly what the object of Adorno's psychoanalytic approach constituted: the individual psyche or the collective ethos "over their heads."

10. In this regard, Adorno's approach had superficial (though only superficial) similarities to that of the psychoanalyst Carl Jung, whose 1945 accusation of a German collective guilt met with enormous hostility when he made it, though to be sure Adorno refers to Jung's thesis of a collective neurosis as "bombastic" *(hochtrabend)* in the text below. When his collective guilt thesis was attacked as unfair and overblown (to say nothing of hypocritical, given Jung's early Nazi sympathies), Jung warned that "naturally no reasonable and conscientious person will lightly turn collective guilt into individual guilt by holding the individual responsible without having given him a hearing." More generally, Jung argued that "since no man lives within his own psychic sphere like a snail in its shell, separated from everybody else, but is connected with his fellow-men by his unconscious humanity, no crime can ever be what it appears to our consciousness to be: an isolated psychic happening." See Olick (2005: 192–202).

11. In a similar manner, Walter Benjamin (1969) bemoaned the triumph of information over wisdom in his essay "The Storyteller."

12. Referring to his notorious statement, written just before his return to Germany (Adorno 1973: 34), that "to write poetry after Auschwitz is barbaric," Adorno wrote toward the end of his 1966 *Negative Dialectics* that "it may have been wrong to say that after Auschwitz you could no longer write poems. But it is not wrong to raise the less cultural question whether after Auschwitz you can go on living" (1973a: 362–363).

13. Again, one of the most famous immediate interpretations of National Socialism that appeared just following the end of the war was Friedrich Meinecke's work *The German Catastrophe* (Meinecke 1950).

14. There are, obviously, some complexities in referring to all those named here as American social scientists.

15. These authors, of course, have not been the only ones with these concerns, as an extensive methodological literature on public opinion research shows. See Herbst (1998).

16. The cynical view is that Horkheimer needed the Institute to appear to be a reliable enterprise involved in the reconstruction of intellectual and scientific life so as to secure future funding. He had apparently learned well the role of the institute director from Paul Lazarsfeld, whose Bureau of Applied Social Research in New York provided one model of how to maintain such an enterprise by serving commercial and political interests, though Lazarsfeld's approach was much disdained by the critical theorists.

17. Much in the style of Adorno's "Aufarbeitung," Mitscherlich made a popular breakthrough with his 1967 book (written with his wife, Margarete Mitscherlich) *The Inability to Mourn* (Mitscherlich and Mitscherlich 1975); but twenty years earlier, he was a much-avoided figure (even Horkheimer declined to give him a position at the Institute, instead sending him to California to work at the Hacker Foundation, where Adorno wrote his astrology study).

18. To be sure, Adorno and Horkheimer were both highly critical of Jaspers's existential philosophy. Jaspers did not think much of Adorno either. In a 1966 letter to Hannah Arendt, he wrote of Adorno: "It seems that Adorno is becoming an authority in the Federal Republic, highly respected. What a fraud. In what I have read of him, I find nothing worthy of serious consideration" (Kohler 1992: 638).

19. Adorno also took on what he saw as the apologetic qualities of Heidegger's postwar writings, particularly in Heidegger's famous "Letter on Humanism," in his book *The Jargon of Authenticity* (Adorno 1973b).

20. That is not to say *The Authoritarian Personality* was not also positively received, most notably by C. Wright Mills (Mills 2008: 84). In 1954, Mills wrote that *The Authoritarian Personality,* "although not well organized and subject to quite damaging criticisms of method, still remains of outstanding importance," characterizing it overall as "perhaps the most influential book of the last decade."

21. Wiggershaus (1995) documents König's generally collegial attitude toward the Institute at the time, but König's attitude seems to have hardened later on. In his 1987 book *Soziologie in Deutschland,* König refers several times to Adorno and the Frankfurt School, and nearly always in negative, even dismissive, tones, as ideological neo-Marxists content with pseudotheory in place of science. Interestingly, *Soziologie in Deutschland* does not refer to *Gruppenexperiment* at all.

22. The question of silence and nonresponse in such work on public opinion, it is important to note, was the subject of a famous book, *The Spiral of Silence,* by the German public opinion researcher Elisabeth Noelle-Neumann (1984). Nevertheless, Noelle-Neumann's own past (which included propagandistic journalism during the Third Reich) did not go unquestioned, nor did her theory of tacit consent (Bogart 1991).

23. For a survey of the range of immediate responses, see Demirovic (1999: 362–363).

24. Améry (1986) indicates in his "Resentments" a familiarity with Adorno's thought; Adorno, for his part, commented appreciatively in his 1965 lectures on metaphysics on an essay by Améry on torture.

25. Hofstätter died in 1994; Hohendahl's book was first published in 1995, though most of it was based on essays published in the early 1990s.

26. The most extensive analysis of the Hofstätter affair we have found is in Bergmann (1997: 283–290), and our account draws on it heavily.

27. Among Jäger's problematic claims is that "it is beyond doubt that the famine suffered by the Germans in the immediate post-war period was the result of a deliberate policy" (Jäger 2004: 158). This claim is hardly supported by a historiographical consensus, certainly not in this straightforward a manner.

Part Two

GUILT AND DEFENSE

THEODOR W. ADORNO

Final Version of the Basic Stimulus
(Colburn Letter)

I WAS associated with several offices of the occupation army in Germany from the end of the war, in which I participated as reservist, through August 1950.*

Most of my assistants were Germans, from the most diverse regions and with the most diverse views. Beyond that, my work brought me together with Germans of all kinds. I believe that, to the extent that one can speak of such things, I got to know average Germans and their opinions first-hand, and especially how ordinary people feel.

Superficial observers say and write a lot of nonsense about Germany. Some think they are all Nazis and bear guilt collectively; others see things as rosy because, as victors, they are in a privileged position and generalize too quickly from their own pleasant experience. Perhaps your readers will be interested in the opinion of a sober GI who is not vengeful, but who also doesn't let anyone pull the wool over his eyes.

I can say many good things about the Germans. They are hardworking

---

*As we described in the introduction, all the discourse analyzed in *Group Experiment* arose in the course of focused group discussions in which some version of the so-called basic stimulus—the Colburn letter—was presented to the participants. As Adorno notes, the putative author of this fictional letter was, in most groups, an American soldier, Sergeant Colburn; when the groups took place in areas that had been controlled by the British, the author's identity was adjusted accordingly. The text we have translated here was included as an appendix to *Group Experiment* under the title "Final Version of the Basic Stimulus."

and only rarely insubordinate. They are clean and orderly, and many give the impression of being intelligent. Of course, I do not know to what extent they are independent or just repeat what they have heard elsewhere. I do not find any indication of unusual crudeness and cruelty, but nor are there many indications that they have taken to heart what was done to people under Hitler. Of course they themselves had to go through so many things—air raids in particular—that it is difficult for them to consider other people's suffering.

Individual Germans seem rather good-natured. Married men are kind to their families and hope to succeed. I think the Germans, who were used to a high standard of living, will pull themselves up again economically. Their splendid technical talent will only really prove itself once they are able to work without restriction.

To me and to most of my acquaintances they are generally friendly—especially the women—naturally also because they think all of us are wealthy.

But this is not the whole story. Despite the past calamity, many think of themselves as better and more capable than us. They do not want to hear anything of the fact that Hitler started it.

They apparently have the feeling that the world did the greatest injustice to them. Whenever something goes badly with us, they become indignant. When we are in a difficult situation, as in Korea, one sometimes gets the impression that they are secretly glad about it and do not think about the fact that we alone protect them from the Russians. Admitting the mistakes of one's own country and talking openly about them appears to be a weakness to them. They are still hostile toward the Jews and use the DPs [displaced persons] in particular as a pretense for one-sided judgments.

Only very few openly admit that they were Nazis, and those admitting it are often not the worst ones. Only a small minority is said to be guilty. In a certain way this is true but in general one finds only very few Germans who unambiguously renounce what happened.

They act especially strangely when there is talk about racial persecution in America. As soon as they hear that a Negro was lynched in the South, they rub their hands together [as if relishing the inconvenient parallel]. I always explain to them that in our case it is a matter of ten or twenty cases a year, while with them it was a matter of millions. In the end, for us lynching is and remains a crime prosecuted by the state. Their state, however, *managed* lynching itself on a vastly greater scale. Certainly they were subject to terror and could have done little more once Hitler was in control. But did they not celebrate him time and again? I was able to convince individuals of all of this, but this is like a drop in the bucket. The risk is that, tomorrow, they will again follow a Hitler or Stalin, and will still believe that such a strong man will represent their interests best.

Whoever is really interested in international understanding must pay attention to what practical democracy actually means and must engage in the long work required to bring it about. One cannot simply plug something else into the space left by dictatorship. Rather, one has to have just as much understanding for others as for oneself.

Only when the Germans accept this spirit will they really be able to make a big contribution.

Preface

THE REASON we devoted so much of our evaluative work to the qualitative analysis is stated in the introduction.* Had we not done so, our report would have lost the richness and substantiality of the material produced by our group experiment. Even the qualitative analysis, despite all the evidence presented, provides only a quite fragmentary impression of this richness. In fact, we had intended to add literal transcripts of some of the typical discussions as an appendix to the publication. Only space constraints prevented us from doing so. Given the current state of the evaluative methods, the real persuasiveness of the qualitative results, their solidity, is conveyed only through knowledge of the primary material: only the living experience of continuous discussions lessens the appearance of arbitrariness that clings to the interpretation of evidence taken as isolated pieces outside their structural context.

It is hardly necessary to note explicitly that we are more than familiar with objections to qualitative analysis, from orthodox American social research. They can be found in Dorwin P. Cartwright: Analysis of Qualitative Material, in Leon Festinger and Daniel Katz (eds.), Research Methods in the Behavioral Sciences, p. 434 ff. The main focus of those objections is the

---

*The full text of the Introduction to *Gruppenexperiment* will appear in the companion volume, *Group Experiment: The Frankfurt School on Public Opinion in Postwar Germany* (Harvard University Press, forthcoming).

argument that qualitative analyses may indeed be correct, but remain merely "expert opinions" unless the analyst can explain step by step to others how he gained his insights. We do not share the assumption underlying this reasoning, namely that every skilled scholar in the social sciences has to be interchangeable with every other one, that everyone should, so to speak, confirm everyone else; this ignores the fact that the subjective conditions for social knowledge are far more differentiated and depend on sedimented knowledge and theoretical insight more than in scientific experiment, which is the tacitly acknowledged standard. The demand for interchangeability in sociology tacitly assumes an identity of minds, and this dooms knowledge to sterility.

Nothing, however, is further from our intentions than wishing to derive a kind of sociological esotericism from this. We do not wish to restrict social insight to the kind of intuition most often imagined by those who think everything other than counting and measuring is an act of magic. For this reason, we not only burdened the qualitative analysis with more evidence than might be advantageous to the report. Rather, we also tried to draw out in every way possible the material on which the analysis is based, and to lay out the theoretical background at least as far as is necessary for understanding how we arrived at the reported interpretations.

The qualitative analyses were designed as monographic treatises. The form and dynamic of our discussants' attitudes toward the topics our research program deemed particularly relevant were examined. The extensive size of those monographs forced us to make choices: we had to be content with two complete texts. The selection caused problems. We could proceed neither systematically nor according to the significance of the investigated topics. The investigation of integration phenomena had to be limited, not simply because it refers to the total structure of the discussions but also because in the same way it provides the formal framework for the problem of conformism and of identification with the collectivity, which substantively were among the most important results.

We decided on the monograph "Guilt and Defense" because it allows us to make tangible that the group method triggers affect-laden utterances stemming from deeper layers of the respondents than the traditional interview method reaches. In addition, this study offers a kind of phenomenology of what the discussants themselves like so much to call the "German neurosis" and will which be cured only when, recognized by its structure, it has been raised to consciousness. This finding seems to us to be much more important than the often odd perspective that our participants expressed concerning the most delicate subjects and that would be misjudged in isolation if separated from their psychic dynamic. Exactly here we have to remind ourselves emphatically that the nature of qualitative analysis is to tease out types of attitudes and opinions, not their distribution. We do not ask, for example, how many people really think about the question of guilt "in a typically German way" but in which characteristic ways they try to master this complex, what role political ideology plays in the process, and how, in the other direction, political ideology is shaped by the requirements of this mastering. Above all, however, we wanted to make clear in the description of what was in the air: the ubiquitous basic stimulus to which every person living in Germany at that time was exposed.

Guilt and Defense

HERE WE give a qualitative analysis of our participants' reactions to the critical comments of the Colburn letter, which refer to concentration camps, terror, extermination of the Jews, [and] the war of aggression. It is clear that these topics are indeed sore spots because the form and content of many of the participants' objections prove exactly what they are objecting to.

More than in any other part of the investigation, this one has to highlight that, beyond its methodological tasks, our study aims primarily at tracing those transsubjective factors that characterize public opinion in the sense already discussed. When the sore spots of guilt are touched on, it becomes especially clear how many of the respondents avail themselves, almost mechanically, of a ready-made stock of arguments, such that their individual judgment seems to play only a secondary role: that of a principle of selection from within that stock.

The qualitative analysis of the material, which uses categories such as defense against a guilty feeling, aggressive projection, and the survival of National Socialist propaganda theses, can give rise to one-sided and unjustified impressions. Completely apart from the question of the extent to which the presented findings can be generalized, it is necessary above all to remember that precisely because the Colburn stimulus was targeted at sore spots, it might have called forth more pointed reactions than could readily be ascribed to the opinions of the participants in and of themselves; that these reactions, much more, were literally provoked. This can be answered in two ways. First of all, the idea of an "opinion in and of itself" is, as we have shown, problematic.[1] By no means do people necessarily hold the same opinion across different situations and most likely think and act differently when these change. The intention was to create conditions that one can assume correspond to the conditions prevalent in the process of forming political and ideological intentions. The goal was not to provide a definitive answer to the question of what the Germans still are or once were. Putting it like this would presuppose a consistent identity, an explicitness and a stability of meaning that hardly exists in present reality. One probably comes closest to the truth by characterizing how particular complexes are processed intellectually and psychologically and drawing conclusions on that basis about certain potentialities, rather than believing statistical reports in which opinion and attitude are themselves largely a function of the dominant power constellations.

In response to the criticism that we provoked our participants with the basic stimulus, we would like to say that it would fly in the face of all psychological theory and experience to assume that all utterances made in irritation are random and irrelevant. What an angry person says when he has lost rational control of his emotions is nonetheless a part of him. It is just as good an expression of his unconscious, latent and self-betraying [*ich-fremd*] psychological potentialities as is, on a less deep level, the supply of preconscious, current perspectives that he shares and that he can assert or reject as a fully conscious being through his own autonomous judgment.

Our study is largely interested in the investigation of this latter layer, of the transsubjective elements that already lie in the preconscious, in the latent dispositions. We abstained from actual depth-psychological interpretation, without rigorously cutting off psychoanalytical perspectives where they imposed themselves.

At any rate, the intermediate layer, which emerges in the investigation, deserves full attention, even if it reaches neither into the deep layer of the individual psyche nor on the other side into the responsible consciousness. At that level, there appears a kind of subjective social-psychological disposition that certainly is not fully in effect in present circumstances, whose current significance one also must not overestimate, but that could again gain unimagined power if it were once again connected to strong objective forces.

However, even those somewhat extreme reactions that we are going to discuss—we know that with these kinds of issues extreme opinions are articulated more explicitly and forcefully than moderate ones—should not be interpreted too primitively. In order to truly understand the guilt and defense complex, far subtler methods of close interpretation are required than it will generally be possible to employ here, where we will be addressing above all the immediately severe [*drastische*] frame of the ideology.

We can proceed from the assumption that we are actually dealing with something like a latent experience of guilt, and that this experience is being repressed and rationalized. Yet it must somehow burden the superegos of most of the study participants. The training in suppressing conscience, which was systematically managed with the greatest refinement, could ultimately nevertheless only succeed somewhat in the narrowest circles of the "practitioners of violence" [English], while the overwhelming portion of the German population was shaped by the moral imagination, however faded, of the liberal-bourgeois world, and still internalized a good piece of it.

The treatment of the defense mechanisms makes sense only under a condition that applies to almost all of the individual defensive arguments, and that must be stated emphatically once and for all. When one fends off guilt feelings and responsibility for what the Nazis did, that does not only mean that one wants to exculpate oneself but just as much that one did in fact regard what was done as unjust and for that reason refuses to accept responsibility. Were that not the case, the eagerness for dissociation would not be necessary.

Even when an apology is offered, it always also contains the implication that one regards as wrong whatever one is seeking to excuse and that one wants to have nothing to do with it. The idea of repressed guilt should not be taken too narrowly in a psychological sense: defense mechanisms are only brought into play insofar as the awareness of the injustice that was committed is conscious of it as an injustice. Of all those who participated in the experiment and found themselves on the defensive, none was prepared to assert: it was right that they were killed. Instead, it is most often a matter of trying to reconcile one's own excessive identification with the collective to which one belongs with the knowledge of the crime: one denies or minimizes this knowledge so that one does not lose the possibility of identifying with the collective, which is the only thing that psychologically allows countless people to overcome the unbearable feeling of their own powerlessness. One can conclude from this that those who find themselves on the defensive, even where they only adopted the rudiments of Nazi ideology, do not sympathize with a repetition of what happened. Defensiveness itself is a sign of the shock that they experienced, and in the process opens up a glimmer of hope.

Close at hand as well is the charge of a procedural circle between the method and the results. The Colburn letter was already constructed on the basis of the unmediated rather than organized experience of ideology. One could thus presume that exactly the ideology whose descriptive analysis is at issue was imposed on the participants by the experimental design, in that it introduced this ideology to them in the first place, and in this way the investigation is illegitimately producing its own result.

The material refutes this assumption. Wherever Colburn's characterization of the Germans is adopted, this happens reluctantly, exculpatorily, and with considerable modifications. The depth of the emotional centers that are stirred by the basic stimulus corresponds to primitive, infantile reactions resembling a child's joy at praise and instantaneous rejection of whatever looks to it like criticism. The basic structure of reactions to the letter is the more or less blind identification with the nation as collectivity, the We that is opposed to other reified collectivities like "the" American.

In the qualitative analysis, we again abstained from attempting anything like a counting-up of arguments, beyond what is contained in the quantitative section.* Not only would the numbers have turned out too small for the individual categories to be meaningful due to the necessarily extensive categorical differentiation, but the account would also be exposed to the dangers of being mechanical and fragmented.

In the following, we give a concise description of our procedure in executing this qualitative analysis. The basic discussion transcripts as well as the most important tape recordings are available for scientific examination in the archive of the Institute. We hope that both well-grounded criticism as well as additional studies will contribute to the further development of the methods applied here for the elucidation of numerous still open problems of interpretation and to the correction or confirmation of our findings.

In this chapter, mainly twenty-five discussion transcripts with 1,379 pages of text were used. They fall into two groups, one of twenty and one of five. The larger comprises those that contained the most statements on the complexes: joint responsibility for National Socialism and the war, joint responsibility for concentration camps and war atrocities, attitudes toward Jews, and attitudes toward DPs. Five additional transcripts were chosen from the entire pool without regard to the problematic of "Guilt and Defense." These are intended to represent those social groups that were least present in the other twenty and thereby to round out the picture somewhat. There was no difference whatsoever in processing the transcripts of the two groups.

The question might arise why only a fifth of the available transcripts

---

*Significant sections of the quantitative analysis are included in our companion volume, *Group Experiment*.

were used for the qualitative analysis of the problem of guilt and defense. The reason is solely that including all of the transcripts would have caused a prohibitive and substantively unjustified expenditure of work. The quantitative analysis of the complete transcripts allows us to check transcripts *not* included explicitly in the qualitative analysis at hand for significant deviation from those statements found in the selected sessions. Whenever that was—rarely—the case, it is taken into consideration in the analysis of the material. In general, however, these spot tests, too, have confirmed that the types of reaction portrayed in the text, and only those, occur repeatedly throughout the discussion material with a rigidity and monotony characteristic of the whole field of political ideology.

The principle according to which the transcripts, especially the first twenty, are assembled undoubtedly introduces a selection bias into the investigation. The quantitative part showed that there is a stronger disposition toward negative than toward positive statements throughout the discussions. According to this, one could expect the sessions in which topics concerning guilt and defense play a great role to be especially rich in negative statements with regard to that complex, and hence a lopsided picture of ideology to emerge. There are, however, numerous statements at hand from groups not analyzed here, but examined in monographs for completely different topics from guilt and defense, especially in the study on the group and the individual and in the linguistic study, and these show the same tendencies.

In all twenty-five transcripts, every passage referring to the subject matter of this study was read in its *context,* and the core of the statements, as well as occasionally ideas for their interpretation, were listed continuously in three files. The notes were then grouped according to the core theme of the statement and also according to particularly characteristic behavioral patterns.

In the first draft, the procedure was that those quotations most effectively illustrating the relevant category were selected; the division between prejudiced, ambivalent, and open-minded statements of participants, however, was by no means mechanically maintained. To be sure, the selection of particularly extreme quotations, in which a category emerges so to speak in its purest form, may give the outlines of the ideology a certain accent that is not quite fair to the attitudes, representing them all too crassly. Where negative statements are presented in what follows, however, it is overwhelmingly a matter of instances of continually recurring themes.

The very extensive first draft of the analysis was compared to the original material, repetitions were removed, additions made, and the whole shortened considerably.

Theoretically, self-restraint was practiced. This means that the interpretation remains entirely in the realm of the participants' subjectivity as it appears in their statements. The varying proportion of subjective and transsubjective factors in the individual contributions to the discussion, as well as the preponderance of one or the other within the different reaction types, we left undiscussed.

It was very far from our intention to investigate the problem of collective guilt, or even, in any sense whatsoever, to carry over an accusatory demeanor into empirical research.

What our qualitative analysis can bring to light are webs of meaning, ideological syndromes. Even if, for the sake of a simpler manner of speaking, we do not repeat each time that we want neither to generalize nor to say anything about the distribution of particular types of opinion, these qualifications apply. Nevertheless, it is possible to make certain conjectures—positive or negative—about whether particular attention should be paid to these in future research.

Thus, one might want to hypothesize and test systematically that social stratification makes itself less, or less consistently, significant for ideological patterns of behavior than one would expect theoretically.[2] While the hypothesis that the poorest groups are most inclined to self-reflection occasionally emerges from the qualitative analysis, this hypothesis is not corroborated by the quantitative findings. In contrast, the qualitative observation that women are more open-minded than men is also confirmed quantitatively. In this regard, it is important to consider that the female ego-ideal, which is still socially accepted and includes sympathy, kindness, charity, and tenderness, plays a role, especially in relation to the complex addressed here.

I. Knowledge of the Events

How the participants in our group discussion stood toward the question of guilt for the National Socialist system, guilt for the war that it unleashed, guilt for the misdeeds that it sponsored with the instruments of total organization, can only be assessed after clarifying the objective facts. Immediately, it would be important to find out whether and to what extent the examined groups knew about the worst deeds at the time they were committed. The answer is extraordinarily difficult. No doubt, the National Socialists tried to conceal the worst not only from foreign countries, but also from the domestic population, by placing the death factories in Poland and having the gassing executed by a small number of murder specialists; or rather, they tried not to let *more* leak out than a vague and panicked feeling of horror. Moreover, the horror itself has produced its own veil—precisely that which surpasses all comprehension could hardly be admitted by anyone, regardless of whether he stuck with the National Socialists or not; it is otherwise difficult to imagine how one could possibly have continued to exist in Germany. The instinctual tendency toward the denial of knowledge, as can similarly be observed for instance with terminally ill people, is certainly connected to the concealment, particularly in the case of those who identify least with the crimes and for whom complete knowledge would have been most unbearable. The more extreme the cruelties became with the help of special cruelty training for the perpetrators, the more improbable they appeared to the consciousness of those who still knew anything of concepts like legal security, humanity, and the inviolability of the person. Commands to stay silent and draconian threats for those who, for example, returned from camps, were more than was necessary.

On the other hand, it seems hardly thinkable, given the number of victims, that nothing whatsoever came to be known, at least during the last two years of the war. Everywhere, Jews disappeared under the cover of darkness; if, in the beginning, they wrote from Theresienstadt, for example, this soon stopped; many members of the Wehrmacht must have seen at least something of the task forces [*Einsatzkommandos*] that also operated outside of the hermetically sealed death camps; and, despite all the danger for those who said something, the pressure of knowing must have been so excruciating that there would have been enough on leave who found some relief in giving at least hints at home. From the beginning the National Socialist era, during which public information was controlled in a terrorist manner, propagated rumor as its tool, for which wars are a good climate in any case; thus, everybody would surely have heard something. But exactly the apocryphal character of what was heard, the uncertainty of horrifying reports that were partly distorted and partly unbelievable, in turn contributed to sweeping away the knowledge through a kind of censorship mechanism. Finally, it is almost impossible today to reconstruct the situation. Everything that back then could have either objectively impeded knowing or allowed it to be subjectively repressed is now used for self-exoneration. It would be presumptuous to decide what of the present claims about knowledge or ignorance is the truth, what comes from psychological compulsion, and where lying sets in.

1. Knowing Nothing about What Happened

While our study must in no way presume to answer the question of how much was known, or even who knew what, it offers enough material for a concrete picture of how Germans reflected their knowledge and ignorance in the winter of 1950/51.

The appeal to ignorance far exceeds the sphere of horror. A thirty-five-year-old lawyer, who participated in a session of self-employed merchants in northern Germany, emphasizes:

> *Sch.*: . . . tat [*sic*] in all of X, with very few exceptions, only the smallest number of people knew before May 1945 that there was a concentration camp in Y. And it's not so really so far from us.

The redundant expression "with very few exceptions, only the smallest number" shows a certain overeagerness, more so since the following sentence renders this ignorance improbable.

Similarly problematic claims of ignorance appear in a group discussion with dignitaries of a Bavarian village. This group is an extreme case, since the discussion came to threats against the assistant, so that the investigator had to fear a brawl. He openly asked the question, who of those present knew about the extermination and at what point in time. This resulted in interjections: "Nobody—nobody—probably heard."

Immediately after those interjections, a sixty-seven-year-old farmer says:

> *L.*: . . . probably heard about Dachau, but one never heard or suspected that people were being killed there.
> *G.*: my relatives—and here I believe I don't have to accuse my mother of lying—even though she lived perhaps five hundred meters from the concentration camp, knew nothing about the concentration camp.

It is difficult to believe that someone to whom rumors about Dachau leaked out knew nothing about what happened there.

Many of the participants unhesitatingly used the fact that, due to the conditions of the Third Reich, the atrocities became known only as rumors. Without authentication to imply that they had not known anything, drawing on the conventional assertion that rumors are unreliable, and in contradiction to the fact that in the Third Reich rumors were the only source of information that was independent of the official propaganda apparatus.

2. Knowing Nothing about What Happened at the Time

In a session with unemployed women, whose tenor was antifascist, the thesis of ignorance appears less starkly, i.e. reduced to the statement that one could not have foreseen that such things would happen. This thesis is much closer to the real conditions, especially when one takes into consideration that before the seizure of power the National Socialists officially emphasized their legality over and over again. They only implicitly let it be known to those who craved them what methods of violence were to be expected, while at the same time making it easy for the so-called fellow travelers [*Mitläufer*] to join the ranks without falling into moral conflict. The following statement is characteristic:

> X.: No, one did not yet really expect it, that it would assume those proportions. I have never paid attention to the Jewish Question, I have to say, I cannot fathom that it ultimately could develop so far. I really have to say that. All that actually only came out later. That was all really nothing for us, otherwise one would certainly not have voted for it.

One could reasonably attribute such statements, in contrast to the previous ones, to the open-minded type.

3. Not Wanting to Know about What Happened

Some open-minded participants state without further ado that they knew something, but they emphasize that people did not believe them. The persuasiveness of this statement cannot be denied easily. In a session comprising politically educated members of work councils, a social democrat and anti-Nazi says:

> F.: I was always an enemy of Nazism—I am a social democrat, and when I said some things I knew for certain, even the community of workers replied: No, this is impossible. They could not think that something like that existed. In my opinion, the bulk of the German people really had nothing to do with the vulgarities Hitler produced and didn't want to have anything to do with them.

This passage openly expresses that, in fact, the vast scale of the events itself became part of the veil that hid them and enabled the consciousness of countless people to dismiss the impossible.

The transition from insisting on ignorance to statements that indicate some knowledge seems to be influenced to no small degree by the group situation. In this process the behavior of the investigator sometimes plays a role, but apparently statements from participants who deny any knowledge at all sometimes do provoke resistance and lead in the opposite direction. Often the conflicts remain unresolved or are drowned in the chaos of discussion, in which, moreover, the responsibility for what has been said gets lost. In order to give a concrete example, a lengthy section of a discussion is quoted below. This section is characterized by the participants' passionate participation in the discussion, so that even changing the tape could not induce them to pause.

> L.: No one, . . . certainly nobody, and the German is supposed to have be-lieved that all the Jews were exterminated, we didn't believe that at all.
>
> J.: Only after the war they said: this one and that one died there and was beaten there.
>
> *Moderator* [hereafter Mod.]: You only learned that after the war? Could I pose a question in return? Now, you also had to deal with Jewish mer-chants, and you knew that suddenly they weren't here anymore. Didn't you think about that?
>
> G.: We certainly did think that their businesses had been taken from them, when overnight he didn't show up, one day . . .
>
> L.: We were told that, somehow, they were moved someplace, and there they had to work for themselves. Just like they go to Palestine today, one thought, they are somewhere in the big, wide world, in Hungary or some-where in Poland, right?
>
> G.: One somehow thought, they can't get a business license, why would he walk around when he doesn't have a business license?
>
> (incomprehensible multidirectional talk)
>
> But anyway, one said they are in concentration camps and have to work.
>
> *Mod.*: I also want to stick with that, gentlemen. Perhaps you could still speak out on that. So, one side asserts that you only learned something about the concentration camps basically in the last half year and probably also about the exterminations that had in fact been taking place.
>
> G.: No, I would have to lie . . . Well, of course the thing was about the Jews: if somebody was in Russia watching the game, then one only knew after-wards that the Jews had been assembled in camps and also what happened afterwards. Of course, one figured out all sorts of things, saw something for oneself. But this wasn't known to the people, the population, for those of us inside, nothing was known.
>
> T.: I was in Riga, at the collecting point for invalids, right. I had furlough there, right, and saw there how they were brought into the factories and were escorted back from the factories, and they had to work there. But not inside Germany. But I didn't know more. During the war, they had to work.
>
> G.: The population in Germany didn't know about that, nothing at all, that the Jews had to do that out there, that they had to work. But those on the spot, they really saw it.
>
> (Interruption: But seen with one's own eyes)

This section demonstrates the relationship between the situation of the group discussion and the admission of knowledge. At first, knowledge is denied, obviously with such threadbare arguments that, apparently, the par-ticipants themselves feel uncomfortable; after the moderator's intervention, however, the participants screw up their courage and unburden themselves through concrete references, which culminate in the expression "seen with one's own eyes." *What* has been seen with one's own eyes here remains, as in many other passages, unsaid. Apart from that, despite everything, ignorance is repeated obsessively.

4. Knew Something about What Happened

In no way does the complex situation always result in the general denial of knowledge being followed by qualifying accounts. Sometimes quite adequate reports occur. Some participants remember, for instance, the fact that, on the one hand, terror largely prevented the crimes from becoming generally known, but that, on the other hand, an atmosphere of horror spread throughout Germany. Wherever such memory emerges clearly, blind apologetics are foregone from the beginning, and the speakers can certainly be counted among the open-minded.

A statement in a group of police officers, in which democratic open-mindedness emerges, can be regarded as representative for the link between a clear awareness of what leaked out and unambiguous rejection of National Socialism:

> U.: Only a few people in Germany knew and only a few people know what happened in the concentration camps. But some things have . . . where I was sent, some things leaked through, and I saw different things, I had to see it and shook my head.

After a statement by the investigator, the group situation leads to a second participant's taking up the view of the previous speaker and relating it to the question of moral responsibility:

> B.: I think that all of us more or less did see something. But what we lacked was moral courage.

In one of the groups most inclined to open-mindedness—high school seniors from a philosophical discussion group, a sort of intellectual elite, that is—the investigator made the effort to determine the question of knowledge and ignorance through intense inquiry and even tried to generate a show of hands.

> Interruption: Take a poll! Count all those who are here and knew it, consciously, more or less . . .
> B.: Most saw something, like I watched the burning of the synagogue down there, but no one experienced it consciously.
> A.: I want to say that I was evacuated to A during the war, and I was quartered at a policeman's place there and could also listen to discussions that this policeman had with other people. One evening the word "Buchenwald" was dropped, and he said that drivers enter the camp with bread and that

all of them were obliged to say nothing about it, and if they revealed something, they'd be punished. This was the only thing I heard about the gassing.

Mod.: I ask for a particular reason. Germans often say: We knew nothing about all those stories. May I ask who actually perceived something about the Jews being killed, about gassing, concentration camps, etc. Who heard something, or didn't?

(Interruptions: Poll! Count!)

Mod.: Yes, that is one, two, three, four, so four gentlemen, who knew something about it beforehand.

H.: I believe that many of our parents knew something, and since we were all in the German Youth *(Jungvolk)* and were children we could have let something slip, so they didn't tell us anything because they were afraid of losing their heads.

F.: My father at least knew something, but never said anything, because, as he points out now, he wasn't allowed to and it would be too dreadful to talk about.

Mod.: The young people again!

U.: It was at least known that the Warsaw Ghetto existed and . . .

Mod.: That's something different.

O.: I saw the central market hall, where thousands of Jews were brought to be carried away to Poland.

(Interruption: We saw the trains to Poland and even Jew-transports that went to Auschwitz.)

Mod.: Did you know that?

(Interruption: That's been said.)

Mod.: Did you know that Jews were deported on a large scale, but not know that they were thereby murdered? One, two, three, four, five, so five gentlemen didn't know anything about the deportation of the Jews. Regardless of whether they were killed there or not . . .

(Interruption: Order, please! Has the number of those present been determined yet?)

(Interruption: Yes, twenty-one!)

Mod.: Who *didn't* know about the concentration camps? Even if only vaguely. Indeed relatively few who didn't know anything about Dachau and concentration camps, etc.: one, two, three, four, five, six!—A good many!—Mr. U.?

U.: I believe I was aware of some details. An acquaintance of ours was a doctor and his wife was Jewish. My father often spoke with them, and he said pretty clearly, even back then, he insinuated to us, as far as possible, after his wife disappeared, that he would never see her again, and he pointed out that none of the Jews who disappeared would get away with his life. I think this was pretty clear.

N.: I still have a certain memory. Once a man was assigned to us and employed as a worker in our company. He had been released from a concentration camp. Upon his release, he was sworn not to say a word. The man was so frightened even to be asked about it, and if even a hint was dropped, he scurried off. His fear indicated that it must have been quite bad.

Apart from the apparent connection between non–National Socialistic attitudes and admission of knowledge, this passage is illuminating in many ways. It starts again with the denial of guilt, but such that the denial already contains the admission—a speaker postulates that most people saw something, but that nobody experienced it consciously. After the word "gassing" was dropped, the participants loosened their tongues. One of them makes a final effort to deny knowledge by shifting it to his parents, who had told him nothing about it—in tune with the understandable attempt of young participants to cite their youth as an alibi. Thereafter, specific knowledge is admitted unreservedly.

5. Response to What Happened

While it is impossible to determine how much truly was known at the time of the terrorist deeds, nobody can claim today that he, right now, does not know what happened. Every detailed treatment of responses to the events and their motivations, therefore, has to discuss whether and to what extent our participants concede or deny the facts. There is hardly doubt that this results in a sharp demarcation between unreformed and open-minded people. To start with, there are those who simply deny the events or declare them exaggerated. They again are capable of rationalizing their behavior in diverse ways. That nobody was there, that no witnesses are to be found—because almost everybody who could testify was murdered, and the eyewitnesses in the Nazi-sphere who survive have every reason to conceal that they were there—is turned into a legal principle for not acknowledging the facts due to the lack of primary evidence. By the way, it is possible to observe in the case of persons with a paranoid disposition that, when confronted with unimpeachable proof during the discussion, they defend their unresponsiveness with an unexpected "How do you know?" Since it is hardly ever possible to offer primary evidence for everything one knows and has reason to accept as true, psychotic characters thus have a certain chance to question the source of knowledge, to exonerate themselves to themselves and, moreover, to impress others.

6. Denial of Knowledge versus Acknowledgment of What Happened

One of the few groups in which blunt differences were truly debated came to an actual discussion of the authenticity of the atrocities. Here, a speaker polemicizes against the reality of the crimes by using scientific phraseology, whereby the visible DPs are counted as substitute for the victims, whom nobody sees anymore:

> M.: If one does a statistical inventory of those people who were in concentration camps or who died there, respectively, and those who run around in Germany today for all intents and purposes posing as displaced persons, it is safe to say that the number has doubled.

Doubling and halving of numbers belong to the basic toolkit of defensiveness. In the following, an open-minded participant argues against this:

> L.: Besides, you doubt, Mr. M., that the number of people murdered in concentration camps actually climbs so high into the unimaginable. I want to ask you then, whether you perhaps do not know that here, from the former *Reichsbank* in . . . , the gold fillings of the murdered were hauled out by the case, not only a few, but countless cases, out of the cellar of the *Reichsbank* here in . . . And considering these cases, it is really possible for one to say— one can indeed get a picture of how many people these alone might have been just by themselves. You said you got to know Auschwitz. Yet, you only suggested this and, furthermore, referred to a talk with a woman whose daughter is supposed to have been in a concentration camp.—Here I want to point out that there were different ranks among the concentration camps (interruption: recovery homes [*Erholungsheime*]). You have to distinguish between normal concentration camps for Germans, concentration camps for undesirable foreigners, and so called extermination camps, where Russians, Poles, and Jews came in.

The first speaker answers not unskillfully in the characteristic "How do you know?" style:

> M.: If I can finally pose a counter-question to the question you've addressed to me: How do allegedly sealed cases with concentration camp . . . come into the *Reichsbank* in . . . , which you cited . . . well, see, let's assume, how do they come into the *Reichsbank*? And when were these cases hauled out, surely by the Americans, right? And this I would like to have clarified by the Americans to begin with, that there were gassed concentration camp detainees inside the cases, which were supposedly sealed, and so on. (Jocularity). That the Americans will have to certify for me, and in written form!

The laughter following the joke about the sealed cases, in which gassed concentration camp detainees were supposed to be found, shows unmistakably how the unconscious of some groups reacts to the events. That in the Third Reich reification was carried so far as to literally "process" humans into things is perceived in terms of that kind of humor that crops up wherever life is treated as death, and such humor spills over into agreement with the murder.

The humanitarian-minded speaker strikes back, but the insane truth he stands up for has a harder furrow to plow than the clever common sense denying it.

> L.: After 1945 every German had a chance to get a picture of it and to see for himself what the methods were by inspecting the concentration camps themselves if he wanted to . . . And I don't know whether you've seen the concentration camp movie *Todesmühlen* [Death mills] (interruption: yes, indeed!), apparently not. I, in any case, have seen it, I also haven't seen the actual cases, but in pictures, etc. But I have also read parts of the Nuremberg transcripts, and you can consult these yourself. They are open for inspection at the American library, it's about forty volumes; everything is laid out with legal precision, the testimony of the Nuremberg convicts, etc. You can inform yourselves of it in detail with authentic material. Close to Auschwitz, I myself saw that concentration camp detainees were murdered, gassed. I frequently flew over the place, I saw the smokestacks smoking and saw the detainees beforehand as they enlarged the runway at our airport. And when they were exhausted, then they were shoved off and pumped into the sky as tiny clouds of smoke. I wonder how these obvious facts still aren't believed today.

After that his opponent advances the objection that, according to the rules of procedure, the discussion is "getting sidetracked too much" and then devotes himself to a positivistic engagement with facts that combines the abstruse and the plausible. His statement as well as the answer to it are quoted.

> M.: I just want to quickly reply to the points at issue right now, in fact, namely I want to proceed from the fact that, as the victor, one can always conjure up convincing evidence. And that one—as you said, who has flown over Auschwitz and allegedly has seen those who built the runway, floating into the sky as tiny clouds of smoke (interruption: Very good. Knocking on the table). How can you actually see that from the air, as an aviator? Firstly, you weren't inside, right? Secondly, one can, of course, make speculations from the air, but one has to prove them in all respects, to begin with. And when I appeal to the Nuremberg court today, I'm presented with files, signed by . . . by names Müller or something, accusations signed, which in no way correspond to the facts. And if I gave 500 Marks for a signature today, I'd like to see someone who wouldn't sign.
>
> L.: I just notice that Mr. M. doubts everything the Allies discovered in German concentration camps, that, moreover, he doubts the testimony of the Nuremberg convicts and, for that reason, questions everything, doesn't he? Probably he even questions whether we started the war in 1939—(M.: Indeed, I would question that anytime!)—and you question that we invaded Poland?

7. Denial of What Happened

In an extremely National Socialistic group of dignitaries from a Bavarian village, it is simply denied that Jews were murdered:

> H.: But those whom we knew before, they are all running around together now.

The supposedly high number of DPs turns into a pretense for acting as if nothing had happened to the Jews. In a group of men from a barracks whose participants possess certain trade union training, we find the statement of a former concentration camp detainee who simply denies the atrocities:

> H.: Earlier we spoke there about concentration camps. I was in Buchenwald, a year and a half, let's say fifteen months. I myself cannot even confirm that atrocities were committed there.
> (Interruption: That's what I wanted to know!)
> H.: Do you know why? Because there were three classes—green ribbons, blue ribbons, and red ribbons. Green ribbons were political, like I had a green ribbon, blue ribbons were possible deserters, and red ribbons were general convicts. I have to say this one thing, the political detainees were treated flawlessly, then there were the general convicts, and they were no longer worth anything. What was inside, anyway?: rapes of women, rapes of children, sexual assault, sadists and all the perversities. As far as I'm concerned, they really could have driven them through the chimney by the millions.

This participant demonstrates Bruno Bettelheim's account of the psychic changes concentration camp detainees go through after about a year— many only survive the extreme situation by identifying with their tormentors, and, in the case of this participant, this identification seems still to dominate today.[1] Cases in point are his moral agreement with the bad treatment of criminals, the pedantic-administrative enumeration of the different prisoner categories, and especially the indescribable barbarism of the expression "drive through the chimney," which, by the way, reverberates with other speakers. That in this way even actual eyewitnesses contribute their part to strengthening the veil has something unnerving about it. The posture of the expert encroaches onto the victim. The former prisoner is retrospectively happy about the tight discipline:

> H.: As I've already stressed, there were exactly three classes, three classes were there. There were real differences. About the third class, I don't know how they were treated, nor about the second class. About the first class, where I was, when we speak about the systems—there was the Prussian system, the drill. Getting out early at five, exercise. Whether it was raining or snowing,

all the same. Exercise, bathing, washing—or bathing, when it was bathing time, cleaning, combing, going to the barber, whether one had lice, or whether one didn't have lice, cutting hair, shaving. Then we went to the workplace . . . There were pigs, anyway. There are pigs here. There were pigs, there were also pigs there. There were. It also once happened that someone wanted to break out, the guard who was responsible for that— was killed. Naturally! If I had been a guard, I would have knocked him off, too, mercilessly, because before I let myself be locked up, he would have to bite the dust. Why is he running away like that! That's how it was.

8. Acknowledgment of What Happened with Reservations

Such participants are opposed to those who acknowledge the events cautiously, with hesitations, in order to come to terms with them—the maybe-sayer. The behavior that is discussed here is epitomized by a participant in a group of unemployed people:

> X.: I'd almost like to say that it seems to us that we have to shoulder this or that atrocity.

The acknowledgment appears to be wrenched from the participants by force of facts, and, for this reason, without their internalizing it. They only admit what they can no longer deny in order to breathe easily again.

9. Specific Reports about What Happened

However, there is also no lack of specific reports as to what happened. Following a participant's advocating the thesis that "the little people never learned what happened in Auschwitz," a forty-five-year-old wife of a miner recounts:

> Sch.: At our neighbor, there was once a Ukrainian and his friend. And the one was such a good person, to be sure. I also worked a lot with him in the fields. And then he had to go away, and then he had to go to another place, and then he returned one day and said "Oh, landlady, you so good. I where now am, nothing good, much work, not much eating," he says, "and cold. A pair of gloves," he said, right? Well, I gave all of it to him, gave him bread to take with him, and off he went. And afterwards the other one learned everything about it, and he said: Alas, my friend in Auschwitz went through the chimney long ago. That's the only thing I know.

Thereupon the discussion moved to Hadamar, the place where insane people were gassed—an act that, according to Mitscherlich's account,[2] led to active resistance in Germany. A second participant plucks up the courage to tell what she knows. She is a thirty-five-year-old widowed midwife:

> A: Well, one time my sister was up in—with the children relocated in Silesia. There was a large camp. The prisoners who were there, they were foreigners, one spoke this way, the other that way. They begged us, all of them were—the long, skinny bodies, starved. But I asked my sister so often: What is that? And in the night—now, the attacks up there weren't like we had them in the Rhine Valley—the whole camp was all screams, but we didn't know what it was until shortly before, that simply everything was haywire toward the end of the war. And then my older sister, it seems, was always very scared and said: "Folks, when the camp is opened, then it's going to be bad for us. They were so nice." Later, the women had to go in there, there also was an old professor, he was also a Jew, the women bathed him. Back then, my sister was still pregnant, she couldn't go in there. So, the oldest daughter had to go there. She had to clean in the camp and to tidy up, yes, this was after the great collapse. And exactly because these were bombed-out people, evacuees, then they were—they were very nice, even those who came from the camps, and didn't harm the others. But then, the peasants in the village, and so on, they had to suffer a lot like the concentration camp prisoners. It was a concentration camp, but in the beginning we didn't know what was in there. I just visited there when I traveled down, but my sister didn't. Then they gave them some bread, etc., when they passed there. Of course, the guard must not have seen that. But they were starving to death. But I always thought, they're just prisoners who've done something. And, in the beginning, my sister didn't know better. Well, close to us, perhaps in these large factories, Krupp, etc., they all had these work units—from the camps. They came out there—that is, marched then, but other than that one did not know very much. If one wasn't near the camp, then nobody knew anything.

The speaker evidently intends her account to display that she did not know anything, but yet, against her will, it becomes apparent that she knew all sorts of things. Her confused, contradictory account can be explained partly by her trying in vain to reconcile ignorance and memory, partly by her being overwhelmed by memory and shuddering to express it. In some sections, like the reference to the old Jewish professor, it seems as if a taboo were imposed on the worst: to name the things means to evoke them, in the spirit of the proverb *speak of the devil and he will appear*.

The most striking, concrete remarks on what people observed themselves is contained in the session of a group with predominantly poor women who are consistently opposed to National Socialism. Several group members lived in a district of a large city where there lived proportionally many poorer, lower-middle-class Jews who were particularly exposed to acts of violence. The session is one of those where the lever effect *(Hebelwirkung)* of the group discussions is most visible:

> L.: We had a lot to do with Jews, and the last Jews were transported from our area in August 1943. And in October we already had in . . . street lots of attacks with massive firebombs. Well, I can only say that the Jew . . . that perhaps in America not as many negroes were killed in one year as were murdered in fourteen days in our area, only in the area between . . . and down to . . . Street, . . . I experienced it firsthand, how bitter it was. This still touches me today, how the death truck came every day and another three, four people poisoned themselves in the morning, people eighty and eighty-one years old. My mother is eighty now, and I would really regret if she saw, when they take them and have them thrown on the truck. A seriously disabled war veteran from 1914, I also knew him well, he's my age, they took his crutches, and so he fell in the dirt, and then they said: "You dog, you've lived long enough," and they threw him on the cart, too. The area where I live now didn't see anything like that and they don't believe it.

The narrative is concluded by another participant who supposedly did not experience such things because they only happened to the poor, an aspect of the persecution of the Jews that has hardly been analyzed yet.

> Ra.: Well, what Mrs. L. told us a little while ago was rather new to me, because I didn't experience such things, because I associated exclusively with West End Jews and was also friends with them. And virtually nothing happened to my acquaintances. Either they are—they had enough money, so that they got away early enough, and—
> (Interruption: These were very rich ones, indeed, these were very rich ones.)

This dialogue develops in the following:

> Re.: I sacrificed myself quite a lot for that, because I myself helped an old woman and prevented—one can say—drove away others and even if I took my blows, here in the . . . district. Only to have a look, I thought: just hop on your bike and drive there. Policemen and everything, they allowed everything. And those who still wanted to drive away to the airport or someplace else had trouble squeezing into the car. They had already been hit with a billy club or whatever.
> (Interruption: When did that happen?)
> (Interruption: I experienced that myself on . . . the way.)
> It was terrible, even the furniture got smashed! What do the kids have to do with it, they hadn't even been born . . .
> (incomprehensible, several people speak)
> One has to thank heaven one isn't a Jew. It was impossible to go out on the street. What do the Jewish kids have to do with it, if even the parents—they

were over eighty—I know a classmate from school, she was gassed, her brother was gassed, he had seven children and his wife, he married a German woman, the mother was gassed and the father was—only a sister returned, she's all alone, all the other relatives were gassed. She was allowed to watch, that's what she told us.

B.: I don't think that's right, that, back then; in the . . . , I've also—that ten- and twelve-year-old children get the people with iron clubs, the windows and "Jew" and spit on and did all that. I barged in there, my husband was with me, and they said: "You look like a filthy Jew, too, you should be taken away someplace special, too!" Then my husband said: "Come on, let's go!" and I walked away trembling. The children followed me and hit my legs with a stick. I won't ever forget that, and that I in . . . the way . . .

Only the tape recording fully conveys the participants' excitement. A third participant remembers a scene of horror:

B.: An accomplished Jewish lady, who lived in the . . . Street, corner . . . , on the second floor, a lawyer, she screamed for help on the second floor, then two young men threw her out of the window, I saw that, that's right. They had her by the legs and threw her out, I saw that, how she screamed for help.

For the participants of this group, by the way, it seems to be particularly shocking that the atrocities that were committed against the Jews also affected those considered to be among the upper class—how in general an executed princess is pitied more than a murdered chambermaid. The respect for the previous social status of Jews is so high that the participant who drives the discussion through her resistance by explaining, she "didn't experience such things," proudly asserts her reasoning that she consorted exclusively with "West End Jews." But the speaker who reports the scene of horror in which a Jewish lady was thrown out of the window also does not neglect to add that she was "an accomplished Jewish lady," a lawyer. This reflection on rich and accomplished Jews seems to indicate that this is not only a matter of sympathy for the victims, but also outrage that the established system of bourgeois society based on property was violated by National Socialism.

II. Guilt

The previous chapter raised the problem of knowledge about the events. Here the goal is to present the result for those who deny knowledge: those who are not conscious of any guilt. The analysis is thus directed largely toward the nationalistic-minded and those who take a defensive posture;

open-minded participants are brought in only insofar as defensive motives appear in them too, although in a different sense. The thesis can be ventured in advance that in the case of the open-minded, on the one hand the defense mechanisms are much weaker and guilt is conceded much more, but that, on the other hand, the whole question is generally not as affectively charged as in the case of nationalists; that they have, adopting the jargon of the discussions, far fewer guilt complexes than those who close themselves off to guilt, and not only in the psychoanalytic sense of the unconscious. In their manifest thinking as well, the dimension "guilty/not guilty" plays a minor role when compared to the others.

1. Negation of Guilt

Often the general negation of guilt that is based on ignorance comes at the beginning of the discussion in the manner of a motto. In this way, the first statement in the just-cited session by the unemployed begins:

> Z.: Well, I agree more or less with the general tone of the letter writer. Then again, the [Colburn] letter has a couple of points that I can't support at all. It is said that the Germans are not as conscious of their guilt as is perhaps expected and desired by the outside world. On this I want to say that the majority of the German people aren't conscious of any guilt because the overwhelming majority of the German people probably acted just like any other people in the world would have acted. Looking at the fact that 95 percent of Germans took no steps against the atrocities that undoubtedly occurred in the concentration camps, didn't join any kind of resistance movements—one cannot conclude from these facts that the German people, in particular, had the impression that they had it pretty good. You have to consider things in light of the actual circumstances that were dominant back then.

The peculiar quality of this statement is that the idea, after lengthy interpolations, is corrupted at the decisive point and falls apart. The thesis is that the majority of the German people is not aware of any guilt. After the theme has been announced, that the Germans did nothing against the horror, one expects it to be argued that one must not infer guilt from this, because no people would have acted differently. Instead, Z says that one must not conclude that the German people, in particular, had the impression of having it pretty good—a thesis that falls outside the framework of the argument. It is thus hardly too far-fetched to assume that this aberration is in fact caused by the unconscious feeling of guilt, which disrupts the speaker's pattern of apology. This aberration stands prototypically for countless other slips.[1]

According to the overview of the material, unqualified denial of all guilt is relatively scarce. The facts have been made known too emphatically for this. Overall, the participants shrink away from putting themselves in the wrong by simply claiming German innocence all too crudely. Defense uses subtler, especially more rational, means, among which reckoning the accounts of guilt (*Aufrechnung der Schuldkonnten* [as in balancing assets and liabilities in a ledger]) is arguably the most important. Also important is being prepared to come to terms with the complex through philosophical reflection and conceptual distinctions, through intellectualization.

2. False Internalization of Guilt

We refrain at this point from developing a psychoanalytic theory of the repression of guilt. Suffice it to say that with personalities that are bound to authority the dimension of punishment and the need for punishment are much more significant than for individuals who are structured differently. From a sociological perspective, the interest in redeeming oneself and Germany at any cost is much lower in the case of nonnationalists than in the case of nationalists. By no means is this to say that the question of guilt is not significant for nonnationalists. But they appear to be more able to internalize problems of conscience, to come to terms with them themselves and to act accordingly, than the others. With these others, the reaction of striking out, putting oneself in the right, emerges right away, and with such an effort they can hardly escape from the critical theme because they could never quite believe themselves. In their case, the motive of internalization becomes distorted: for example in a group of army officers, where the reference to guilt is directed against "propaganda," meaning against all accusations against Germany from outside. Subjectivism fuses itself with relativism: if the measure for guilt is solely internal, who can decide on its objectivity?

> *Sch.*: This one sentence also stuck with me, how everything else was treated by the previous speaker concerning the attitude of the Englishman[2] that, according to him, we do not have a feeling of guilt for what has happened. I want to mention one thing. What is guilt? After all, guilt is something that has to come from inside, this feeling of guilt. Guilt cannot come when an outsider comes and tries to make clear propagandistically and journalistically: Guys, well, you're really guilty, don't just feel guilty, but we want to impose this feeling of guilt on you from the outside. That's the first thing. The second is: What is the measure for guilt?
>
> *Mod.*: We have to interrupt . . . May I briefly summarize? He said, the feeling of guilt has to come from the inside and cannot be imposed from the outside, and, moreover, that the measure for guilt must be intrinsic.

Sch.: The measure for guilt is pretty much subjective, that is, based on feeling. Legal scholars say: guilt has to be connected with law. But what does law mean? What was shown to us in the Nazi period, that's supposed to be law? We were actually shown that law is power. Not only what's in the code of law, gentlemen, law actually is power, that's undoubtedly clear, because if accuser and judge are the same person in court, then this isn't law anymore, it has to be power. How can one argue we are to have feelings of guilt if we presume guilt to be power, guilt to be based on law, and law, in turn, to be power. What becomes of our concepts? Who feels guilty for the millions of our fellow countrymen who were pushed out of the East? Who feels guilty that in the immediate aftermath we had damn little to eat, that people froze to death, and that people died? Who feels guilty for that? No one! Because in the courts, let's talk for once about the Nuremberg trials. We said: what do you want from us? Others did similar things. Nonsense, it was said, not up for debate now, but your guilt is up for debate. For abstract concepts there just has to be a general measure of value that is universally valid. It's possible to say: You bad Germans. You are guilty now. Now we sentence you. Everybody else is not guilty. This also applies most of all to those gentlemen who are used to following their oath of allegiance. How can one presume—it's unparalleled in history, as it appears to me, that the generals are sentenced in front of a tribunal, the party was, the generals on the basis of their oath, on the grounds that they did their duty—this is the basic principle of every soldier, of every civil servant—that men have been sentenced to death based on their acting in compliance with their duty, and, even more, by hanging, one of the most ignominious manners of death that can befall a soldier. Well, did one have even the slightest understanding for this on the side of the occupation powers, so that one now cannot say: You all on one side are guilty, we are better than you—and then make it even worse. Where were the psychologists? Now, I come to something Mr. Z. said a little while ago. We are accused: You don't have sympathy for different people. Well, who's had sympathy on the other side: we want to show you how to make it better. And then they start to do it just as we did it and perhaps even worse. In our case, at least the appearance was preserved. At the Nuremberg court, no one even tried to preserve so much as the appearance. I want to add to that, to come back again to the matter of guilt: Is the matter not to be assessed purely in terms of propaganda? Because the ally who was still a friend at the Nuremberg court, who was judge and accuser in one, has been propagandistically made world enemy number one in the course of three years. Isn't this perhaps evidence in our favor, demonstrating that the majority in America hasn't been enlightened at all, or is enlightened only little by little by the relevant propaganda in order to be manipulated toward the positive or negative side. The majority of Germans didn't even know what happened in the concentration camps. It was withheld from us or, if something seeped out, we were so influenced by the propaganda that we had to approve of it.

Sch.'s insistence on responding to the problem is unusual. It is difficult to decide whether he concerns himself with it in such detail because he is seriously striving for clarification, just in order to construct the defense more effectively, or, finally, because he is unconsciously fixated on the problem and cannot disengage from it. The facts are probably approached most closely by assuming that behavior like that of the participant is not really influenced by one or another of those factors, but that these factors themselves belong first to a conceptual scheme of classification that seeks to impose psychological order on the phenomenon, and to be sure in different layers of the ego, while in it all of these aspects coalesce and cannot actually be distinguished from each other. That here inwardness purely and simply plays the role of ideology is revealed in the words of the speakers. The same one who says there that guilt must come from within reproaches that, in contrast to the Nuremberg trials, "in our case, at least the appearance was preserved."

Apart from the fact that the Gestapo, which suspended all legal guarantees, can hardly be credited with preserving appearances, the claim that preserving appearances would be a higher moral category repudiates the demand for inwardness as the showplace of authentic feelings of guilt.

3. What Is Guilt Supposed to Look Like?

In more than one case, the critical reflection on the concept of guilt takes the shape of a formalistic dodge. Accordingly, a participant asks, seemingly unconcerned by any evidence, with pointed guilelessness and naiveté:

M.: In what way are we supposed to be guilty?

The demand to specify the term, in other words to state in what respect there could be talk of guilt, gets muddied up with the rhetorical question which denies guilt by implying that it is impossible to specify what it consists of—a technique, by the way, reminiscent of certain rules in contemporary logic. Beyond that, he speculates where complicated matters are involved on the effect of a single, unexpected, very precisely formulated question that demands a concise answer, maneuvering the addressee into an awkward situation and confusing him. Posed emphatically, questions in general often contain an aggressive element.

Later on in the same discussion, a critique is made that one is "summoned to a confession of guilt," again under the formalistic pretext of asking what then such a confession of guilt is supposed to look like. The justified aversion toward ideological performances, empty public confessions of guilt, is exploited in order to avoid the controversy about guilt at all:

> H.: But now the story always appears, as if the Americans in general or any one of the other foreigners says: Now, finally, admit it, just admit it finally. Well, he admitted it: now he's going to be put away anyway, like one always says in court: just admit it, say it, it's the best you can do. Then he thinks, maybe I'm getting away with it scot free. No, now he still pulls half a year. If he had told everything fully, then they might have put him away for three-quarters of a year.
> (Interruption: That can't be right.)
> Va.: That's how it looks if we still believe we are the only well-behaved, kind-hearted people and that, after having murdered millions, we now start crying Lord Jesus, because now the others are striking back? If I box someone's ears, and he gives me a big one or even two back, the way they did, then I always have to tell myself: I actually provoked him.
> H.: But he can't want a confession on top of that.
> L.: I don't believe he wants a confession either, but it's mutual, we still provoke other nations by acting as if we didn't do anything. Above all it looks—I don't want to return to a topic we already discussed—as if we are not at all ashamed of the Jews. There are still many who say, it doesn't matter, they should have gassed many more. Unfortunately these voices were stronger than those who honestly tell themselves: It was really an outrage.
> H.: This could be the reason. So one doesn't ask, and there is the answer: [We] aren't guilty at all. So, in the opposite direction, what should we say then, or how should we formulate this confession of guilt?

Apart from the telltale slip "we are not at all ashamed of the Jews" (instead of: of the crimes against the Jews), apparently once again at the bottom of it is the opinion that guilt is so internal that it cannot be demanded from outside. This idea of morality in the sense criticized by Hegel, however, in the end serves the interests of the guilty party. Since he has to settle it only with himself, he is absolved from the actual responsibility within society, and the religious intensification of the authority of consciousness leads ultimately to relativism.[3]

In one of the discussions the concern for "how this feeling of guilt is actually supposed to look" shows its true face—the feeling of guilt is idle chatter:

> K.: And I'd still be interested how the feeling of guilt, which he [Colburn] has missed among us Germans, how it . . . despite those things, which all weigh on the German people and still weigh—and especially the youth gets to really breathe again maybe not in the foreseeable future due to these consequences . . . I can't quite figure out . . . , what this is supposed to look like, what form it's supposed to take.

Mod.: Well, I think in the form . . . that we are not supposed to act better . . . than the Americans, in spite of their beating us, as Mr. Colburn says. And that we are to make up for all that we did in foreign countries and to the Jews. And that we are not supposed to be rebellious. And that we should not pity ourselves. And that we have to try to make up for all of it.

B.: I believe he meant it that way, but my opinion, repeating the word you quoted, is that the whole feeling of guilt has just been idle chatter.

Here defensiveness works in such a way that the actual talk of the question of guilt, which was popular for a short time after the Second World War, just as after the first one by the way, is used to discredit the feeling of guilt itself as "idle chatter." The latent meaning is that one is innocent, since nobody can impose a feeling of guilt from outside.

In the same group, it is argued that since it is impossible to "imagine" the German feeling of guilt, discourse about guilt is futile. If this argument were pursued, one of the consequences would be that one would have to infer the absence of guilt itself from the absence of consciousness of guilt.

K.: Well, I think at least this group—if we dare to return to the starting point—that Hitler bears the responsibility for the world set on fire etc. and therefore also the German people per se, that this is firmly rejected by at least this group. I'd be interested—and I'm very sorry that I can't ask the writer how he actually conceives of the German feeling of guilt.

The same use is featured verbatim in a session of female refugees:

D.: May I ask straight away how you imagine, or how the people who are convinced of our general guilt, conceive of us arguing against that guilt, because all of us, I can probably say that on behalf of all of us, didn't know anything about atrocities, nothing.

The question "how do you actually imagine?" leads to the other's being accused of estrangement from the world, of lack of realism; had he only been there, had he only seen how impossible it was to do something, then such phantoms would disappear. The phenomenon corresponds exactly to what depth-psychology terms the externalization of the superego. Disputing subjective feelings of conscience, denying one's own guilt and German guilt in general, get mixed up together associatively, with ornate illogic.

In order to put the discussions about guilt in the right perspective, it has to be emphasized that defense against guilt per se cannot be equated mechanically with nationalism or psychological repression. There are expressions of defensiveness that, in context, convey exactly the opposite meaning, especially those in which the concept of guilt is assayed more closely. As evidence, a passage from a group of teachers is quoted:

> F.: I'm guilty of not having been rebel enough to go to a concentration camp. In 1933 I was a resolute opponent of Hitler, but never such a rebel or conspirator that I was imprisoned. Also, I wasn't caught. Thus, I'm a fellow traveler and am guilty of following. I ask myself in which of those famous years I incurred personal guilt, at any rate seen from the perspective of today? In which year, on which day, in which month did I do that? Or would it have been human duty to be more active? But then it also has to be said, with the consequences for the family, etc. That's probably the question that many, many from my ranks asked themselves. But I don't know any moment in which I failed. It's not failure if I also took the life and the existence of my family into consideration.

To start with, here the acknowledgment of guilt does not have that formalistic tone that serves as a prelude to the phrase: the matter is settled. The sophistic element in the effort to discredit the problem of guilt per se by demanding to specify year, month or day, where the nonactive one is to have incurred guilt, however, cannot be overlooked; the passage sounds like a weak echo of Zeno's paradoxes. On the other hand, however, the defense that martyrdom, which open and active resistance against the Nazis would have meant, cannot be expected from an individual is true and substantial.

4. A Small Clique Is Guilty

Only hard-boiled National Socialists go so far as to deny the fact of extermination. In the process, however, the less decided—and only those of them who grapple with moral problems at all—encounter the task of constructing the guilt for what happened as plausibly as possible so that they come off as flawless.

The principle of authority allows for shifting everything to the top leaders, who are no longer alive. A kind of negative selection is presumed, for example, in a session of unemployed women.

> B.: One is simply speechless—the majority of the German people, because brutality is not part of the German people in that sense; they're certainly a good-natured sort, so that they would take the freedoms from others or torment them in that way.
> Mod.: It's always only a question. He who worships power is not always so good-natured.

B.: No.

Mod.: Well, absolutely not, despite good nature?

B.: These weren't good-natured people up there, up there special sorts really
came together.

The phrasing "these weren't good-natured people up there" does not
lack grotesque humor. The indulgence of that utterance continues in the
following, where the knives are drawn at once for the wives of these "elements," which leads easily into self-exoneration:

> B.: When you read the newspaper today, for example, let's say the *Neue
> Illustrierte*, how they write about it now, Mrs. von Schirach and Emmi
> Göring and the like, then you get the impression from those accounts that
> those high personages who were in government, that they also entirely dis-
> agreed with these—well, exaggerated, that they also tried to get Jews freed
> and to support them. But that, as individuals, they could do just as little to
> stop it as we could . . .

In a strongly National Socialist-tinged group of male refugees, in a long
and inflammatory speech, a speaker takes up Goebbels's expression of an
"atrocity fairy tale" and, after limiting guilt to the "clique," goes on to an
undisguised glorification of National Socialism:

> R.: Finally, I want to say that all these atrocity fairy tales about National
> Socialism one can read in the magazines, that these are for the most part
> overblown stories written out of pure sensation mongering, that there was
> really only a small clique who committed these atrocities in the National
> Socialist state.

The partial truth, that the execution of measures of terror and extermination were indeed reserved to a very small circle, develops into falsehood,
since this small circle was supported by the trust of a large majority up to
the last two years of war and since resistance against the terror measures
did not assert itself effectively, while in other sectors of social life, especially in the economy, tacit consent prevailed despite the form of dictatorship.[4] The thesis of the small clique is only plausible as long as it is isolated
from those processes; seen in the context of the historical process, it loses
much of its persuasiveness.

Apart from the fact that the Nazis had assigned the execution of the
murders to a limited circle,[5] the whole political and organizational way of
doing business in the Third Reich aimed at differentiating the population
into followers and elite troops, not much different from the scheme of denazification. Totalitarian regimes are, as Franz Neumann has trenchantly

demonstrated on the level of political analysis,[6] paradoxically pluralistic. This permits the masses to identify with or distance themselves from the regime as needed. However, where a totalitarian regime breaks apart, the majority can then shuffle the atrocities off themselves as what "they" committed and by renouncing horror and bad conscience, while it is much easier for them to keep faith with the advantages the regime offered. This sinister connection has to be penetrated if one wants to fully understand the problem of defensiveness. A participant in a group of officers puts the whole mechanism in the simple formula:

> X.: What the small circle of the Gestapo did was unknown to us and, therefore, we couldn't take any steps, because we didn't know anything.

5. Innocence of Particular Groups

There is another twist of a per se accurate insight that uses the virtuosity with which moral defensiveness develops and that is perhaps equivalent to the degree of unconscious guilt one has to repress: that in a world split into nations or national power blocs, lacking a superordinate and independent authority under international law with sufficient instruments of power, the victor is right and the defeated is wrong. This formal insight is used to discredit the substantive question of guilt as undecidable from the outset. Since it is established that the victor blames the vanquished—this is roughly the inner structure of this train of thought—nothing can be said about guilt and innocence on an international scale. On the basis of such argumentation every judge is rejected as biased and if possible the tables are even turned—one assumes the role of prosecutor as soon as the judge, whose impartiality is doubted, expostulates about what was perpetrated in the Third Reich. In the process, every possibility of self-exploration supposedly perishes.

Youth, generation and similar vague categories often play a role where responsibility is to be shifted from certain social groups, be it that one blames a generation for something bad, mostly the older one, or that one wants to let off another one, mostly one's own, from all evil. The innocence of youth is emphasized in a Bavarian group:

> R.: By and large the big mistake is made here of condemning the youth. I don't believe the youth had any possibility to struggle against it anyway, that one could have . . . stopped . . . the racial hatred or the persecution of races . . .
> B.: Well, of course, it has to . . . be noted: back then we were I believe . . . six or seven years old in the year of 1933; grew up with *Heil Hitler*. And then, I

believe, I can say . . . something about . . . since we all came together from . . . and the area . . . for example, crucifixes weren't removed from the classrooms of the so-called Gau [district] . . . without a doubt it was to the former *Gauleiter* [head of district], he had trouble with the *Führerhauptquartier* [executive-headquarter] back then.

E.: I absolutely agree with you, but I can remember the year 1938 . . . when the shop windows of Jewish stores were smashed and how the crowd objected.

B.: Did you object?

E.: Not me!

B.: Did you join? . . . you? We can be quite honest. Who did join the objections? Me, if I had objected, my father would have smacked me!

Sch.: I also believe that back then around 1938, when the persecution of the Jews basically started, who among us, that is, we as youth, virtually kids back then—back then we actually had no reason at all to really act or even to participate. While today it is something completely different, when we ourselves see that what people do is somehow wrong, while back then, what happened there basically didn't concern us.

In the same session the abstract notion of youth is used in a glorifying manner:

B.: The step was first taken in 1948, when, I don't know, when a youth council in Munich invited the whole youth of the world—representatives of course—to the international youth meeting in Munich. There was a lady from India and also Jewish youth, and we as representatives of German youth got on very well with them.

I think it's not a problem for youth. I can remember conversations here with Jewish adolescents who completely shared our view. They said we have to understand each other. And the people who . . . were in Munich, they got along pretty well. I believe it's a problem of the older generation. In the same way, I think we as youth have to sharply reproach the older generation for the whole thing between 1933 and 1945—perhaps even from earlier, from the Wilhelminian era.

E.: I fully agree with you.

K.: That injustice took place, this at least is understood by the youth to a high degree and—that what could be corrected . . . that we were of course ready to take the first step, and not only in some sort of gathering like happened in Munich, but time and again, that we, the Germans, have to be the ones to reach out first again and again; but a feeling of guilt in the sense that we are everywhere and always the ones who are guilty for all the bad things that happened during the war, that even as youth, who in the abstract have no blame or virtually no blame at all, if we may say so, that we, still, perhaps for all eternity, have a feeling of guilt, which, from our point of view, per se has no justification whatsoever.

Pf.: Yes, to the point raised by Mr. K., one thing must certainly be added: The question of guilt, or that which is always laid on our doorstep, that we are to blame for everything; the question of guilt and the hatred was generated by the Americans shortly after the war when it was always said: Nazi bastard! Right . . . ?

The argument used here is the counterpart to the more popular one that where there's smoke, there must be fire. It operates with a sort of probabilistic logic: After every war it is said that the Germans were guilty, and this really cannot be the case. Rather, every matter has its two sides, and this remainder of an ingrained "common sense"–conclusion [English in original] implicitly brings about the bold extrapolation: thus, we are innocent.

Just like youth, women are supposed to be particularly innocent. This is expressed in a general way in the first sentences of the already mentioned group of female refugees:

D.: In one of the comments it was said: We Germans haven't yet taken to heart, or, much more, we haven't yet taken the bad of the Hitler time to heart, enough that we feel guilty about it. And I have to respond completely openly and honestly that we German women feel that we are free of this so-called guilt—as I know German women and talk with them about it. I just don't agree with it.

F.: I'm of the same opinion. We are really unaware of everything that happened, and we always only wanted the best, we women. And I also don't feel any guilt.

Group innocence is urged further in a group of female unemployed. The investigator points out that especially during the first years of the Nazi regime much about the notorious deeds committed in the concentration camps leaked out. He immediately receives the response that women cared little about politics, followed, as if self-evident, by the conclusion that they had believed in those rumors as little as in the legends of ritual murder:

F.: But I believe . . . it might be that the men knew it. I want to say, we women, we cared less about politics.

Mod.: There was no talking about it at home?

F.: No, politics were indeed discussed. Nothing was known at home either. One imagined concentration camps as prisons, a kind of prison from which you can't write. Some sort of prison. But what happened to somebody in there, we didn't know. And that they got little to eat, that was the only thing known. But we didn't know any more about all those concentration camps, and that there probably, well that there were longer punishments. More wasn't known about this.

Sch.: Yes, I have to say, when I heard later that really bad things happened there, nobody really discussed it, because it was severely punished. At the time, I believed them to be slanders. I never believed it, when I heard references to it. I didn't think the regime, us Germans to be capable of doing something like that . . .

Mod.: Despite the Horst-Wessel-song [a song encouraging revenge for a Nazi martyr] and all those nice songs, you didn't believe it?

Sch.: No, I didn't believe it, that they . . . something like that, if one heard it about the Russians, probably . . . but I thought that in our case . . . completely impossible.

H.: We also didn't believe the Jews were abusing Aryan children. Well, you can't really believe everything you hear, I really have to say.

6. Collective Guilt

Throughout, individuals' attempts to fight collective guilt are much more affectively charged than those to evade individual guilt. Standing behind the rejection of the collective guilt thesis is not only solidarity with the people and, presumably, not only the political interest in avoiding unpleasant measures that could result from the collective guilt construction. A prime motive is probably also an individual's urge not to be drawn in, for example through party affiliation, but to save one's neck from the collective noose.

As American research has shown, participants bring up attitudes for which they have a bad conscience, but do not advocate them as their own, instead hiding them behind the formula "people say" [English]. Occasionally, similar effects also occur in the discussions on the question of collective guilt, for example in a group of unemployed, in which the participants compensate for their own powerlessness with huge generalizations [*(gigantische Theoreme)*]:

L.: My colleague, Mr. M., spoke about militarism and also about war. Who actually is to blame for the war, and is Hitler to blame for the war? I have to say, from the chitchat among comrades: We heard discussions that Hitler is not to blame for the war, but America, and that America tried to send Hitler to Russia as a advance force, so that Communism would be fought in Russia, in the interest of America, and so that National Socialism . . . When the mission in Russia was fulfilled, America would automatically grab Russia. Germany would in this way have fulfilled its task, which was given to Hitler. Unfortunately, this didn't succeed, and so the political situation is such that the social question is difficult to solve. The social question is not per se a national question, but an international question for all peoples, who have to be connected. In other words, Germany as the country in the middle of everything would have to send representatives abroad, to the different foreign countries and deal with the question everywhere. But since there are several opposing currents, I assume the social question is almost impossible to solve. And the foundation of democracy, of course, which is based on solving the social question. So, complete democracy is impossible.

Z.: But a collective guilt, as Niemöller [Pastor Martin Niemöller, who advocated for an admission of collective guilt] said in his day, and which is also to be rejected, does not exist.

The apocryphal construction "that America tried to send Hitler to Russia as an advance force" is merely a pretense for an extremely nationalistic thesis. From the fact that the "social question" is characterized as an "international question," it is inferred that "Germany as the country in the middle of everything would have to . . . deal with this question everywhere," in other words solve it in the sense of a Hitlerian Europe. Toward the end, the unsuccessful logic is again characteristic for the issue. The participant remembers Niemöller's familiar statements about collective guilt. He presupposes that indignation about these statements is solid and thus formulates: "as Niemöller said in his day, and which is also to be rejected"—in other words, the rejection of collective guilt takes place by stipulation through association with the name Niemöller before they actually judge it, and only then, as a *causa judicata* [matter that has been settled], the judgment follows later that this collective guilt does not exist.

This, together with the wording "and which is also to be rejected," leads to an issue that one often encounters in Germany, but is difficult to describe and even more difficult to grasp theoretically, and is merely referenced here as a social-psychological problem because it is closely connected to the question of today's political ideology. It is this *communis opinio*, be it real or set by the speaker or made up, this demeanor of presupposing ahead of time and without particulars that everyone is in agreement, that serves to push aside actual awareness of everything that is troubling. Everything is treated with a wink as collectively settled, and the affirmation of consensus substitutes for insight into the issues. The phenomenon of "group attitude" described in the section on group and individual may belong to the same complex.[7] Psychologically it is supposedly a matter of those moments in which collective narcissism, the desire to belong, finds its fulfillment, in that the individuals who are dominated by the desire to have something behind them speak as one and form something like a collectivity. In such moments they feel so strong and at the same time so protected against everything coming from the outside that their rationality is switched off. One does not even need to discuss it or even to think at all anymore. The judgment of the group usurps the judgment of reason.

The question of collective guilt is such a sore spot that whoever does not share the established opinion is treated as the bird who befouls his own nest. This could be the reason why there seems to be mutual consent in the case of the majority of participants as concerns this point of the discussion.

7. War Guilt

The outrage over the assumption of collective guilt easily connects to the rejection of war guilt and the "leave us out of it" *(ohne uns)* theme.

> A.: Nevertheless, I dispute the collective guilt of the German people for the war, because it has been over for years. If the German was absolutely guilty, then absolute peace would have to reign now, because the German doesn't have anything any more. He can't do anything, and he doesn't do anything, he also doesn't want anything. But still, absolute peace hasn't arrived yet. To the contrary, in my opinion, there can't be any talk about peace whatsoever today.
>
> Mod.: Miss A., I don't quite understand what you mean. We had a war, and we experienced it because we were dragged into the war by Hitler. And now belligerence continues. These things simply are a consequence of somebody's having started it. Now it continues. If something is set on fire, it continues to burn.
>
> A.: Yes, but if the fire is extinguished, and if it still continues to burn in other places, then the one who initially started it can't be guilty.
>
> B.: Yes, that's also true. If we, let's say, hadn't had Hitler and hadn't started a war, then Bolshevism would have been there anyway and would simply have rolled over Germany. And then America would now already have Bolshevism, which only we stopped, which we stood against in the war, and the world opposed us. And now we're supposed to fight against the same enemy together with the world after all, also, so, again stand up to Bolshevism, against which we actually made this war for which we are blamed, and for which our military leaders have been tried. And now they want us to get enthusiastic about that again. We are supposed to fight the same enemy again. The majority of the people don't understand the logic.

If nothing at all helps anymore, the whole factual course of world history is suspended and another one is constructed just to be able to make clear in this flimsy way that things would have turned out this way anyway and that because of this the talk of guilt has no basis. But even such impudent conceptual maneuvers can support themselves on the basis of the most real tendencies, if not from the past reality then from the present. Few arguments hold the same penetrating power as the one that maintains: today one needs Germany's military capability against Russia while in his time Hitler, instead of being helped to defeat Russia, was attacked on the flank.

It deserves to be emphasized that there is no lack of participants who concede the German war guilt *sans phrase* [without qualification]. Such statements are not rare. The willingness to take responsibility for the war seems to be greater than to do so for the atrocities committed by the Nazis. An example from a progressive group of trade unionists will suffice at this point:

> B.: Well, colleague H. is giving us a lecture on National Socialism. In and of itself, I assume that we have gotten away from our topic, because the topic here was the question of the guilt of the German people . . . The argument was simply that only Hitler was guilty. Well, on this we do agree: Everybody. There is absolutely no one here who is of a different opinion.

This passage, which remained uncontested, probably expresses the *communis opinio* of this group to some degree.

Often, war guilt is treated as in the format of a school essay of the sort "external circumstances–deeper cause," in which the attack by Hitler is actually admitted but then revoked through circuitous speculations. One of many examples, taken from the beginning of a session conducted in an encampment:

> R.: Well, he . . . spoke about Adolf Hitler, that we started the war. This is quite well and good. This also can't be disputed, but who actually started the war? Did the people start it, and who is the guilty one now? Are we, the people, the guilty ones or are they, over there in America, the guilty ones as a people or who is the guilty party now? Because it's only the ones on top who have the money in their hands, and who thus have the corresponding power. Whoever didn't obey went to the concentration camp. We couldn't do anything about it.

Under the compulsion for defense, logic falls apart once again: that Germany had started the war "can't be challenged," but "who started the war?" Apparently, the latent idea is that "who" is unspecified and that one must not think about the people in this regard. Of course only the entirely unspecified suspected "ones on top, who have the money in their hands," are mentioned as culprits.

8. Measure for Guilt

In the group of army officers cited above, the measure for individual or national guilt is discussed, and the establishment of definitional problems is followed by the conclusion that, since the concept cannot be grasped in a clear-cut way, all of us are more or less "guilty." Pseudophilosophical thoroughness of conceptual clarification is here a comfortable and at the same time narcissistically pleasant pretense: since it is supposedly impossible to agree on the conceptual form, the thing itself is supposedly invalid:

> *Sch.*: I'm convinced that, when we raise the topic of guilt, we should define from the outset what is to be understood by guilt, where is the standard for measuring individual or national guilt to be found, and aren't all of us more or less guilty? Don't we want to establish that as a foundation before later judging? Because how can I render a judgment? For that I would need a standard according to which I can judge. If this standard is completely confused by those who want to bring it to me.

The evasive function of such comments is obvious.

A passage from the already mentioned Bavarian dignitaries offers something similar. Here foreign policy guilt is distinguished from moral guilt before both are rejected:

> G.: Are we dealing here with moral guilt or guilt over foreign policy ? If it's a matter of moral guilt, if the question refers to the moral aspect, then . . .
> H.: Belongs in the confession box!
> G.: . . . then this doesn't belong, I believe, in this place tonight, because the Americans are plainly just as guilty in the moral sense, in my opinion, are just as bad or good as we are. If it's a matter of foreign policy guilt, then I believe the events have already overtaken this question, because if you call on a people to join the same army to which you belong in order to fight a world-enemy, then the question of guilt is moot because in that case it can only be a matter of equal comrades in arms.

The passage is extraordinarily informative. It almost seems as if, in the haste of defensiveness, the art of conceptual distinction reverted to the old sophistic craft of making the weaker thought the stronger one. At first the distinction between moral and foreign policy guilt sounds as if it comes from the pedantic approach of an academic lecture. But it is not in the service of clarifying a complex subject but of compartmentalizing jurisdictions, in which the division of labor takes over the moral sphere and in the process dissolves it. Organized religion is supposed to be responsible for moral guilt: to the confession box, and then the dignitaries are excused from any further worry. The "foreign policy guilt," however, is—not entirely without justification—ascribed to the constellation of real power relations, and in this manner the thesis that this kind of guilt is moot is deduced from the fact that the policies of the Western allies toward the Federal Republic have changed. With head held high, the subject [thus] strolls through the battleground of murdered concepts.

In a session of Christian youth workers, the investigator asks whether the question about guilt is settled and receives the answer:

B.: Yes, without doubt it's settled now.

The speaker then specifies this in a way that from the start sees only the tactical aspect as relevant; by the same token, the objection of another participant follows directly on it:

B.: Because if we're now told again: Well, now you have to take the blame, then nobody will enlist in the Wehrmacht. It's quite clever now that one says, sure, your crime, we'll let you off for it. But immediately after that, well, but we do need soldiers.

Sch.: Well, I believe, either it was a crime, and it was as much a crime five years ago, and then it still counts as a crime today, or it wasn't that much of a crime to begin with; and we don't have to ignore it so generously today. If at the time . . . if it really was a crime, then it is still a crime today. But if it wasn't as big a crime as it is seen to be today, then we don't have to so generously cover it up just because at the moment they need us again.

Once again, B. applies the very effective theme of defensiveness mentioned above and cleverly spots the weakening of the moral position of the Allies due to the change in policies toward Germany. His partner stands his ground, but is confused to some degree, as the phrasing "or it wasn't that much of a crime to begin with; and we don't have to ignore it so generously today" indicates.

III. The Self-image of the Participants

Many speakers justify their position toward the complex of guilt by considering their own nature.[1] Such considerations carry special weight because they occur spontaneously and point to critical self-reflection. At the same time, such considerations themselves help with defense. With them, not only is guilt dismissed by referring to actual or imaginary social powerlessness, but also subtly by referring back to one's own personal suffering. It would thus be premature to construe such statements, without further ado, as genuine self-reflection. These too can degenerate into the stereotype that fends off consciousness of actual responsibility, insofar as the subject reifies itself as an object of pathology without seriously applying the implicit criticism of the subject to himself. By the same token, such defensive theses contain elements of truth. If numerous participants characterize themselves or the Germans in general as sick in whichever sense, they are confirmed by uncounted symptoms of confusion and bewilderment that occur in the discussions and accumulate particularly when the really critical areas, the concentration camps, the atrocities, the murder of the Jews, are discussed.

1. The Germans Are Sick

Our participants were incited to self-reflection by the basic stimulus. The Colburn letter spoke of the tendency to fend off the consciousness of guilt. Occasionally this statement of Colburn is immediately accepted. This is how it appears in such cases:

> G.: The German's reaction to it is perhaps not really sincere. But it's like, if you reproach somebody who himself feels guilty for it, repeatedly, over and over again, then he'll defend himself somehow. Maybe this reaction is not really sincere at all. That's why the American doesn't have an honest impression of how we ourselves think about those things. In part, we'll insist on our defense even if we don't always believe that we are innocent and that we really did do a lot. That's why he doesn't have the right impression of us.

The alleged derivation of the defense mechanism becomes a part of it. The insight into the repression of guilt leads to the magical transformation of the guilt itself into a "neurosis":

> U.: The impression probably has to arise for every foreigner, like Mr. C. said, we're immediately on the defensive, we're like the man who was in the clink once, has a criminal record, and walks around saying: "Yes, you accuse me of that, but there are lots walking around who have done exactly the same, and they don't have a criminal record, and I do, I think it's completely unfair." We are still in this kind of neurosis, which is easily explainable, that in fact affected everyone. From this typical defensive position we convey the impression that (a) it wasn't that bad, (b) others did it as well, (c) circumstances etc., and then the usual story—we didn't know. For a lot of foreigners this produces the impression—either the Germans don't think it was that important at all and are basically still adherents of the past system and simply don't want to say it. At least they don't have a deep feeling of guilt—What Mr. C. said was to my mind quite right: "What's the good of pointing it out to him over and over again. Then one will react sourly to it, and then you go from one defensive attitude to the next defensive attitude." So, instead of being overcome, the neurosis is intensified.

According to the logic of this discussion, overcoming the neurosis means nothing other than not having any feelings of guilt anymore, regardless of whether they are justified or not. The word neurosis plays, as technical termini often do, the role of a magic formula: its mention is supposed to solve all problems, without even becoming clear whether the speakers associate a clear idea with the concept. At any rate, it is only a matter of the appearance of self-reflection. The theme has been adopted from the everyday jargon of psychology that something is out of order with oneself, that one has complexes. In the process, one has the feeling of having moved forward, without in fact having taken the trouble and the pain of finding out what actually could be wrong: the empty reference to the problem of one's own ego functions merely to cast off responsibility from oneself. Apart from that, the passage is thoroughly ambiguous: it does not make clear whether the participant agrees with Colburn's reproach that the Germans are always in a defensive posture or whether he himself is obeying the defense mechanism. The first possibility is at least more likely.

The insight into one's own defense mechanisms seems to increase with the degree of political enlightenment. In a session with industrial managers, a participant quite clearly answers the reproach of the Colburn letter that they are taking the guilt lightly, that they are distancing themselves from it all too easily:

> U.: Good, then I'll put up with it. One doesn't like to talk—if we are talking about a nation—about the bad things one once did. Perhaps it's a psychological reflex that is expressed here, and then one doesn't judge appropriately.

In the context of anti-Semitic riots, a female participant from a fashion school group reflects on the defense mechanism:

> N.: But in this respect he naturally sees a certain nervousness with us, because, naturally, we have a completely justified vulnerability on this point, because we actually committed a rather serious offense in this respect in the past twelve years, and then bad conscience naturally gets stirred up much quicker, as if up to now it hadn't been a problem for us.

The "completely justified" is striking. It certainly implies that there are grounds for bad conscience on the basis of the guilt; the phrase "completely justified vulnerability" attracts attention, however, again basically in the sense that one could demand that the wound shouldn't be poked. Three times the speaker emphasizes how "natural" all this supposedly is.

Evidence for this would be the way in which the idea of German sickness is first coupled to the plea for understanding and then to the self-interest in better treatment:

> B.: You already started the German reeducation [original in English], the education of all the Germans, wrongly. You haven't treated them as a sick people's soul—because the Germans in themselves are sick and the sensitivity we

have rests in part on this psychological sickness—but instead you've punished them as naughty children. This is not proper democratic education. One would have to approach them with a feeling of gentleness, at least for the broadest mass. An entire people cannot be bad, just as an entire people cannot be good, instead the whole is an average of good and bad characteristics, and the mass is then formed by propaganda and led by a few personalities, in democracy too. Here's the psychological mistake he [Colburn] points out to his compatriots, that they closed-mindedly approached the entire people with the feeling that the German people are bad.

The distinctions introduced by the speaker between a "psychological disease" and the claim the German people were "punished as naughty children" is highly problematic. For the psychological disease resides in precisely those infantile mechanisms signified by the term "as naughty children." How little the discussion participant is concerned about his defense of the supposedly sick Germans against the punitive policy is obvious from the contemptuous passage about the average and the mass, which "is formed by propaganda and led by a few personalities." While he attacks the Americans for approaching the Germans with the prejudice that the German people is bad, he practices the same prejudice in all naïveté.

2. No Duty for Self-Accusation

A participant in the group of Bavarian dignitaries understands the question rationalistically. In his case, defense is not a matter of psychology but motivated by concrete interest. But exactly this allows him to behave without inhibition toward the question of guilt:

> H.: Pay attention, now. I believe, when we talk about moral guilt there, I want to serve as interpreter, how someone might think when he goes to bed in the evening and has the blanket over his head, so that nobody sees or listens to or thinks about him. This was the entire people. So he personally shuts out everything and thinks . . . and reasons: "Now, we've killed so many Jews, now we Germans—it is without doubt the German who did it—now they behaved this way in Greece, they behaved in such and such a way toward the partisans in Russia, etc. in France, etc. It was a dirty affair, and we should be ashamed from top to bottom." The man will certainly say this for himself. But when he sticks his head from under the blanket, he certainly won't say anything about it, especially not over the border, because he says that this confession will be useful to the others, even when it comes with the best intentions, insofar as they say we've got it in black and white and now the consequences will be drawn from it. No one has to incriminate himself. That's a widespread legal principle.

One's own reaction is dictated solely by political considerations, regardless of moral duties.

3. People without Space

Occasionally an effort will be made to help the vague awareness of a German abnormality to a less contorted expression and in the process to derive this abnormality itself from objective circumstances, though not without the ideology of "people without space" [a Nazi trope] playing a role.

> H.: I still want to say the following: We mustn't forget that we lost the war and that the powers opposed to our people brought about an even more difficult predicament than before. I actually want to use the expression that Germany is a powder keg, that is, it's virtually an art to feed 50 million or even many more from this little piece of soil that we live on. The nations who want to be a model for us and who tell us, you have to be more decent and more democratic, more understanding, they live in much better conditions.

Instead of the highfalutin discourse of collective neurosis, which by the way has also been advocated by authors like C. G. Jung,[2] here the simple reference to the "overheating" of the German condition appears connected with the plea for "understanding" for the Germans.

4. Dependency

The psychoanalytic theory of neurosis boils down to the diagnosis and interpretation of infantile character traits. In the apologetic self-diagnosis these play no unimportant role. One knows the story of the child who fell, hurt himself, and rushed to his mother with clenched fists and cried accusingly: you didn't watch out for me. This attitude, which is particularly relevant in the shifting of German guilt abroad, is already intended in the participants' self-assessment. To be neurotic and irresponsible means, for them, to be dependent.

The recourse to one's own childishness appears for example in a session of student fraternity members. To be sure, democratization rather than the Nazi period was being discussed:

> N.: If I belonged to a dictatorship for centuries up until yesterday, I can't be a free democrat tomorrow and I can't judge this democracy with all its good and also partly bad, I can't find my place in it at all. I have to be introduced into it slowly. And, to my mind, the Americans have failed to do that; maybe if he had expressed this desire to convert us to this free form

of government with good will, rather than not seriously or too quickly, if he hadn't in this sense left us on our own too soon, and we don't have the necessary experience or even the necessary critical abilities toward the matter.

The nonsense that "If I belonged to a dictatorship for centuries up until yesterday" can be explained by the strong desire to reclaim the situation of dependency for oneself as well as to cling to it as much as possible. This wish allows the speaker to forget that, viewed historically, Hitler's regime is the only case of a real dictatorship in Germany. More important, however, is the complaint that "the Americans" have "left us on our own too soon." It is completely legitimate to assume that not only is this an expression of the wish to be protected from and to remain free from having to make one's own decisions, but moreover also of the deep and certainly unconscious disappointment over the change in American policy, over the fact that the occupation power did not impose its authority as forcefully as expected.

The conclusion that is drawn from the putative or actual pathological state of Germans is always the plea for understanding from other countries. These are psychologically maneuvered into the position of the parents, on whom the child depends, whom it trusts, and from whom it expects forgiveness. Basic matters like the fact that many Germans had been nourished by the Americans for years do their part as well. But as soon as one characterizes oneself as sick, dependent, or psychopathological, the other nations appear to lack the necessary psychological understanding that is postulated on that basis. Not only is it said countless times that they have a false impression of the Germans, but foreign countries are regularly accused of this supposed lack of understanding.

The structure of the Colburn letter, which first makes positive statements about the Germans and then offers criticism, provides the most convenient starting point for this purpose. A passage at the beginning of a session with a girls' group, mostly refugees and orphans, is characteristic.

> I.: Yes, well, the speaker, at the beginning he's very polite and wants to respect us, but then suddenly somehow—well, he attacks us, he asserts several things about the master theory (Herrentheorie [presumably theory of the master race, Herrenrasse]) and the Jewish problem. And so he says that we still have to be educated *(erzogen)*, and foreign countries say this all the time too, that we've still got to be educated to become democrats.—That's pretty much the general attitude and the general understanding of foreign countries, always that we just have to be educated.
>
> Mod.: Well, you say that he attacks the Germans in the letter. Is this really the case?—

K.: Yes, I want to say to this that he has a very good talent for observation and that we can almost entirely agree with him. Of course, he starts a bit clumsily, at the end, inasmuch as he attacks us very hard. And we can't really put up with that.

Mod.: And why do you think we can't put up with that? Miss K. said that he is really telling the truth, that he has observed well. So we wouldn't have to have any guilt feeling at all or mustn't feel attacked. So why do you believe we feel attacked?

I.: Well, just because we don't want to accept a lot of things.

Mod.: Well, then what? Can you say it concretely? You are certainly thinking of specific things. Miss I.?

I.: I mean, he claims for example that we alone are responsible for the outbreak of the war.

Mod.: Yes.

I.: And naturally we refuse to accept that. Since we also know that foreign countries made preparations for war, we can't simply declare that we alone are to blame for the outbreak. We simply refuse to accept this.

Mod.: So Miss I. disputes German war guilt. Right?

I.: Yes.

E.: No, she doesn't deny war guilt. I mean she doubts . . . that only we are entirely to blame for the war.

At this point the insight into one's own defense mechanisms counterbalances the actual defense: it is as if the substantive truth of the claim that one is innocent derives from the natural law that people reject guilt, and it shines through that "the American," who "attacks us very hard," is in the wrong because he is committing the psychological error of thinking the Germans have to be "educated."

5. The Victor Is Responsible

The charge of a lack of sympathy emerges absurdly in a group of neighbors in which the roles are entirely reversed: after one fails oneself, one idealizes the others, and because they aren't worthy of it this leads to complete inversion.

B.: We made war and everything inhuman one can think of! I expected something completely different from a bringer of peace, see? That they still let people starve when the war was completely over. My sister always emphasized, my brother-in-law died of hunger. I assume so too . . . he still spoke with my sister and said: I'm finished. So, he starved to death, I know that for sure.

E.: My view was also: Particularly the American occupation, it would have generated much more sympathy if it perhaps had somehow supported the German

civilian population or at least the poorest people with food and so on . . .
it came too late, the realization came too late, much too late in my opinion,
in my opinion it was nothing but a punishment agreed on by the Allies.

The demand for sympathy shows here particularly strongly the infantile
model of the appeal to the parents. It is expected, as if it were self-evident,
that the conquerers would nourish the conquered. The prospect of "generating more sympathy" is held out as the reward for this. In the consciousness of this participant, the situation has already completely turned itself
upside down: the occupying power should not only care for the well-being
of their charges, but in addtion, moreover, should court their sympathies.
This inversion is quite common.

Shortly after this, in the same session, it is repeated again just as emphatically, perhaps as an aftereffect of that statement:

> *Th.*: Every now and then, one hears the comment in the streetcar and
> everywhere among the people: They should just make us completely into a
> colony . . . They should just Americanize us, so we finally know where we
> stand. There are so many who are indifferent too. The German has become
> so indifferent through the long-term . . . oppression and . . . bad experi-
> ence that he has had, that he is pretty indifferent to the fact that he has no
> national feeling anymore, he just wants to have peace and quiet. He doesn't
> care whether he's practically an American or a Brit or whatever. He just
> wants peace and quiet so that the years of war and the years of hunger will
> be forgotten, so that he gets some peace.

Once again, things are turned upside down: the German people is supposed to have been oppressed and to have had bad experiences. In the
seemingly disdainful wish that the Americans should just make Germany a
colony, however, the depth that presumably stands behind all such statements breaks through again: not only the wish to finally be released from
all burdensome responsibility, but also for the authority of the nourishing
father who proves himself as an authority by being tough on the children.

We should call attention to at least two specific aspects of the problem
of sympathy. One peculiar thought, which at times finds itself associated
with the reproach that there is too little understanding for Germany, is that
for whatever reason other people have to be better than the Germans. If,
in the opinion of the participants, they are not, this is used as a trap against
them. Sometimes the conclusion runs: if democracy is supposed to be better than us, its members have to behave better too; if they do not, this is evidence against democracy:

> *V.*: If someone already made mistakes, then others are supposed to make it
> better and not make even bigger mistakes.

To begin, the bad behavior of the occupation power is construed in a thoroughly unsubstantiated manner; the members of the democracy are then equated with the system itself without further ado, and the infantile objection is then also raised against them that they should be a model, without the question of the behavior of the Germans under the occupation even arising.

However, this idea is in no way limited to wildly nationalistic groups, but also occurs in rather matter-of-fact *(sachlich)* groups, as in one of the refugee groups:

> B.: On the other side it has been the case that the West, in the form of America and the other states, wants to teach us to behave humanely, and in particular they place human rights *(das Menschenrecht)* and international law *(Völkerrecht)* as the highest principle. One has to say, however, that in the past things did not proceed exactly according to this international law and according to these human rights with us in Germany. Now, of course, it's different . . . now America is trying to make up for it, and I have to say, they are at pains above all to soften the resistance of France and also of America and to win over these peoples for us too and in this respect to change minds. However, it is the case that if you want to proceed according to human rights and international law, then one may not make the mistake in an occupied country of showing them exactly the opposite; instead, you have to be at pains to treat these people especially and pretty precisely according to these human rights and this international law. And for this reason, the Americans were often criticized by the Germans that the Nuremberg trials—to mention them again—and these other war criminal trials, and the denazification measures showed us exactly the opposite of human rights and international law. They acted there exactly as Hitler and the other dictatorial power holders—namely, they took revenge (interjection: Yes!) and condemned people who hadn't committed any criminal act, without any regard to the person concerned, but simply on the basis of a certain membership in a party or on the basis of holding some office, or charged them because of their livelihood, just because they were in the NSDAP [Nazi Party] and perhaps had a small appointment.

The principle of rational law and humanity should explicitly benefit a group that prided itself on overriding these principles—very similar to the way in which, before the seizure of power, the National Socialists in Germany very skillfully exploited all the legal guarantees handed to them by the parliamentary system to overthrow the very same.

In contrast, in a group of high school seniors, the demand for understanding is advocated more in the sense of leaving alone *(Gewährenlassens)*:

> Gö.: They should really leave us alone. It's been emphasized that we are slowly developing ourslves in a forward direction, and for that reason I reject too deep an inquiry into our behavior.

The logic that because of the slowness of German development "too deep an inquiry into our behavior" is rejected deserves to be particularly emphasized. The defense mechanism takes advantage of a kind of intentional superficiality.

6. One Had to Have Been There

The other peculiar argumentation is that German affairs can only be judged properly if one was there. This motif assumes approximately the following form:

> Z: He [Colburn] can't judge any of this because he can't recognize the whole mass psychological effect, the whole science isn't that advanced yet, secondly because he did not experience this vortex in its time and place—regarding the defensiveness of the Germans and the distancing—I'm of the same opinion. If it is held against you all the time, a certain instinct for self-preservation comes about emotionally.

This defense makes the participant into an expert who judges the state of a science that is foreign to him. Through the deflection *(Reflexion)* that during the war not a single Englishman or Frenchman was there freely, everyone else besides the interested party is supposed to have the right to judge knocked out of his hands. The insistence on living experience becomes a maneuver.

In regard to the Nazi era, the same argument is advanced in the session of [female] fashion students.

> Z: We Germans have our major faults, but also our positive sides. I would claim the same about the Americans . . . They are a young generation; as something young, they don't have the burden of an old culture and its advantages and disadvantages, and that is also the reason in part for their strikingly honest openness. They came to Germany, have also now experienced National Socialism, got to know National Socialism only at a distance, never the core, the center of National Socialism. Because in the last analysis it is an inherently German affair and an affair that is very closely connected to the entire German existence. And they made various mistakes for which one can perhaps forgive them when one looks at it from their viewpoint: they won, they came to Europe, there were 1,001 problems—and not only Germany—they started the whole denazification, probably with the best intentions, but psychologically wrong.

What happened in Germany is supposedly an internal German affair that one can only understand firsthand and that perhaps does not concern other nations at all—the ideology of noninterference that was prevalent in the first six years of the Nazi regime casts its shadow. On the other hand, however, the Americans are supposed to have made "mistakes," for which, with all manner of caveats, "they can perhaps be forgiven."

IV. The Reality behind Defensiveness: Truth and Ideology

The participants who manifest the general tendency of defensiveness against the accusation of guilt, only give themselves over only to untamed imagination in extreme cases. Mostly, they use real factors that they fuse into the context of their purposes. In psychology, this process is called "rationalization." However, it would be superficial in social analysis if one were to assess such themes only on the basis of their psychological function and to ignore their actual content. It is of considerable importance for the understanding of contemporary German consciousness to determine which aspects of reality lend themselves to ideological deformation.

1. Propaganda

In regard to the real factors called on by the speakers who find themselves on the defensive, and not only these, one must think above all of the role of Nazi propaganda; of the seductive power that it possessed in the years before Hitler's takeover; of the exclusion of every other influence under the dictatorship until the population was intellectually fully at the mercy of the Goebbels apparatus. It was terribly difficult and required not only detailed political information but an independent self to resist the pressure of the propaganda. If this state of affairs is today put in the service of defensiveness, it does not in the process become untrue per se.

A twenty-three-year-old medical student, for instance, says this:

> E: First of all, I also think what Mr. A already said, that propaganda played a pretty big part. Because I was fourteen or thirteen back then when I watched the movie *Jud-Süß* [a Nazi propaganda film directed by Veit Harlan]. When you saw that—really how all that unfolded—you could instinctually get angry and get the impression these must have been bad people.

Considering that every counterargument was left out, and that under the conditions of the contemporary culture industry a great deal of people are only able to distinguish between reality and the contents of propaganda with great difficulty anyway, the truth of this utterance is all the more illuminating given that this student was still mostly a child during the war. He described the decisive aspect of the propagandistic effect to which he was exposed, namely that the Harlan film did not just operate with anti-Semitic theses, but directly demonstrated the wickedness of the Jews visually and aurally. It certainly required a significant measure of intellect and conscious resistance to escape from the effect of what presented itself so plausibly as direct evidence. The propaganda power of this film rested precisely on its not appearing as propaganda but as a picture of a reality.

Particularly consequential, of course, was the effect of propaganda that referred to the successes the Hitler regime enjoyed from the takeover to the 1942 reversal in the war. The belief that an endeavor is legitimated by its success is, despite all moral objections, a commonplace of Western civilization. Precisely here, National Socialist propaganda was able to connect to themes that were in no way brought into the world by Hitler:

> Sch.: But this was pointed out again and again in print and writing, that absolutely no other governmental form or government could manage something like that. That's the way it was.
>
> F.: Now this American also says on top of this that the Germans always spoke of "We," and that they were always trying, so to speak, to defend their own nation. Well, that's probably what every nation does, at least I would assume. And it is also after all through success that a certain self-confidence in the German people came about. And it is also clear domestically that people went along when they could see successes, in terms of the economy and also foreign policy. This naturally awakes a certain idealism, a certain excitement, particularly in younger people. On top of that came the restoration of military sovereignty, which particularly inspired the young people. Many of them cheered and said: Thank God, we can at least speak our mind again, we have something standing behind us. People didn't think too much about what would follow. But through the whole thing, the government seemed to be so firmly entrenched that there really weren't any resistance groups in the country anymore.

Particularly striking is the phrase, we could "at least speak our mind again" after "the restitution of military sovereignty." For nothing was more impossible under the dictatorship than to speak one's mind, and the participants stress this often enough anyway. If one might follow the language further, there is a sort of compensation phenomenon: precisely because as an individual one was not allowed to speak one's mind, one adhered to the belief that one could speak it as a collectivity—namely through the mouth of the dictator—to other nations. Hence the surprising phrase.

A high school senior estimates the propaganda as less ideological:

> F.: Back then, the German people were continuously worked over in a modern dictatorship for twelve years. The propaganda worked full speed, and

I still remember something that Goebbels said in his "Do You Want Total War" speech [February 18, 1943] in the sports stadium. He said at that time he had the masses in such thrall that he could have had them climb the trees around the stadium if he had wanted to. He did not have responsible and judicious Germans around him, but people who surrounded him in a typical mass psychology. Now, after the war, much has changed here in Germany. But one thing remains, and persists today, namely most people's fear of all politics. We know so many of our generation, and also here in our circle, who say: I will never join a political party or a political group. We can also immediately see if we look at German youth organizations that only a minimum are concerned with political questions, and this really is a task for those in responsibility, those politically interested, to awaken the interest of the German people in its entirety. Just yesterday evening the radio . . . conducted an interview in which three apprentices, a student, and others were questioned about this question, and the general answer was: We just can't accomplish anything, and everything we do is in vain.

Here full insight is gained into the manipulative character of what is generally understood by the term mass psychology. The realization also applies that the fall of Hitler did not change all that much in the anthropological conditions for this mass psychology.

Because the Hitler propaganda always had to cover up the contradiction between its content and the real interests of the masses, it was, like the general technique of agitators, essentially of a psychological kind, and its power was psychological as well. This seems to be evident to at least the more educated of our participants, as is said in the following statement:

> H.: A great tragedy lies over the whole thing because the German people is decent. It's neither better nor worse than other peoples, but was really misled by a Pied Piper of Hamelin who had very good ideas at first, which unfortunately nevertheless weren't really put into effect due to human deficiency; this German people then knowingly faced death and stood and fought on the front and in the homeland like no other people.

One may recognize in the comparison between this statement and the one treated earlier that substantively identical ideas can serve completely different tendencies, psychologically and factually as well, and as a result must never be interpreted in isolation.

THIS speaker, too, perceives the psychological power of the agitator Hitler—thus, the image of the Pied Piper of Hamelin—, but here it is merely used to remove responsibility from the people, who faced such supposed magic powerlessly. In the process, not only is the people itself glorified, but the Pied Piper is credited with "very good ideas at first." This never gets around to the actual critique of fascist propaganda techniques.

2. Terror

Nazi propaganda is described as irresistible and is probably to a great extent experienced as such. In the process, the propaganda immediately foreshadows the terror into which it actually crossed over; it is rightly said that the concentration camps were directed as much at those outside as inside; that they were the most effective means for advertising the omnipotence and omnipresence of the system. Again and again, reference to the impossibility of resistance appears in our transcripts, sometimes in an apologetic context, sometimes with shame and sorrow.

In the mouth of the open-minded, the theme of powerlessness appears with the accent that one would like to have done something but was not able to under the pressure of terror, whereas the nationalists present the impossibility of resistance abstractly as a given fact, without even ever seriously having aired the idea of resistance.

The following passage is characteristic of the way powerlessness is actually experienced by most:

> E.: You really couldn't do anything against it. What would you have done anyway?
> (Interruption: Back then, we already stood . . .)
> We were muzzled. Whoever opened his mouth ended up in the concentration camp.
> (Interruption: Every one of us . . .)
> But it accomplished nothing. I experienced that in my own family. You had to hold your tongue pretty well, otherwise all of us would have been hauled away.
> *Mod.*: Through denunciation in one's own family?
> E.: No, no. My stepmother was Jewish; they took her. She never returned.
> *Mod.*: When was that? During the war?
> E.: In 1943. My youngest brother, my stepbrother, he was seventeen years old at the time, they took him because he was a half-breed.
> *Mod.*: Well, and you also never heard anything about him?
> E.: He wrote until the end. He was in Monowitz (?) near Auschwitz until the Russians moved in, and since then we haven't heard anything. But we couldn't do anything about it. If you opposed, you were already gone. And that's how it was everywhere. One can't say that individuals lacked civil courage; they just wouldn't have achieved anything with it.

This female participant does not stop at establishing powerlessness, but criticizes the popular concept of "civil courage" with the justified thesis that under total terror this concept loses its meaning. Here, powerlessness is not used for the purpose of exoneration; much more, the speaker imagines the situation of the resisters, with whom she identifies.

The theme of the uselessness today of individual action is melded with the reference to the Nazi terror in the following statement:

> D.: That's exactly the sad thing; with Hitler it was really that we were chess pieces. And the regime was just so strict that we couldn't do anything else. We were chained and gagged in such a way that if we protested or wanted to protest in some way then we were either stuck in a concentration camp—that is, would have been stuck in a concentration camp—or, depending on what our crime in the Hitlerian sense would have been—we would have gotten our heads cut off. So, depending on how big our guilt would have been in terms of rebellion against Hitler, one would have either turned us into stiffs or put us in concentration camps for however many years. And the American, that is to say, well—the Englishman says so too—we should have revolted. Well, how about the instinct for self-preservation, because, let's say roughly—I can't give the exact percentages—but perhaps if everyone who didn't share Hitler's opinion had revolted, that would certainly have been a large part of Germany—then surely a quarter or a third or I don't know how many would have to have been hanged.

With the reference to the instinct for self-preservation, the simplest and most decisive aspects of the situation under Hitler is expressed. Nevertheless, the comparison to "chess pieces" still occurs just as much in reference to today's situation as in reference to the dictatorship. It is significant for the problem of guilt that individuals are not only actually dependent, but regard themselves from the very beginning as dependent chess pieces, identify with the situation, and in the process strengthen it even more. Apart from that, it comes through at the end of the quotation that, given the large number of dissenters, resistance would perhaps have been possible. This is just not said openly.

The identification of individuals with the social power, which here is at least virtually criticized, is nevertheless rather often put forward positively by our participants in the sense of the notorious maxim that we are all in the same boat. In a session carried out with North German trade unionists, a forty-eight-year-old lawyer explains:

> M.: . . . in addition in the war one was naturally in a community under siege, and was now convinced, now you can't break rank anymore because your sons and your fathers are at the front and have to bear—so that afterwards we were all in an emergency situation from which we could no longer escape.

This theme leads in some cases to a glorification of collective discipline, which covers what was done by individuals. This argumentation is particularly familiar in the ideology of the so-called soldierly man, whereas it is by the way striking that much is said about the sanctity of the [soldier's loyalty] oath, while the question of whether this oath was sworn freely, out of the sense of personal responsibility, or under the threat of terror is hardly ever mentioned.

Thus, a fifty-four-year-old unemployed and unskilled worker acknowledges:

> H.: That's exactly the question: To what extent can I follow an order out of internal discipline and internal necessity, and to what extent can I not follow it. For me an order is also a big thing. I think in this way like a soldier. For me the order has to be taken as important and serious, for me a command is not a question of blind obedience.

The distinction between blind obedience and inwardness that makes the order one's own is questionable, if the content of the order is of the sort that requires blind obedience to be executed. On the one side, the speaker wants to shift responsibility with his reference to the order, but, on the other side, free himself from the accusation of blind obedience; he does not in the process notice that he is trapping himself between two opposed theses. Here, by the way, a mechanism is at work to which Nietzsche pointed in *Human, All Too Human*.[1] The tyrant is able to distance himself from his atrocities insofar as he does not commit them himself, hardly ever sets eyes on them, but leaves them to his henchmen, while these think of themselves as mere executive organs of an order and tremble for their own life if they do not obey: thus, all participants come off with a good conscience.

In a session cited several times with unemployed women, among whom the tendency prevails of shifting the blame to men and exonerating women, a particularly ghastly episode is wiped away by the idea of discipline, without the legitimacy of the discipline itself ever being called into question. The relevant passage is reproduced here:

> B.: When my husband got leave, he told me that, in Kraców or someplace—I don't know where he was—Jewish women were shot there with infants in their arms. So then I said to him: "And you want to tell me that this is true?" Then he said: "I saw it myself." I didn't want to believe that from my own husband, that German soldiers are capable of shooting women with children. Then we were in a restaurant, and my husband met an old comrade there, and then my husband told him: "Tell my wife, she doesn't believe me." I didn't want to believe German soldiers shot women with a child in their arms. I didn't—despite the fact that two were telling me—my own husband told me, I didn't want to believe that. People said: They com-

mitted some sort of crime, perhaps killed a German or something else. That's the reason why she was shot.

D.: I want to respond that the German soldiers who carried that out or had to carry it out, that they were told by Hitler from up there, or by the Generals, that they were told stories about the crimes these women committed so that they would develop enough anger or hate or whatever to shoot these women, so that they would have the courage or whatever you want to call it, to shoot these women. They must have been told some sort of crime.

H.: They simply had to obey their military order. Their personal attitude toward the people and their personal brutality were completely irrelevant.

Mod.: Yes, but look, this problem you're just raising. You say it's simply obedience; this always leads back to the point we started from—should obedience go so far that one can order us to commit crimes?

D.: No. One mustn't think that the soldiers were simply told that this woman committed this or that crime, in other words were simply told lies just in order to give the soldiers the grit to kill this woman.

A.: They didn't tell the soldiers a thing. They told the soldiers: She's to be killed, that's it. They just weren't allowed to object. A soldier has to obey. Where is it going to lead if a soldier does what he wants to . . .

(Interruption: Yes, certainly!)

In times of war? A soldier, he has to obey. Other nations do just the same. They'd shoot us dead too, they also obey orders of their . . .

Some things in this passage deserve closer examination. First of all, it is clear that the theme of the supposed guilt of the Jewish women who were shot with their infants in their arms first appears only later in the conversation between the speaker and the German soldier—whether it was because the soldiers wanted to protect themselves when they noticed their horror or whether it was because they insisted on such a theme for the sake of their own peace of mind. According to this scheme, the murdered must have been guilty the whole time. The hollowness of this guilt legend is also acknowledged immediately, but the story is turned around in such a way that the soldier[s] must have been told something about the guilt of the victim in order to anger them—a barely more plausible assumption, for in general whether the soliders are in the right mood to kill is not taken into account in orders. This is then brought up in the further course of the discussion, but now the debate about whether the soldiers had to obey blindly or had to be given reasons for their actions distracted from the sore spot of the murder of the women. At the end, all this results in a posture of defensiveness: after it is established that the soldiers simply had to obey, the argument extends to the assertion that other soldiers also had to do the same: "They'd shoot us dead too."

3. Generalizations

In order to make transparent to at least some extent the connection between truth and untruth on which defensiveness draws, one has to take into account a mechanism which the examination repeatedly hit on: conscious or unconscious misuse of truth itself as ideology. Themes that in themselves are justified appear in contexts in which their truth content functions solely to distract from the offense committed, to relativize guilt and innocence, and, from a supposedly higher standpoint that takes the subject out of his actual situation, to excuse him from any concrete responsibility. Within the social context, there is hardly any argument that, separated out and isolated, would not be useful for such purposes, as there is no idea, even be it entirely true, that cannot transform into illusion and lie if hypostatized and removed from living experience. The significance of using truth as ideology for the apologetic technique as well as for an individual's instinctual economy can hardly be overestimated. The subtle crossovers from true premises to false conclusions all too easily elude counterargument in the heat of discussion. The partial truth of an argument promotes trust in the rest and for the goals, however questionable. Psychologically, though, truth as ideology helps to produce a good conscience. One is relieved of the discomfort of lying, which leads to conflicts with the superego, or, much more, it is easy to repress the discomfort of lying if one can make the lie plausible enough to oneself that conceptual effort is required to uncover it. In general parlance, this phenomenon is referred to as habitual lying. The material of the group study is rich in examples of its phenomenology.

We know the role that cliché, rigid and therefore false generalization, plays in totalitarian thinking. Anti-Semitism, which transfers a number of negative stereotypes to a whole group with no regard to the persons concerned, would be unthinkable without the method of false generalization. Even today, the collective singular used for foreign peoples—the Russian, the American, the Frenchman, a usage that entered everyday speech from the army—is evidence of this. The collapse of fascism and its system of false generalization has opened many people's eyes to this practice—so far as it concerns themsleves. It seems to be a law of present-day social psychology that what one has practiced oneself is always what makes one most resentful. The unconscious motives for this, closely related to the projection mechanism, need not be discussed here; suffice it to say that, as soon as one has condemned false generalization, it is easy to distance oneself from National Socialism, and that once this has been accomplished without too much cost, it is easy to put oneself in the right and to make yesterday's persecutor today's victim, as for instance is practiced in "The Questionnaire" of Mr. [Ernst] von Salomon [a popular autobiographical novel that mocked the denazification process, accusing it of the same logic the Nazis had employed].[2]

Whereas one generalizes about foreign peoples without any inhibitions, every criticism of German actions is rebutted by pointing out that these are false generalizations. The basic stimulus was constructed in such a way that the critique was advanced with extreme caution and meticulously avoided or qualified collective generalizations. Nevertheless, many participants objected to it because of its supposed generalizations, and in this way the accusations of the Colburn letter are indirectly confirmed, insofar as the effect leads to precisely those patterns of behavior identified in the letter. The underlying scheme is: "Colburn reproaches us for wanting to fend off consciousness of guilt, that's a false generalization, not all of us are like that"; from this, however, things move inconspicuously to the denial of the deeds themselves, in other words of exactly those events to which that consciousness, whose absence is denied, would have to relate.

Quite characteristic is the speech of a forty-five-year-old merchant:

> *I.:* I think one has to credit the writer of the letter for one thing: First of all, he made the effort to delve into a foreign country and into the attitudes in this country and maybe also—you also have to take into account the year of this letter. I believe we would also basically make the same mistake of wanting to generalize things too quickly after a quick look in a foreign country, and as far as that one perhaps shouldn't criticize him too much. But the fact, also already mentioned by the gentleman before me, that things are portrayed falsely here with certain generalizations, I actually want to agree with that. The assessment of individual people is not and cannot be different in any country at all; because in any country they range from the worst to the best quality of character and inclination, of ability and talent, all types. In what percent and in what combination they appear and in the process shape the face of the country, that might be the decisive question for the country. But then we also come to the conclusion that in general people are not so extraordinarily different if one draws a big circle, in other words includes the population of the country as such. In our opinion, he made the most mistakes in political insight and political judgment, and left a lot out in the process. If one talks, for example, with English merchants about politics, and about the policies of Hitler, then you realize that you can talk with them just as objectively and calmly as you can with any other people who we would consider reasonable. I'm only talking about the English here because it's an English sergeant. His criticism of the defiance and the collective defensiveness against all bad characteristics, this is really a completely inevitable result of the mistake of generalizing German war guilt, and in this way it is simply the defense of the injustice piled over

us, on us, after we previously probably also created an extraordinary amount of injustice. The generalization that Germans are perhaps all too willing to run after a strong man like a flock of sheep, this—I believe—is so absurd that it hardly needs to be discussed; that's my personal opinion on the matter.

In the decisive spot, there is an equivocation: the speaker talks about "the injustice piled over us, on us," and it remains unclear whether he is thinking about wrongful accusations or about wrong done to the Germans themselves. In the sense of the preceding criticism of false generalizations, the idea extends all the way to judgments about the Germans; with the af-terthought: "after we previously probably also created an extraordinary amount of injustice," however, the argument switches over into the sphere of real injustice and into the offseting of guilt accounts. At the end, the German inclination for strong men is disputed merely apologetically. "It hardly needs to be discussed," like everything embarrassing; caution or bad conscience, however, leads the participant to the qualification: "that's my personal opinion on the matter."

The stereotype of "the" German is particularly unpopular with our speakers. As soon as they get wind of it, many turn into skeptical nominal-ists. Thus, a fraternity student says:

> *E.:* I wanted to say, the notion of "the German" is quite problematic . . . well . . . one simply throws the term around. I studied in Switzerland for two and a half years and got to know many foreigners and so at times thought to myself: "What actually is the German? How different is he really from other people?" And now we have—we live under entirely dif-ferent conditions than in America, and certain racial assumptions exist, but it is not my impression that the differences are as big as one perhaps is mak-ing them out today. We simply grew up under different conditions, but that there is such a big difference between the German person and an American person or a Swiss person or an Englishman, I don't have that impression.

It is unmistakable that there is a tendency here to push the opposite of stereotypes—the emphasis on differences—so far that relativism results; that it should be impossible, due to the supposedly vast, but the again lim-ited, differences to measure one person with the same scale as another.

Against widespread or resurgent anti-Semitism, it is asserted above all that one must not generalize. In fact, the stereotype, the granting to judg-ment autonomy from the experience that gives rise to it, is one of the core pieces of anti-Semitism, and any self-reflection requires avoiding it. On the other hand, it is also apparent here that the criticism of the principle of gen-eralization stands to a large extent in the service of defensiveness. Further aspects of this psychological background can be found even in critical statements against generalization as well; namely the inclination, in the name of such critique, to construe according to the well-known scheme two different classes of Jews and then to condemn one of them again according to stereotype. An argument such as the one against generalization, which can turn not only against the stereotype but also against every thought that transcends immediate conditions, has no specific content as such and can take over the most diverse functions, depending on the context in which it appears. It is not only Jewish-friendly groups in which anti-Semitic generalizations are spoken against. It is put this way in a session of Christian working-class youth:

> *E.:* I think a fundamental mistake is being made here by talking about the Jews, that is to say, namely that one is generalizing completely crudely. I've had experience with Jews too, and I have to say that while there are indeed black marketeers among them there are also very decent people.
>
> *Mod.:* Mr. M. is also confirming this now.
>
> *E.:* And I also had the experience that not only Jews participated in the black market, but by the same token even more racially pure Aryans.

It conveniently goes hand in hand with this that certainly many Germans took part but that, nevertheless, "foreigners and Jews" played a special role. When Colburn, for his part, turns against generalization, he finds no sympathy at all. There is a sentence in his letter saying that the agitation against DPs is unjustified, because before the currency reform everyone who could engage in profiteering did. This gives participants in a group of inhabitants of a Bavarian village occasion for wild calculations that end in an anti-Semitic tirade:

> *G.:* Then we'd like to get back to the letter, because it actually says there that, the Jews actually write, every German profiteered. I believe the Jews profiteered much more than us. Certainly every German knows these days, I might say, that only one-tenth of Germans profiteered and nine-tenths certainly did not profiteer.
>
> *J.:* Yes, I think so, too. There were . . . among the Jews there was not 1 percent who didn't profiteer, because actually all of them profiteered.
>
> *L.:* One mustn't understand profiteering as, I mean, if someone, anyone secured something he absolutely necessarily needed . . . Let's say it this way, the other, the profiteer, he wants to get rich, while the other, he only wants to live.

The phrase "the Jews actually write" is obscure. Apparently the Colburn letter is being attributed to Jewish sources. The clichéd thinking is evident in the rhetorical figure: "among the Jews there was not 1 percent who didn't profiteer, because actually all of them profiteered." The justifying sentence is completely incapable of fullfilling the function with which the speaker burdens it; for one thing because the predicate "they profiteered" is identical with what is to be proven, namely the fact that they profiteered, but also because its own total content contradicts the thesis, even if it is ever so slightly qualified. Beneath this logical misconstruction lies this: One cannot say of even the smallest minority of Jews that they did not profiteer because it is said to be part of the constitution of "the" Jew—established by the stereotype—to profiteer. At the end, then, an arbitrary contrivance *(Hilfskonstruktion)*: since there is no way to deny that Germans profiteered as well, they are completely arbitrarily, and without even a conceivable possibility of differentiation, credited with wanting "only to live," while the Jews wanted "to get rich."

Even in the very open-minded group of high school seniors, the critique of generalization, which is in itself justified, takes on a problematic accent. The following passage is an exemplar for the subtlety with which true insight is refurbished psychologically for the purposes of defense:

> L.: I want to tie in with the previous speaker and say that one should be careful about making generalizations. This applies especially to Mr. Colburn as well as to the previous speaker, who, for example, held German science responsible for Hitler's being able to come to power. I believe that this German problem has to be regarded from a wholly different perspective; because the German question is actually far more difficult than, for example, American democracy. If one follows history, it is far more difficult, already purely on the basis of Germany's geographical location, to make a clear determination. And so I want to emphasize especially that the pyschological side of this situation has to be emphasized as well: why it came to all that. We must not infer generalizing attitudes from single utterances. When the previous speaker spoke of particular professional groups or scientists who are being blamed here for something, it is actually the case that in Germany precisely the question of democracy has to be viewed from an entirely different perspective. What was the situation after the First World War really? We have to take this into account, and so, when the previous speaker talked about America in comparison, when he said: sure, America is a democracy in which something like this could not happen, that a dictatorship could gain power. And so no generalizations, no holding entire professional groups or whole peoples or nations responsible for something.

The admonition not to generalize leads here to the demand to understand National Socialism historically—and to excuse it. The presumably unconscious will not to let the transition appear abrupt causes the speaker to insert a lengthy passage of more or less contentless sentences. It is particularly important to the future college student to whitewash "the sciences" by means of protest against generalization.

4. Reference to History

Granted, the appeal to history often occurs with a particular intention; the unemployed manual laborer cited earlier says:

> H.: The question of who was the biggest criminal: It is so terribly easy for the winner to depict the defeated as criminals. This is something I reject. Naturally I do not approve of what Hitler did in the end when he was in the corner that the others rounded him into. Certainly not. But I refuse to run after them, or once again save the asses of those who only throw dirt on us, label us as criminals and now hold us responsible for the whole guilt, which stems from entirely different casues that are buried much deeper.

This statement is an especially striking demonstration for the misuse of truth as ideology. For the fact that the causes of National Socialism are buried deeper than in the supposedly criminal nature of National Socialists is certainly true. However, the vague, abstract and nonbinding reference to the "deeper causes," which themselves are not elaborated, here serves the purpose of moving on to the counterattack. The speaker acts in such a way that, on the basis of the accusation against Germany, he now himself construes a guilt, that of "throwing dirt on us," and opens a sort of counter-ledger. The distortion of tracing Hitler's deeds back to the "corner" into which the others "rounded" him is characteristic.

The argument, once uttered, continues to have an effect throughout the session. Much later a participant says:

> Z.: The problems that history raises will always come up again and have always appeared again. We can learn from history that wars always existed. And in my opinion, there is no apparent basis that could lead to there being no more wars. In exactly the same way as the last war was waged, there will be wars in the future. And now it is a cheap fact that the victor rises above the vanquished and imputes guilty motives to him. Such methods are a subjective basis for judgment. We have to free ourselves from this. We can't continue anymore to stand on the subjective standpoint, but somehow have to get around to a different notion of history, which perhaps finds its expression in saying that the wars that have taken place, the problems that have to be solved, are in the last analysis historically necessary, if they've appeared. They are not to be traced back to the guilt of some individual . . .

(Interruption: Very true!)

or to the guilt of a national group or of any other social group; rather, they emerge from the structure that the population happens to have here on earth and on the basis of the fact that it continues to develop dynamically and collapses . . .

The "deeper causes" to which reference is made here are unsurprisingly superficial: that experience teaches that there will always be wars and that, for this reason, no specific responsibility at all exists. The recourse to highly unjustified general historical and sociological laws, themselves based on fascist ideology, functions in the sense of a determinism that acquits every individual and every group.

The individual's well-founded foreboding of being at the mercy of historical forces against which he himself cannot do anything is dissolved in a notion of destiny that damns the individual to passivity and at the same time unburdens him. In a cosmopolitan women's group, a participant says "War would have come either way," in order to launch an offensive using the old ideological theme of foreign envy in the name of this resigned observation:

Pf.: Germany was just too diligent, worked too much. We overtook them, and they didn't want to admit it. In my opinion this is likely—
L.: You're right, Mrs. Pfeiffer.
H.: This plays, I believe, a role in every war.
W.: I'm of the same opinion too, that it would have happened anyway, the war . . . we lived in peace too long.
Mod.: You believe humans can't bear to live in peace for long?
W.: That's not what I wanted to say, but twenty years—if it had taken longer, it would have happened anyway, even without Hitler.
Mod.: Even without Hitler? For what reason?
W.: Because the people wanted it. They really did want to have war. 1914 it was always said . . . 1939—when is the war—1939, 1938, 1937 it just was always seething that there would be war—They had prepared, they actually wanted to try it out again!
Pf.: And now you're talking about war again.

The notion of the inevitability of war here has taken on some obsessive quality. The group repeats the same thesis over and over again in stubborn compulsion, without somehow getting beyond the mere assertion.

The picture becomes more complicated through the influence of the popular cliché of the—mainly British—envy of the rise of a striving Germany and the thought of war as a capitalist escape hatch. A member of a refugee-group says:

K.: . . . this didn't for me begin with Hitler, this didn't for me begin with the First World War. This goes back to the previous century, at the end of the dividing up of the colonial world, when we Germans as a cultural nation tried for once to have some land somewhere too, that's when the Englishmen's hostile attitude toward us began. Back then they didn't want to have us in the world. On top of that was the intelligent but just as much diligent German worker, who was later seen as the most hated man in the world. This contributed to the outbreak of the First World War. And that is where the avalanche was set off, and not with Hitler.

Similarly, a speaker in a neighborhood group:

Pf.: What was actually going on with us? Here was a Hitler, who supposedly started the war. Certainly, he started it. But why did he start it? Kaiser Wilhelm as such actually started the war too. It's strange that the Germans should always start. I'm convinced that one simply doesn't want to let the German come up, that one just looks for reasons and in Adolf Hitler found a man who is not politically mature, who just fell in. The war would have come anyway, whether a few years earlier or ten years later. But one would not have let Germany grow big.

Again it is supposed to be "strange" that the Germans always start the wars, and this regularity seems so unbelievable to the speaker that he smells baseless denunciation behind it and then takes refuge in the even more unbelievable construction that "one" had picked Hitler because of his political immaturity so that he could for no reason provoke a war, which suited the future victors very well—a fantasy of truly paranoid style.

But the thought that the rise of Germany was feared is so deeply entrenched that it is not restricted only to the aggressive nationalists, but is also found in participants who are striving for a balanced judgment. Thus, a police officer says:

W.: I believe, then, to be purely guilty or purely innocent, that does not exist in this case. There is only a predominant guilt. My opinion is that Germany bore the greater part of the guilt for bringing about the war. Because without doubt as far as I know we violated existing agreements by attacking Holland, and so forth, and we trampled on neutrality. I also believe this was done intentionally in Hitler's policy. And obviously the world was in an uproar about this. But it is also understandble, on the other hand, that we were not completely innocent. So, after we overcame the aftermath of the First World War and recovered economically, we became big competition again—so again the capitalism—which meant a danger, and so in the end it came to all these entanglements. Naturally, we did want to become bigger again. So for instance the population numbers increased, and we needed more space, we still need it today. And the world did not want to allow that we could get this space. And so the question of guilt is, well, shared, but I believe the larger share lies with us.

5. Pseudosocialist Posture

In the session of a group of men from a barracks, an old socialist idea about the connection of war and capitalism is put forward in the following form:

> N.: And I myself believe that the American, still before the war with his capital, whether it was Opel or General Motors or somebody else, with his capital, first helped Germany get back on its feet, that it came to a point that it was capable of leading a war, and then afterward sold Germany out as the ones responsible for the war, that's a very risky business. And generally it is exactly like that: one cannot hold an individual person responsible for what happens in world politics as a whole.

The economic explanation of the wars is being misunderstood here as if the wars were business ventures of some influential firms or other. A monstrous intrigue of individual entrepreneurs whose aim is supposedly to put the Germans in the wrong is being alleged. Even the political commitment to socialism does not protect against the paranoid structure of such thinking.

Finally, we point out that the true nature of this socialist-disguised way of arguing reveals itself at times by being paired with anti-Semitic phrases; this is also the case with the same speaker:

> N.: But one also has to say, somehow they take, they take advantage of the strengths, the strength of the peoples, in order to play one against the other. And I'm convinced whether above this a much bigger power has to reside, that it is, like Mr. O just said, the high finance, which is often associated with Jewry. Mr. O. said that. One almost has to believe that they steer the fates in the same way, in order to pitch one against the other.

Toward the end of the same session, it comes to a confused demagogical speech in which everything that has been presented here gets mixed up together:

> B.: Back then Mr. Gromyko, the assistant secretary of state, said in Russia: "The American lost the war politically and economically by occupying Europe."—We only ever discuss one problem; What is there?—What is here? We have not talked at all about the main reasons and some people have absolutely no idea what is going in the world. This is about true socialism! And this is called communism! Lenin said: "What is communism, and what is socialism on the beautified tour of Teutonism *(Germanentum)*, that is the well-being of the international proletariat." And in this sense you can ask any nation. If today I am going beyond myself, that has to be written down, what I say here, so that a ridiculous lie will not be made out

of it. In this sense, the man upstairs, who governs everything, rolled with the golden ball, he rolled it the wrong way through the roulette. And I tell you today: Most people don't even know what it's all about, namely about socialism! And the proletariat inside, in the whole world, suddenly wakes up and slays the beast of prey, in other words capital. They are going to strike down the power of this selfish beast of prey!, in that they rattle the weapons among themselves! And Mr. Lenin—er Stalin, like the democracy that never exists, whether in America or anywhere else where they're still fighting over it, where they still are, whether it is the Federal government, the Federal administration or anything else! The people now gave them an example with the guidelines! Now we're awake. Now socialism speaks and woe to you if you do the wrong thing. Then comes the cowardly social-ism, the communism. We're now going to show you what's going on here. You clogged up *(verkalfakert)* our International with the young as well as with the old Jews. This stops now. He belongs in Palestine. Before the Internationals!, where he belongs! And socialism, with its rifle at the ready, is going to tidy up among itself internationally and wreck this beast of prey. That he understands himself as international, that's what I'm trying to es-tablish.

And further after an interruption by the investigator:

B.: Stalin is a Bolshevik! A robber and murderer! He's going to be devoured by his own people, once it gets going, you understand? When the people fi-nally wake up. The nations among themselves, the nations will agree with each other and will say: "So, our socialist aspirations will wake up interna-tionally and devour this plague, which today has put us on the lowest step! That's why we have hands, and hammer, sickle, as the others already said. And when that doesn't work there, and if it doesn't work, we still have axes, right? And when we catch one, then we're going to shove him where he belongs. Then we're going to crush his throat with this hand, so that he'll be thrown down into the abyss!—Sure, we don't want to drag it out here, they should only . . . these things that, that they chop up every-where . . . Look: Why does the American cry today! No living person cries today like a nation. That is the American, because he says: This flood from above, it has secured itself 100 percent, it took us by surprise, and we, to-gether with all the Germans, are going down in Noah's flood. But from it-self, through the inner revolutions which come into existence there, there is a fight to end all fights, there is a fratricide, let's say, all the survivors are so-cialists. We are going to build ourselves a new state. That is the socialist state, and whoever offends against this state again, comes to the tree of life—that is the gallows. We will build it there, and he'll be hung.

Only the audio tape gives a sufficient idea of this speech, which is deliv-ered in highest agitation with a vehemence reminiscent of Hitler. Herr Bauer, a stocky apoplectic, had remained silent during the whole session, and only at the end did his pent-up emotions break loose. There is reason to assume that among those who remained silent or spoke little, there are more participants of his type. That in this case we are dealing with someone who is paranoid in a clinical sense cannot be doubted. But at the same time, we can peel out from all this nonsense a few rational motives: the sense of economic connections as a reason for the war and the hope for socialism as the only way out of the entanglement. Insofar as the speaker is trying with these themes to penetrate behind the mere facts to get to the essential, it is as though the thoughts emancipate themselves from experientially learned control and run amok. From the intuition into the origin of the war in social conditions arises the depraved fantasy of a conspiracy of dark powers that aim at ruin; the dream of socialism is mixed up with wild threats against exactly those Jews on whom these threats were realized, and in the end nothing remains except the naked drive to destroy. Truly symbolic for the entire sphere to which the speech applies, and which still smolders, is the definition: "the tree of life, that is the gallows."

V. Defense

When the truth or at least elements of the truth are processed by the defense mechanisms, a displacement takes place throughout. One transforms one's own guilt into the guilt of others by taking the mistakes these others have made or are supposed to have made as the cause of what one has done oneself. This mechanism, however, has a well-known psychological side: that of projection. One's own urges, one's own unconscious and repressed, is [*sic*] ascribed to the other. One thus lives up to the expectations of one's own superego, and at the same time has the opportunity to release one's own aggressive inclination under the heading of legitimate punishment. The projection mechanism is manifest in paranoia, in the persecution complex. The inclination to project, however, extends far beyond the psychotic sphere and occurs in all possible degrees in normal everyday behavior. During the Third Reich, in America projective inclinations were regarded as the absolutely key phenomenon of the German mentality: The book *Is Germany Incurable?* by Richard M. Brickner[1] interpreted the entirety of National Socialism from the perspective of a collective paranoia. It cannot be investigated here whether political movements can be adequately explained with psychiatric categories or whether the tendency toward pathological projection is especially strong in Germany. Yet the material of the group study is nevertheless rife with examples of it. The speech by Herr Bauer discussed at the end of the fourth chapter is espe-

cially pronounced, but by no means an exceptional case. It must nevertheless be remembered that the material presented in the following pages must
not be regarded entirely as projective in the strictly psychological sense.
The projection mechanism is inherently connected to rationalization, and
in face of the virtuosity of rationalization it is often difficult to distinguish
between the instrumental effort to exonerate oneself by opening up a guilt
account for the partner and the unconscious as well as obsessive transfer-
ence of one's own inclinations and urges onto others, on the basis of which
one assigns blame. One may really only speak of projection in the truly
psychiatric sense when the condemnation of others takes on traces of the
delusional imagination. We have not organized the material according to
the scheme of distinguishing such pathological projection from more or
less rationally chosen counter-reproaches, but according to the themes to
which the accusations are attached.

1. Projection onto Foreign Countries

In one instance, the tendency to projection is discussed by the participants
themselves in connection to the Colburn letter. The inclination to seek
scapegoats is thereby at first justifiably assumed to be universal, but from
there an almost imperceptibly slippery transition is made toward the denial of guilt. The connecting link, usually, is a single word. The mechanism
of association substitutes for the thought. If the Germans look for guilt in
others, this is part of the general human inclination to deflect guilt onto
others. Precisely this expression makes it possible to accuse the outside world
by virtue of the same mechanism that "puts everything on the Germans."
The very informative passage reads:

> Gö.: The inclination to shift the blame to others is actually also in the human re-
> lation of one individual to another, not only in that from nation to nation . . .
> I believe that many people see the scapegoat more in others than in them-
> selves.
> I.: Well, I meant, for the outside world it is really easy now to somehow shift
> everything onto the Germans since we lost the war. We really can't defend
> ourselves properly at all.

The expression that many people see the scapegoat more in others than
in themselves leads here to psychological defensiveness: the projection
mechanism, to be sure, is recognized, but insofar as one subsumes oneself
under the scapegoat rubric, one's own guilt is also handled like a mere
delusion, rather like talk of the German neurosis.

The exculpatory accusations against the outside world are not without their truth content. They are indeed often advanced by intelligent and progressive participants, as for example those in a working-class youth group:

> E.: And I believe Hitler would never have come into power, that is to say by 1935 it would have been time enough that the major powers, the Allies, would have intervened, when Hitler had become too strong, that is to say in the truest sense of the word, when Hitler got too fresh. We found out in 1938 in Munich where the decision really fell. And today we are in a more or less similar situation . . .
>
> S.: I believe foreign countries allowed Hitler things that they would have flatly refused his predecessors. For example the naval pact and all those things. They were flatly denied Hitler's predecessors, invasion of the Rhineland, etc., and all those things.

The aspect of truth in this argumentation is just as compelling as it is powerless in regard to the question of German responsibility. Naturally, one cannot speak here of paranoid tendencies. Even if the wrong that one committed oneself does not get any smaller in the process, it is nevertheless comforting and as a result belongs to the most popular argument that the responsibility for Hitler and his misdeeds falls to his proctors. In the process, the role of the outside world in regard to Hitler is retouched at will: toleration is turned into unconditional active promotion.

At times reproach of the outside world is concretized with reference to the good relations between foreign diplomats and prominent Nazis:

> U.: Foreign countries, Mr. François-Poncet, for example, or the English ambassador in Berlin, were much better informed about these events from their espionage divisions than the average German, let's say, party member. And yet, Mr. François-Poncet as well as the English ambassador took part in all of Hitler's receptions. I don't know, there were more than sixty nations that had ambassadors and envoys and whatever in Berlin. For what reason, if at the time they were really convinced that it was wrong and that it was a crime and it didn't suit them, why didn't they pull out their envoys? Then we would have become confused, at least those who were not 100 percent pledged to National Socialism, and we would have said: Wait a minute, if they are leaving, what is actually going on?—We thus had to assume that everything was completely in order. Mr. François-Poncet hung around with Göring, he went hunting with Himmler, the same man whom he supposedly already knew in 1938 to be a killer. If I'm a reasonably decent guy, I don't sit down at the table with a murderer.—
> (Interruption: Quite right.)

Something completely analogous is found in the discussion among police officers cited earlier:

U.: Had one made the same concessions to the Weimar state on the part of England, France and also other countries as one later made to this Hitler, then things would have been better in the Weimar Republic. The diplomats who later came to Obersalzberg, they were already too late, because they only came when we had a *Wehrmacht* [army] and thus Hitler could pound on the table. Only then did they come and still at that time wanted to try to prevent the upcoming war. But it was already too late. They are guilty insofar as they withheld every concession from the Weimar Republic, and judged it entirely selfishly, namely Germany's situation, and did not, so to speak, give it a lift, the young German democracy. And afterward one had this Hitler, and then afterward the concessions on Austria. England even said: I'm not interested if Hitler occupies Austria, Austria is a German country. Just let them take it, afterward, like it was taken, and the non-German countries were next, then the knife was at the throat, and then there was the most extreme consequence, that of going to war.

In the same session, one of the sorest spots is touched on with the ingenuity the apologists display throughout:

B.: Aren't we looking at this thing in too short a time frame? If America back then had judged the situation better, if the entire world had judged the situation better, if they hadn't made a Herr Hitler presentable by establishing embassies, consulates, etc., given international receptions, etc. And anyway, maybe there is guilt precisely for the non-European countries. And they didn't even grant asylum to the people here in Germany who fled, we might as well say who gave up their existence, and then granted them asylum to a very small extent and only if the financial conditions were there. Practically speaking, it was the case that in fact the poor suckers stayed in Germany and had to endure the whole misery, the whole peril, concentration camps, etc. etc. But the people who could afford it, they were gone, they were acceptable again over there. For those people, one granted asylum. That was not only the case in America. I know of a case in Sweden where they sent back over four hundred people. And that's the heart of the problem. America should contemplate the fact that for the most part it, and not only the German people, made a certain Herr Hitler viable in the first place.

The toleration of Hitler is explained by civic solidarity, only with the strange accent that he who is supposed to benefit from this solidarity, the German dictator, is thereby implicitly exonerated.

2. Humiliating Peace of Versailles

Besides the argument that others bear the responsibility because they tolerated Hitler, the cliché is still in effect, unbroken and unshaken, that the entire nationalist reaction, and not only Hitler alone, used after 1918. The humiliating peace of Versailles is supposedly responsible for the fact that Hitler rose to power. So, for instance, an export merchant says:

> Z.: To quite a large extent, National Socialism was also the product of the conditions that were imposed on us through the peace of Versailles, and that were allowed to persist for much too long. It is therefore not the fundamental tendency toward totality, but it was the conditions created by the peace of Versailles . . . that provided the foundation for National Socialism in the first place. The same applies today.

In a group of teachers, one simply talks about the "shameful treaty" *(Schandvertrag)*.

> F.: This famous peace treaty is still a "shameful treaty" in the mind of the Germans.

In a group of army officers, Hitler is unambiguously traced to Versailles:

> H.: Unfortunately, Versailles was supposed to pin the guilt for the war on us, and this in some ways contributed to the birth of Hitler, one can certainly say that.

One is not in such a rush to leave the past behind when it can be used for defense.

3. Liberation of the Germans in the East

A businessman from Upper Silesia does not mention Versailles, yet he wants to ascribe the whole disaster to the injustice that was done to the Germans in the East, and otherwise to the First World War in the abstract:

> B.: If we are talking about the causes of this war and about the effects of this war, . . . then the cause of this war is certainly not German totalitarianism, or whatever you call it, or Hitler, but the cause of the war was certainly the First World War. And if one goes back to the causes, one can always infer the effects from them. And you yourself already mentioned before about Gleiwitz, that we attacked Poland, etc. Well, then, what was the cause? The cause was clearly that millions of people were sold to Poland because of the lost First World War, and that America, England, and France agreed to that. I myself was born as a Pole, and grew up in the so-called Polish homeland. Well, over there it was such that we Germans were treated as second-class people, we were chased like animals into the mines, we were good enough for any kind of work. And, naturally we were eager to get out of

this piece-of-crap country, I want to call it, Poland, to get back to our homeland where things had been better for us before. Because every person wants to live where things are better for him, that is to say, where things were once better for him. Had this revenge not been taken after the First World War, certainly no Hitler would ever have come to power here, and the Second World War would not have broken out. But the cause for the Second World War was the unjust treatment of the German people after the First World War, was the sale of German land to Poland and to all the other countries, was the dismemberment of a so-called national unity. If one wanted to get rid of national unity after the First World War, one should have gotten rid of it entirely . . . not only in Germany. It was therefore not the case that we attacked Poland, but that we as the motherland had to strive . . . to represent their life chances, give them a boost and remedy these abuses.

The seeming rationality of the initial considerations about the complexity of the causes of the war and the treatment of the German minority by the Poles introduces the extravagant thesis that "we did not attack Poland," but represented as "mother country" the "life chances" of the German "countrymen." The content of this statement is also mirrored in the speech of a former *SS* man from a group of refugees who clings staunchly to National Socialism:

R.: You initially said that it's proven objectively that we in fact bear the guilt for the Second World War. I, as an inhabitant of the borderland, well perhaps twenty meters from the Russian border up in the Baltics . . . can only tell you that for Germany an immediate threat was created in that moment . . . when the Russians took over the two states. In that moment, armies upon armies were assembled in the two states, as one could hear again and again from the immigrants and emigrants. I experienced that myself right up against the border: heaviest artillery, tanks, soldier after soldier, until one day they finally closed the border; and that in this moment German diplomats succeeded, like a very good electrician, an electrician who doesn't even exist, to combine a positive pole and a negative pole, that is to say in this case Bolshevism and National Socialism.—I don't believe, though, that one says to these diplomats today that they were drunken revelers. Back then we also had diplomats who had good heads. Back then we were forced to start this war because we had no other options. In the East we were literally choked, and what would have happened to us East Prussians if the Polacks had dwelled (*gehaust* [has a very negative connotation]) among us? . . . We would have been exterminated root and branch.

Following a confused description of the situation in the East before the outbreak of the war, which culminated in a defense of Ribbentrop and of the German-Russian pact, the attack on Poland is depicted as an act of self-defense, as the only alternative to being "exterminated root and branch."

4. Bulwark against Bolshevism

Very similar to the theme of the liberation of the Germans in the East is the long-lived ideology of Hitler as a bulwark against communism, which is cited here in the form in which it was raised by a forty-one-year-old female secretary:

> D.: It . . . is, I believe, criticized by the Americans and the English that we, how shall I say . . . well, attacked the Russians looking for a territorial expansion, but Hitler only came up with this to prevent Bolshevism from spreading to Germany. And that the Americans did not recognize this enough is proven by the fact that they did not pay enough attention to the Russians. In this regard, I believe, Hitler had the right perception that he had to create a bulwark against the Russians. It is not so much a matter here of territorial expansion as of an incursion into the Eastern sphere— how should I say—to not let it come into Germany.

5. Yalta and Potsdam

In a group of female refugees the Allies' guilt account is charged with "allowing the Russians [to] come in that far."

> D.: Well, it actually is the case that they bear the entire responsibility for that, because in the end they undertook the fragmentation of Germany . . . And that's the source of our horrible poverty now and of our squeezed [i.e. densely populated] life and—it is certainly blameworthy how in the end they have had to occupy here so long, because, if Yalta hadn't gone as it did, if they hadn't let the Russians come in so far, things would perhaps look very different for the German people.

In the same spirit, reproaches under the clear influence of Nazi propaganda are made against Roosevelt in the group of Bavarian dignitaries:

> G.: The Potsdam Treaty, in my view, was also signed by Mr. Roosevelt, and as far as I'm informed, he agreed to it without any significant counterarguments. And the Potsdam Treaty was surely the source of many evils that we are experiencing today domestically. Thus the entire refugee question, the ceding of the Eastern German territories to Russia and Poland, to say nothing of the division . . . of unified Germany into two entirely opposed halves. This was all the result of the Potsdam Treaty, and not only Stalin but Churchill as well as Roosevelt participated in it.

M: We didn't know how the Hitler regime was going to work out just as one couldn't know how Stalin was going to work out. They have incompetents just like we had.

G.: Not only that, but they had to know on the basis of their much greater experience and their reading materials . . . how Stalin gradually consolidated his power in Russia. He had it from the very beginning, that is beyond doubt, but that he killed I don't know how many people in Ukraine, namely the indigenous population, the farmers, whom he either murdered or banished . . . it was, as far as I know, in the millions—I can't say for sure. These facts, which we little people knew, the diplomats—the foreign diplomats—had to have known for a long time, and I still don't understand today that at the time they assessed Stalin lower than Hitler, when they made an alliance with Stalin against us.

The distortion lies in the fact that while the Allies are reproached for their—involuntary—alliance with Stalin, it is repressed that Hitler had actually made an alliance with Stalin in 1939, and that in the end it was he who attacked Russia.

6. Air Raids

Authentic cases of projection can be found where actions supposedly committed by others apparently do not correspond to the facts and at the same time remind [one] of one's own guilt. That air raids on open cities were started by the German air force is forgotten and the guilt for total warfare is shifted to the English:

R.: I think that the English people absolutely alone are to blame for the World War, for the Second World War, that came about and that the guilt becomes even greater because the English started the devastating air attacks on our civilian population.

In different groups, the guilt of Hitler and the National Socialists is regarded as liquidated by the air raids; thus, in the workers' council group:

Pf.: I'm sixty-three years old and was able to watch two world wars. I myself never participated. After the First World War, we recovered more in the first three years than today after five years. At the outbreak of the Second World War, or before the outbreak of the second war, a terror was organized in the Nazi regime that could not be opposed by the man in the factories, the coworker. The terror was so vast that we were ordered to all kinds of festivities and events. After the horrors of the war began and the big air raids here in . . . came, as we could watch here from up close—so one can really not speak today of German guilt, because those were not, in my opinion, strategic targets, that one in this way without further ado . . . that one just leveled entire villages.

Often, the participants begin exact calculations, for instance by pointing out that bombardment of cities toward the end of the war was already no longer militarily necessary. The following discussion passage from the group of police officers is characteristic of this:

> *J.:* One thing I have never forgotten in my life, . . . apart from the Nazis' be-ing the biggest gangsters who ever existed; only gangsters could knock off people in such a way. But that the American is so humane, that is also not the case. I was in the air force and participated up close in the all-out attack on . . . It is 100 percent that the Americans knew that on that night 250,000 to 300,000 refugees had been taken into the city and that there were about a million people inside the walls of . . . Back then the Americans came and set the whole city on fire in the night. The population had no idea how to behave in an air raid. After the city was on fire and the population, which had no training at all, the second wave came and threw explosive bombs into it. And during the day, several hundred American long-distance fighters shot into the crowds. And the next day, we heard "250,000 dead in . . ." This is a fact that cannot be denied. Where did the Americans get the moral superiority to create such a bloodbath? . . . I talked here about . . . , because it was completely obvious that this didn't have anything to do with the final victory, which the Americans could have had at any time. I under-stand when they bombed the other cities, because Hitler actually had con-verted every house into a war machine.—I understand, the Americans did not know where construction was going on, where war material was being made. Hitler did that too; but in this one instance, they acted unfairly; they should have showed some human sympathy.
> *Th.:* The Nazis at least have the excuse that they were aiming at industrial centers when they bombed over there. But it was certain that . . . was no in-dustrial city, and . . . one has to assume that they intended to commit a crime in this case. It really cannot be described any differently. Because there were only refugees in there, and the city had never been attacked be-fore, because nothing was in it. One can't just forget that . . .

In fact, the claim about the military insignificance of X does not go un-opposed. A speaker says:

> *U.:* As concerns the attack on . . . , I experienced it . . . from fifteen kilometers away, and in fact I myself . . . I barely got out on the passenger train, in the evening at a quarter to seven, and at half past seven the first attack came. That was the English . . . as far as I know . . . the next midday the Americans came and on the next evening another English attack came. But I knew the situation in . . . and I'm honest enough to say that not only

in . . . refugees too, but there was also a lot of military in there. Because . . . was not at that time very far from the front. I came from the Eastern front, and we . . . marched through, on a bright midday, on the twelfth of February. At that time . . . was entirely intact. Then we said: There hasn't been any war here. It was not very far away from . . . , when we already heard the canons. It was the Russians. The attack came in the evening . . . and one did hardly anything to protect the people.

7. Mistreatment of German Prisoners of War

A fifty-four-year-old commercial clerk (refugee) says in the course of a long plea:

Pf.: When the Americans so . . . innocent and so upright with their so-called international law fuss *(Völkerrechtsgeschrei)* that they let loose on the world, then we may not overlook that probably all of us, at least the men, were soldiers and maybe also experienced an American prisoner-of-war camp, that we experienced infractions that in no way have anything to do with humaneness and or with international law. I myself was in a stalag during the war . . . and I can tell you on the basis of my experience that I was shocked about the Americans' understanding as regards the Geneva Convention, as regards the Hague Convention, and so on, that they recklessly defied every, even the smallest human emotion, that they didn't hesitate to beat doctors who wore the Geneva emblem and so were visibly marked on the outside, that they reduced the light-duty barracks, the infirmary . . . that contained five to six thousand people to one hundred, and so on. These are all things that, in the end, it is just as common in the American army as in the German that higher authorities who were supposed to attend to the condition of the imprisoned didn't take any notice of. I only mention this in passing in order to say that in the end the lapses that took place during a combat operation have in the last twenty years— I have to say, because I experienced the [First] World War and wasn't aware of such behavior from combat soldiers—that a certain brutality has taken hold.

This participant accuses the Americans of inhumanity, but his own attitude toward humanity is given away by the term "international law fuss," which belongs to precisely that layer of speech from which the term "humanitarian foolishness" *(Humanitätsduselei)* stems. The conclusion that, in the meantime, a certain brutality took hold, leads to a leveling of all guilt; through the war "the people just became so brutal."

As further illustration for the accusation that the Americans treated war prisoners brutally, the statement of a refugee who was captured in Africa is cited:

N.: . . . in the first years in America we got six thousand [*sic*] calories a day. We got army rations, we ate wonderfully. But what happened then, after 1945, when we lost the war and the Swiss commission entered and said they now resigned their mandate . . . and we were left entirely at the mercy of the Americans. . . . What happened then was more than horrible, and I can imagine that if one speaks here of concentration camps, that one certainly experienced nothing worse in a concentration camp than was done to us.

In the same session, the same speaker gave a blatant example of projecting guilt for wrongs committed onto others:

N.: As prisoners, we just had to forget . . . above all, when the war ended in 1945, they turned us over, I have to say it completely openly, to the Jews in the States—it was high officers, or the so-called provisioning manager or these caretakers *(Betreuer)*, as one could call them—we probably would have called—there they were called caretakers. These were Jews, largely German emigrants, and they were naturally the most repulsive people that existed. They immediately put us on a starvation ration, brought us photographs of Buchenwald, we had to look at the pictures under the watch of armed guards. We had to watch the most horrible films, then they dug out the dead who were allegedly from the concentration camps, and how they carried around the dead bodies. And then if somebody occasionally closed their eyes—most had their eyes closed, you know, and didn't want to look at that at all—he got hit in the back with a club so that he would wake up again and so forth. That certainly was not democratic.

Thus, it was not the *SS* people who were brutal, who tortured the Jews, but the Jews who supposedly forced the Germans to acknowledge the crimes of the *SS*. It appears "natural" to this speaker that German emigrants were supposedly "the most repulsive people that existed." Here the National Socialist way of thinking is present unbowed.

8. Period of Hunger

In defeated Germany, famine was pervasive. Without American help it would have turned into a catastrophe. This help is often forgotten and instead the "Amis" are reproached with true or imagined episodes from the beginning of the occupation era. Thus, from some participants in the neighbors' group:

P.: I have to say directly, did the American government not know about that? Why did it tolerate that? In my estimation this whole hunger period— thank God, it only lasted for half a year—was ordered from the top down. Later on I had the opportunity to talk to an American soldier, because I was assigned to the kitchen. And he told me that as Germans we should be made to feel what we did to the others. So this was inhuman too. It was ordered by a government that at the time on the other side was paying attention to humanity.

B.: . . . at that time—as the American invasion was happening, my sister told me that my brother-in-law was simply starving. Because they only got a loaf of bread for eight days. And then, where we were, in the Rhone, the American soldiers took the ham from the farmers, cut out just the raw meat, the fat they threw away, tread on it, soiled it—I don't even want to say it—so that others couldn't use it. We were evacuated to an inn. It was run by a friend of my husband. Sometimes the American guard came into the pub room. Then they unwrapped their bread, and when they couldn't eat anything anymore, they spit on the bread and bit into it afterwards and threw everything on the table, so that no one could eat it anymore.

G.: I found it wrong, even if they had defeated us. They came in here and let the whole people starve. That's really a crime against humanity. And with their calories! The people didn't even have them [the speaker is referring to calorie limits imposed on Germans, which they couldn't even fulfill]! I don't want to know how many people died there, old and feeble people. And only so many calories, and only just calories. And the people didn't even have them. They were forced to steal.

In a group of Bavarian farmers a comparison is made between the supposed kindness of German soldiers and the sadistic brutality of Americans:

J.: In the whole East we never saw that from German soldiers, even from the SS I never saw it, yes, that—we threw a piece of bread to a Russian, he looked so starved, we threw him bread. And, in contrast, right in front of our eyes when we were starving, they threw it in the dirt in front of us and stomped the cigarettes into the mud. They bit it right off from the white bread: look what I have, yes, what kind of a master I am in contrast to you, you are merely a less worthy people.

Among the functions of such stories is not least that so-called concrete examples have a substantially greater probative value than general claims, and that, moreover, stories like that of the defiled bread and the cigarettes thrown into the mud are libidinously charged by the participants themselves. Truly paranoid in the process is that experiences that do not fit into the scheme of the persecution complex are remodeled in such a way that the system is correct anyway. The participants saw that the American soldiers were no brutes. But they are unwilling to concede at any price either that, in the first place, there was no moral obligation for the victor to help the German after all that had happened, or that in the first months of 1945 the supplies on hand were presumably not sufficient. They want by all means to have been persecuted and tormented and for that reason they invent an order from above, from mysterious powers, that allows them to reconcile their friendly experiences with the soldiers, the memory of the hunger that they did actually suffer, and the shifting of their own guilt onto others. In this spirit a statement from a refugee group runs:

> *Th.*: In my opinion, it was simply a punishment, generally agreed on by the Allies, that one let the Germans starve for two years, three years, perhaps even . . . I've heard that initially they wanted to let us starve until 1952, and then broke that off. I think half of our people would have starved then. Because of that the Americans forfeited very wide sympathies.

Again, it seems self-evident to this speaker that the Americans have to drum up sympathy among the Germans and not the other way around.

9. Lynching

Under the heading of projection, lynching stands at the top. Here the nationalistic participants spot an analogue to the racial persecutions the Nazis committed, and turn the facts on their head. The latent idea standing behind the statements about lynching is simple: You murder Negroes *(Neger),* so you cannot reproach us for having murdered Jews, if not even: You actually showed us how. Apart from that, the frequency of the lynching theme is probably explained by the Colburn letter's pointing out the difference between cases of lynching in the [U.S.] southern states and the extermination policies of the Third Reich. However, only the theme as such, and not the difference, is reacted to.

The following statement from the session with fraternity students is manifestly absurd:

> *O.*: I still wanted to respond to the comments of the American, who simply said that in our case people were murdered in concentration camps by the score, while in their case, if somebody is lynched, it is a crime. This, to my mind, can't be compared at all, that's something completely different. If in our case, in the Third Reich, a man had been lynched, he would have been convicted in the same way as over in America, because that would have been pure murder. What happened in our case, that was in the last analysis behind closed doors. That was something entirely different, it can't be compared.

In line with a specifically German tradition, moral and institutional categories are fused here. When in America a mob takes things into its own hands and exercises mob justice by lynching, then this is murder and a crime. In the Third Reich there were indeed hardly any such more or less spontaneous actions, but merely "extermination measures." Yet, because those lacked the character of individual spontaneity, they are said to be less condemnable than the excesses in the southern states. An apology is thus made out of this in the session of fashion students.

> B.: I believe that this was part of the plan of National Socialism from the beginning, that the Jews slowly but surely would be chased out of Germany. But I think that, at the bottom, the . . . racial problem back then namely between Germans and Jews and now in America between Negroes and Whites is completely different. Because back then it was actually desired . . . It just was a matter of the government against the Jews, while in America it was less by the government, this race hatred . . . than the individual American against the individual negro that had perhaps been around for centuries . . . It is completely different. That is what is so disappointing in and of itself in the case of this hatred against the Negro. The individual American hates the individual Negro. This is much worse than a mass's turning against a race, because the mass doesn't have as much feeling of responsibility as the individual.
>
> Z.: . . . Now I also nevertheless believe—this is why I absolutely do not want to compare this lynching with racial condescension *(Rassendünkel)* because even in the time of the persecution of the Jews in Germany one must not underestimate that the Jew is not for the German what the Negro is for the American, not second class ["second class" in English] . . . I had many many Jewish acquaintances, and I also know from him [*sic*] the standpoint about the majority of the Germans and the opinion. For this reason, it really interested me as a human being that despite persecuting him, one treated the Jew the same and, to be sure strangely, not as a second class [in English].
>
> (Interruption: No, not at all!)
>
> Well one didn't look at it from the human perspective; one treated him that way because he wore a yellow star, because of nothing but purely external reasons.

That as a private person one did not treat one's Jewish acquaintances as second-class humans is summoned up as a defense for what the government did. One could pass over this bizarre form of defense—that mass murders without hatred are less grave than individual crimes of hate—as a mere eccentricity if other groups did not follow the same line:

> F.: It is still another difference that in fact in America lynching was committed by the population itself, while here it was hardly the case that people on the street attacked or hanged a Jew, or such a thing. Instead, the actual persecution of the Jews happened directly because of the state and a large portion of the people . . . didn't become aware of it, even during war. I can

remember it exactly. I was in Emden at the time. There the Jews—apart from the incidents in November 1938, of course—were assembled later on for a transport. And wherever one inquired it was said: "The Jews are going to Poland now, to eastern Poland, to Lublin, etc. There a large reservoir is being created," right, "and all Jews shall be deported to that place." One couldn't simply assume (!) that all those people were supposed to be executed. That's just out of the question.

There is not only method to madness, but again appeal can be made to a kind of pseudorationality: from the fact that the crimes were not committed spontaneously from the bottom, but "directly by policies of the state," one made it particularly easy for the population to evade the inconveniences of conscience. That it did not succeed totally is, to be sure, indicated by the "couldn't simply."

10. Alien Races

The distinction between in- and out-group is the decisive social psychological substance of racial doctrine. A group of German Youth Association members proceeds to its examination following a discussion of lynching:

I.: I believe you can reduce the basic theory of this—of every racial doctrine to a simple common denominator, that there are differences between all races, without thereby making a value judgment. If you take a hand and poke a piece of gold wire into a healthy finger—perhaps during work—this piece of gold wire will begin to fester after a short time. This does not mean that the piece of gold wire is less valuable, because it is good gold and as such precious metal; and on the other hand, the finger is not bad either because it now starts to fester, even though it was a completely healthy finger beforehand. Only the two things together don't get along.—I think that's what in the end moves people to make a distinction between races; a distinction that is rather directed against the intermingling of races than concerned with making value judgments about any race and, hence, the defamation of a colored race or rather of colored races against the white race.

While here an understanding, value-free standpoint is pretended in the abstract, the familiar comparison to purulence gives away the unconscious type of reaction which underlies it.

11. Displaced Persons

In the group of teachers inclined to psychological self-determination, a participant notes very accurately:

I.: True, isn't it, we Germans shift our hate to the DPs.

The DPs did indeed play a central role in defense. It is hardly saying too much that, throughout, they function as scapegoats and are used to justify retrospectively what was done to the Jews, or at least as an appeal to extenuating circumstances. That the diatribes against the DPs continued even when only a very small number of them were left in Germany indicates that the subjective mechanisms that need this theme are more important than the actual situation from which they sprang. The reproaches overshoot every mark and are mostly not even substantiated. The list of statements against DPs is by far the longest of all that emerged in the analysis of specific contents of defensiveness.

One speaker identified the DPs as violent criminals, an accusation raised only rarely against Jews:

> *Pf.*: It is simply the case—it's not merely the Jews, it's also the DPs. I personally know of a case of a taxi driver, he had a fare to the Landsberg camp for four Jews, and just when he demanded the fare, he was knocked down, and only with the help of the MP [Military Police] could the thieves be rounded up. That's the Jews who still live in Germany today.

Psychologically this seems to be a matter of projection of the acts of violence that were committed against the Jews. The element of truth is presumably provided by the excesses of liberated foreign workers and similar groups immediately after the war.

The more the so-called indigenous population considers itself indigenous, the greater the fury they show against the nonindigenous, and blame them for the fact that they were displaced; thus, in a session of Bavarian farmers:

> *Mod.*: May I ask: Do you now still not deal with Jews commercially?
> (Interruption: No, no!)
> *L.*: If the old Jews were to come back . . .
> *G.*: But they aren't coming . . .
> *L.*: If the old Jews came back, at any time, any time again.
> *J.*: If one of those who had been here already came, then yes. But what's coming today, that's all just Jews, that's not a single German, he can't even talk German, or only broken. Yes, then I'm immediately afraid, I'm afraid right away. Because they've got something completely different in mind. They only want to scope out whether there are any opportunities for theft on the farm. That's just the way DPs are.
> *Mod.*: So you mean, the Jews or a DP who comes to your farm, who from the very beginning is clearly a DP because of his language as such, then you are automatically afraid because you don't know what will happen?

J.: Yes, because I don't know what's happening at night. They only come around in the day to scope things out, because I say every decent man goes back where he came from.

L.: The Jews, in part it's foreign Jews who are here. That's why the hatred for Jews is so big among Germans.

G.: So where did they actually come from?

J.: Thousands came here. We don't need the foreign Jews. The old Jews can return, nobody would do anything to them. Why do they come to Germany at all?

It is difficult to imagine that those participants really do not know that the DPs did not come to Germany out of insolence: likewise that, insofar as they come from the East, the possibility of going back where they came from is largely cut off, which one of the discussion's participants specifies with unimaginable cynicism as a criterion for a "decent" person. It is also characteristic, moreover, that a distinction is drawn between "decent" Jews, who are equated with our—namely the German—Jews, who cannot return anyway because most of them are dead, and the indecent, who are distinguished because they can't speak any German. All over the world, this division of the Jews belongs to the arsenal of anti-Semitism.[2] The archaic hatred against the foreign per se merges here with the anti-Semitic stereotype and Sadism against those who have nothing.

The archaic theme of hatred against the foreigner as such, in particular against the sinisterness of the foreign language, also features crassly in the women's group comprising refugees and orphans:

I.: What I mean is, the Eastern Jews after the war, they also didn't make themselves especially popular. It was actually mostly the people who couldn't speak German properly at all, that's already disagreeable, and then they mostly were involved in black marketeering.

Mod.: Wasn't everybody involved in black marketeering? Or was it only Jews who were involved in black marketeering?

I.: No, I don't exactly want to say that, but they attracted attention in particular, when they did their black businesses. In Munich and also here in . . . certain streets were known where one mostly met Jews. Yes, they are particularly skillful in business affairs. You can't take that away from them.

Mod.: Not only in business affairs.

D.: Perhaps all this anti-Semitism is even more effective in Germany because the German in himself is actually hardworking, and, I want to claim, also honest to each other. Exactly in contrast to the character traits of the Jew, who, in himself, is lazy and lets others work for him.

I.: Excuse me, but . . .

D.: Yes, and also tries to swindle others in business, Christians in particular, the nonmembers of his race, and perhaps this is why a peculiar hatred exists in Germany.

One's own position and one's own language are set here as the absolute—if someone does not know German, this is already "disagreeable." The acknowledgment of Jewish skillfulness in "business affairs" serves, as usual, merely as thin cover for the stereotypical accusation that the Jews are lazy and let others work for them, while the Germans are honest and are "in and of themselves," i.e., by nature, hardworking. The old anger about the necessity of having to work and about any kind of oppression finds an outlet in the fantasy that a hated and entirely powerless group is doing too well. Hence, the fact that the displaced had been supported in some ways by the Americans arouses particular hatred. The question is not even raised whether the expelled, who barely escaped the most horrid destiny, have a moral right to such protection and the modest advantages that were granted to them.

Even that the Americans immediately gave the half-starved concentration camp inmates something to eat first is counted against the DPs; and the indignation against this leads to an anti-Semitic tirade not even lacking a dramatization of a fictive swindle:

N.: I believe the American also made a big mistake, when giving the Germans a start governing themselves. Above all, he opened the concentration camps. We just heard, blue, green, red, everything that came out of there. The American didn't differentiate. He just let everyone out. The concentration camp detainees, at first they were all the men. They came into the driver's seat and got all the fat ration cards, they got more to eat. They also had more money, right? A whole bunch of Poles—we have the sorry lot still running around today—the Polacks are all over the place. So we really don't like these people. But I don't know, I can ask everyone here, when there is an attack somewhere around here—four weeks ago they tried to beat me up in the forest, three Poles—when there is an attack somewhere around here, the Poles are behind it, this riffraff. Either they never behaved differently in Poland, in any case there has to be a reason they put this riffraff under lock and key. But that one granted these people privileges here and then exchanged money with them one-to-one in the currency reform . . . What has become of them? Even today, they are the worst racketeers. There are still Poles and Jews in . . . street, and so on . . . Yes, one should really start sweeping out there first; that's the right place, and people shouldn't give us a hard time. It's not our fault! We're fine workers. We go to work early, come home in the evening, and earn our money with our bit of work. The fat cats with the briefcases, they go . . . I can remember: shortly before the currency reform, there were still Jews from X running around, and they still asked: "Do you have a Mark? How many?—I'll give you 10 percent!" and so on. They wanted, they got the Mark exchanged one-to-one, regardless of how many they had. Whether he had fifty or a hundred thousand Marks, he got it. They built department stores from it.

The speaker is still living completely in the National Socialistic conceptual world: he dismisses the Poles, the so called Polacks, with terms such as "riffraff" and "racketeers." He does not distinguish between Polish DPs and Jews, whom one rightfully "put under lock and key."

The discrimination against the DPs carries a specific meaning for defensiveness. Anti-Semitism is retrospectively made into a consequence of their behavior. In this way, on the one hand, the existence of a German anti-Semitism in the period in which the worst happened is discussed away; on the other hand, the anti-Semitic tendencies that are noticeable today are justified with supposed Jewish guilt. Only today, according to the argument, is there even anything like anti-Semitism in Germany, and the accusations against the past appear at the same time to be nothing and legitimated ex post facto. Again, this theme appears most visibly in the groups of Bavarian farmers, who are incapable of more subtle rationalization. Thus, the village dignitaries with whom we are already familiar speak out as follows:

L.: Now we've got hatred for Jews, it didn't exist at all earlier!
Mod.: So you believe the hatred for Jews is greater among you now?
J.: Earlier we didn't have it at all. Back then it wasn't big, we didn't have any of it.
(Interruption: We just had a certain hesitation with the Jews.)
Especially the farmer in the country, who was financially a little shaky, right, and somehow needed money . . . they liked to do business with the Jews.

It would require closer examination whether this theme finds a particularly fertile breeding ground precisely in Bavaria. One can imagine that the Jews, who had lived there for centuries, were indeed mostly integrated in the population; that additionally the farmers viewed the creditors in many ways positively—even if with an ambivalent undertone, as rings through in the sentence: "We just had a certain hesitation with the Jews"; and that nevertheless the whole hatred of a still relatively economically closed group is turning against that which is experienced as foreign and unassimilated.

A particularly pregnant formulation of the claim that the DPs initially created the hatred for Jews can be found in a Bavarian farmers' session:

L.: And that's why the hatred against the Jews came back again. Before, it really wasn't all that strong. The Americans believe and claim that it was Hitler who impressed the hatred on us. That isn't true at all; rather, it was only afterward, as we got to know them, what all they do, after the war. They were allowed to steal a car or a typewriter or whatever, went into the synagogue, and nobody could catch them anymore. But we knew they

were inside. That's true, isn't it? Even the country folk didn't believe that
100 percent. That's why the hatred against the Jews came about, not because of Hitler, but on the contrary, we all felt badly for them.

The truly delusional quality of this passage consists in the confused idea
that "stolen typewriters" were dragged into the synagogue. Regardless of
the temporal order, this farmer also explains and justifies the anti-Semitism
with what was supposedly done by the Jews, after the millions were already murdered.

12. Concentration Camps Not All That Bad

In the equating of DPs with criminals, fantasies of punishment sometimes
come into play: they should go back were they came from, into the concentration camp. At times, this is stated explicitly:

> M.: I want to say about the DPs that, among the DPs, as Herr B. already said,
> there are elements who truly belong in jail, and one can even say: they be-
> long in the concentration camp. And if we assume that in the concentration
> camp such a large number of people were murdered, I want to say about
> that that I know Auschwitz in part. (Interruption: Kapo! [prisoner who
> worked as a guard]). No, I wasn't one of those, who perhaps . . .
> (Interruption: Behind barbed wire, or . . .)
> . . . no, not that either, I was there neither behind barbed wire nor as a guard.
> But I want to say one thing, and that I want to, what for instance a woman
> told me when I was a prisoner in Holstein, and I want to quote it verbatim,
> what she said: "I personally do not know what happened in the concentra-
> tion camps, but I ran across burning asphalt with my child in the air raid
> nights." And this kind of thing I know how to judge, and not what the con-
> centration camps are accused of in the abstract. And I believe if one were
> to conduct a statistical tabulation of who was in the concentration camp,
> of who runs around outside here, then as far as I can tell this number has
> not only doubled but even tripled. And one should show the people, that is
> to say the number of people who died in the concentration camps.

In this peculiar construction "I know Auschwitz in part," the participant reveals the need on the one hand to appear as an expert—even be it
an expert of horror—but on the other side not to embroil himself. The
story that is cited of the woman who ran with the child in the air raid
nights over the burning asphalt is apparently supposed to compensate for
the horror of the concentration camps. The demand raised at the end, with
the gesture of a fanaticism for truth, that one should show the people who
died in the concentration camp, of course, cannot be met and is a mere dis-
traction maneuver.

It is among the most scurrilous findings of the investigation that the well-nourished condition of the concentration camp detainees is mentioned repeatedly in an apologetic manner.

Thus, for example, in a refugee group:

> U.: A Jew once came from Buchenwald perfectly well-nourished, impeccably well-dressed, who had an emigration permit for Shanghai. Back then, he needed a certificate of clearance from the finance administration that he did not owe any taxes to the Reich. I later read about the atrocities that supposedly happened during that time there, and I can almost not believe this up until today because in that case this man would not have been so well-fed, because he was quite rotund and perfectly normal, neither beaten nor anything else.

This theme appears in an extreme form in a barracks meeting:

> E.: Well, whoever saw the detainees right after collapse only saw that they were well-fed people.

13. Jewish Revenge

The behavior of the DPs and of the Jews after the collapse is interpreted by some as thirst for revenge, and this thirst for revenge is frowned on in the name of a humanity that was not exactly highly regarded during the Third Reich.

> K.: Well I believe the embitterment, well, it is coming from the Jewish circles, mostly from there. If the Jews today infer a right to commit injustices from the fact that a wrong was committed against them, and that they then . . . now do the most unacceptable things, you know, and especially in such a time, as was already emphasized before, when it was really a matter of the necessary food and so forth. Any person would be somewhat touchy about this, and one naturally reacts to it. And I believe this is an essential point.

Especially those emigrants who returned with the occupation forces are accused of thirst for revenge, and this is listed as a cause for harm:

> B.: One has to add—and this is a particularly sad role—the role of the German emigrants. The things they said about Germany abroad and the depiction—humanly understandable: they did lose all their wealth, some of them lost their relatives in Germany—that's what did it, that the image of Germany and the German people that was imprinted onto the minds of the ordinary people was completely distorted. Well, you cannot expect that from one day to the next, now abruptly in a few years, this man changes this distorted image, which is still being distorted by his local press—

please, look at the foreign press, look at the French press. The man, therefore, tried over time to change his opinion. The accusations that we raised this evening against the occupation forces are indisputably justified and right. There is no doubt about that. But we want to concede that the entire occupation force is indeed infected and riddled with German emigrants, came to Germany with the wrong assumptions, and for years treated us according to these notions, which were in fact propagandistic, and which were kept alive in part through their own experience and the newspapers. What is depressing for me is that even today, after all these long years, the occupation forces still cannot, in the crucial hours . . . switch faster.

Two things deserve attention in this statement: first that the participant concedes that the behavior of the emigrants is "humanly understandable," without drawing even the slightest consequences for that: the negative image is indeed distorted. On one hand, it is discussed that the sinister aspects of the past "were kept alive in part through their [the emigrants'] own experience." But on the other hand these aspects are called "wrong assumptions," and it is surmised that the occupation forces were "infected," as if by a disease, by those to whom one at the same time acknowledges having done something. But then it shines a bright light on the speaker's state of mind, almost six years after the fall of Hitler, that he blames the emigrants because even today, in the period of the Cold War with Russia, the occupation forces have not "switched" quickly enough. The participant, a former officer, is tacitly convinced that the Germany for which he presumes to speak is actually of one mind with today's America, and that only regrettably did the Americans not implement solidarity with German nationalism to the full extent quickly enough.

In a mostly conciliatory youth group, the putative "Jewish thirst for revenge" is also discussed:

> *Pf.*: And now we're back to this point . . . It is true that those Jews who are actually of good will and who actually want to rebuild . . . they went to Palestine. And the others, those with a thirst for revenge—so not all of them who are still here, but some of them—and who perhaps want to fill their pockets again, they are still staying here right now and basically want . . . to make the most of their thirst for revenge against us Germans. And . . . when . . . Colburn . . . says there: . . . The Germans are becoming bitter against the Jews again, I believe that has its justification in that it is not generalized to the Jews per se, but limited to the Jews who are in Germany right now and who are doing these things . . . who now are basically taking out their thirst for revenge on us.
>
> *B.*: Yes, it was basically the case that in 1946 we had wanted a good agreement, a good understanding with the Jews, and the Jews basically spit in our faces.

Guilt and Defense — *136*

The most obvious thought never occurs to this naïve participant, namely that he is presumptuously asking the Jews to forgive and forget the horrors that exceed all imagination just because a vaguely defined youth is of good will.

14. Reparations

However, if it is a question of reparations, the geniality stops:

> *Sch.*: Doctor, you posed the question to us whether we feel inwardly moved to compensate for something. Then I really want to ask: Do you think we are obliged to compensate for something materially or only ideally?
> *B.*: I completely believe that whatever we could make good to the Jews, they have already abundantly taken. I'm just thinking of the constant statements and constant material questions of a certain Herr Auerbach in Munich.*

The construction of the Jewish thirst for revenge is the mirrored knee-jerk response of numerous participants' behavioral pattern. The Jews are criticized for insisting on the appearance of justice because one does not want to make up for the wrong, especially when it is a matter of returning Jewish property.

Rarely is the duty of compensation simply denied; rather, it is completely acknowledged formally, but is made illusory through qualifications and caveats. Hardly any idea is absurd enough not to be employed if it is a matter of retaining one's own property. A statement from the Bavarian dignitaries' group indicates that because the severity of the crimes precludes reparation, one can evade it just as well as the concession of guilt:

> *H.*: I remember, for example, the Bavarian minister president Hoegner already said once: "Yes, the Jews should just come, we'll gladly accept them," or: "We did wrong, but we want to make up for it." I mean, the practice is actually there already. The evidence that one has a compensation ministry, that one has a law, and that one does this much. But one should not demand something extra any more, one should not go on and on over and over again and say even more: "Now, admit it and finally say it, and so on, and go through the history again and again anew: it is now almost balanced out

---

*Philipp Auerbach, a survivor of Buchenwald and Auschwitz, was Bavarian "State Commissioner for the Welfare of the Victims of Fascism," and was in charge of the State Restitution Office at the time the research was conducted. He was often attacked for his uncompromising stance as well as for being a self-promoter. In 1950, following a state audit of his office's finances, Auerbach was charged with embezzlement, arrested in 1951, and tried and convicted in 1952 in a trial tinged by anti-Semitic remarks from the judge.

already. Such heavy things, one could not, one cannot measure them at all, and it is really also clear that it is balanced out to the dot on the i, and those who had losses and damages will feel it until the end of their lives.

Unambiguous statements in favor of compensation are rare. Where participants own up to it, they are, revealingly, free from the guilt complex, like a participant in a group of workers' council members:

K.: My opinion is really that one should not talk about guilt at all, from any side, but should actually only think about reparation here, from all sides, because all of us are guilty.

15. Drawing a Line under It

The wish not to have to talk about guilt any more—to a certain extent, the idea that after the great bankruptcy all accounts are settled—is in many ways blended with specific resistance to reparations. In a group of former army officers it is said:

A.: But out of the entire problematic of this discussion about this letter the necessity absolutely emerges that one now . . . that the complex entanglements of guilt that run through all nations . . . that they would finally be dissolved like the Gordian knot, that one wipes the slate clean of all accusations with regard to any kind of pasts, that one also lets the pasts disappear that attribute guilt to the German people in some way, and in the same way we here in our German people have to let go of the justified guilt accusations against the Allies.

The youth group, from which a bit about the question of the compensation for guilt has already been cited, concludes that all guilt has already been atoned:

K.: I don't want to provide the letter-writer with more material again, so that he can say again that the Germans pity themselves. But I want to say, nevertheless, if we really were guilty, and this guilt has to be atoned for somehow, then I at least see in everything the German people had to go through, and all the horrors and the financial sacrifices and material sacrifices and also other kinds of sacrifices we had to make, then I already see in those things a kind of atonement, if it was in fact at fault.

In a different youth group, the BDJ (*Bund Deutscher Jugend,* [Association of German Youth]) session, the demand to "draw a line under it" is raised guilelessly with reference to the claim that many had not known anything about the events:

Z.: I want to switch back here to the Nazi time, where also a very large percentage—and I believe especially in the small towns, where not everything
got through—didn't know anything about these methods in the concentration camps; or if in fact one or the other thing was said, that he would
simply not have believed it because he didn't see the person to whom this
happened. And that's why one may not speak then about collective guilt.
Naturally, I don't want to start that whole thing over again today. Draw a
line under it! But I also want to say: every person should first think before
he condemns another.

In the face of the horrors that the population experienced in the later
years of the war, horrors that ran together into a single picture of unartic-
ulated terror with what was committed by the National Socialists, it is obviously extraordinarily difficult for many of our participants, and certainly
not just for the nationalist and fascist leaning ones, to complete the
thought that they had something to make up for even still now. It is as if
talking about the guilt in the collective spirit today violates the deeply
rooted idea of the equivalence of crime and punishment. With respect to
this elementary fact, the reference to the German guilt or to the disentan-
glement of responsibilities all too easily takes on the quality of something
invalid and ideological. Only against this background, rather than in isolated psychological observation, can the defensive themes be evaluated
correctly. One must not misrecognize the psychic energy at work there—
the repression of guilt and the narcissism of identifying with one's own
group. One must understand that it is almost impossible to expect the population that experienced the catastrophe to generate a spontaneous feeling
of guilt, while at the same time in the other direction the desperate defense
against any feeling of guilt represents the symptom of an extremely dangerous social-psychological and political potential.

VI. Elements of National Socialist Ideology

As we have already occasionally mentioned, many of the substantive
themes of defensiveness exhibit rudiments of National Socialist ideology.
The immediate expression of these was often subject to an internal censorship at the time of our study, though also certainly to an outer one, the fear
of unmasking oneself politically. For this reason, National Socialist theses
changed shape somewhat in the postwar situation. The indoctrination during the twelve years of totalitarian information, propaganda, and education went too deep for it to be wiped away through a defeat that not only
caused disillusionment deriving from the fall of the Reich from its domi-

nant position in Europe but conversely also produced legends of past glory. But themes of this sort dare to come out into the open only occasionally. Mostly they are disguised as problems that one claims to have been made aware of through Hitler, as supposedly historical insights and such things, or are at least taken out of their explicit context. What lives on are fascist theses that shed the elements that are judged by the participants to be too objectionable. It is obvious that not least Hitler's failure contributed to the modifications. Often, the participants find a compromise of the sort that they distinguish—as often occurs in neofascist literature—the supposed ideal core of National Socialism from its misuse or the glorious early years of the Hitler dictatorship from the later "decadence." In all of this, one has to consider not only that fascism was forced on people from the outside by a propaganda machine, but that the receptiveness to totalitarian systems was built into the psychology of the individual through sociological, technological, and economic developmental tendencies and continues to exist to today. We cannot usually distinguish with our National Socialist experiment participants how much it is a matter of the inheritance of fascist ideology or the expression of that persisting anthropological disposition.

1. The "Good Sides" of National Socialism

A compromise between National Socialist leanings and the inhibition against saying something that goes against the power relations that are still considered in effect is the reference to the good sides of the Hitler regime, which is apparently considered justified, voiced in the trade union group:

> M.: There is no doubt at all that millions of people stood on the streets and waved, no matter whether it was a simple worker or . . . I've often thought about those things, because I never went there myself, and I found a solution, which Stefan Zweig, who himself is one of the persecuted, mentions once. Stefan Zweig says: "Hitler decreed the yellow star for me, and then almost all Germans said: It's not right to mark people like that. Or, he decreed that Jews may not use the trams. Then the Germans said: It's not right. Then for a while they did nothing else except to end unemployment, build streets . . . that is, did positive things. Then this crime that was done before disappeared from Germans' memory. This alternating system: do something bad, do more good things, alternating like that so that finally people got used to it."

That a Jewish witness is invoked for the supposedly good sides of the Nazi regime—by the way with a shift in emphasis in the relevant quote, which highlights the propaganda tactic rather than the thing itself—deserves to be emphasized because it happens again and again that experiment participants with fascist tendencies fall back on the true or fictitious statements of Jews as justifications. Apparently, it is considered particularly effective if one can appeal to the voices of the victims themselves, be it even with the most outlandish constructions. The popularity of a figure like Victor Gollancz in postwar Germany is explainable by this mechanism.* If the victims themselves understand us, the latent thought runs, then nobody else has the right to reproach us, and even we ourselves do not need to. It is this social-psychological phenomenon that places the generous gestures of the formerly persecuted in an ambiguous light.

If the bill for the economic upsurge was presented little by little only after 1939, this is expressed in the naïve consciousness in such a way that a time in which Hitler did good was followed by a time in which he caused harm—by the way, corresponding quite similarly to the traditional image of many tyrants, especially that of Caligula.

At times, this kind of on-the-one-hand, on-the-other-hand reasoning determines the mood of entire discussion passages, as for instance in a women's group from a Hessian village:

> N.: It is certainly true that, in Hitler times, poor people were supported—and today—not even the devil gives anything to the poor people.
> Sch.: We had a home, and today we have to make our way in the world . . . on the one hand, it was better, and on the other, it wasn't.
> A.: Well, in the long run, it would not have worked out well with this Adolf Hitler either. It was a much too harsh program, because then he would certainly have had to let some things go. Sure—he helped the working class, he helped the peasants, even a lot, he also did in my profession—he did a lot, the child tax credit, and so forth, . . . right—and that did make a big difference. But . . .

Nonideological statements, in which the former and partially continuing popularity of National Socialism is attributed to material interests, are in no way rare in these kinds of contexts. In a women's group in a barracks camp we hear:

> Z.: Well, for us at home, we had, for example, eight children, we fared quite well during the war. The big boys got soldier's pay, and for the children we got child support, and then we built a house of our own and we had it re-

---

*Victor Gollancz, a British publisher and Socialist, was well known for his criticism of the Allies for their treatment of Germany, in particular for food shortages, which he characterized as an infraction of human rights and a threat to Western values.

plastered, and then we paid it off and everything, whereas today we can't do anything anymore.

W.: I also have many children, we also fared better during war than today, and of course we were bombed out, and so we have nothing anymore, and we can't buy anything new anymore these days.

B.: I think the women had a lot more protection . . . we had a lot more protection as women with children than we do now, when one is alone, with no help from anyone.

Similarly, in a different group of women:

H.: That was after all the main reason why he won: back then we had great unemployment. He promised everybody wages and work, and that's why, maybe, initially, he was so popular. There was plenty of work to go around.

also in the group of high school seniors:

H.: Hitler came and got rid of the misery . . . and, that swayed many many people to follow that system.

and in the group of women from which we cite a lot:

O.: . . . that Germany finally through the horrible misery and unemployment of the years 1929, 1930 and 1932—and that so and so many hundreds of thousands killed themselves in desperation. One doesn't talk anymore about suicide *(Selbstmord)*, but of altruistic death *(Freitod)*. That was brought about by the misery, and then the people found work, and so they were initially quite content.

As much as the National Socialist notion of national community *(Volksgemeinschaft)* served ideologically to deceive the people about the character of the dictatorship, this nonetheless actually offered them the awareness: We are being taken care of. National Socialism exploited with greatest skill the contradiction of the late-liberal society for its purposes, that on the one side the individual is responsible for himself and his material destiny, and on the other hand is mostly rarely capable of it in reality. In exchange for the deprivation of freedom, short-term security was at least granted, and the memory of this period still lives on today. Any attempts to overcome Nazi ideology that miss this fact, and above all do not draw real consequences from it, themselves succumb to the danger of being futile ideology.

In general, the speakers resist acknowledging that the recovery from the economic crisis in the first years of the Hitler regime, alluded to in the last quotes, had its foundation above all in the borrowing *(Bevorschussung)* against precisely that war that led to the catastrophe. The memory of the good times persists, isolated, quasi-unsoiled by the negativity, and pseudo-gratifications like those offered by the KDF *(Kraft durch Freude* [Strength Through Joy], a Nazi leisure organization that provided entertainment and tourism for the working classes), still seem to hold their propagandistic value. In a North German refugee group it is said:

> R.: All of us, the big majority, the way we cheered back then, and we did cheer, nobody can deny that, and there sure was reason to cheer, because there were very few who were not doing well. And at that time only those who were against the dictatorship, against National Socialism from the beginning fared badly. Those fared badly. Today, only to mention one example, no worker can afford to go to Madeira on a KDF-steamer, also these days nobody can afford to somehow walk up to the manager at work and say: I won't work any more for this crappy pay. Back then one could do that. I experienced it myself as an apprentice. Back then the German labor front stood behind you.

Similar things are articulated by a neighbors' group:

> U.: Because I think, except that the war came, many good things were also done right. For instance streets were built, and so forth. And I have to say right off the bat, everybody lived well.

The phrase "except that the war came" is telling. The war appears as a sort of an industrial accident *(Betriebsunfall)*.

2. No Parties Anymore

One remembers how effective the Nazi slogan of the fight against corruption was and likewise that against "party disorder" *(Parteiunwesen)*. These propaganda themes also survived the Third Reich.

In the relatively progressive group of high school seniors, it is said:

> H.: There are probably many people who say, all these people who sit in Bonn . . . if one of them is sent to Strasbourg, everybody there gets to have a Volkswagen or even a Mercedes. Those are expenses. It's like that . . . today if . . . a dictator were in the position—and a man actually would come who would decisively put an end to the unnecessary expenses, who stands above the issue, who decides the outcomes, who works faster and less self-interestedly, without regard for the party, etc. Because every step that is taken today happens in contrast more or less with partisan pressure, with an eye on the votes in the next election for the party.

The pettiness that counts even the "Volkswagen" of the government members as an excess is part of the reserve fund of fascist propaganda in the same way as the lie that the dictator who represents the interests of a highly particular group is acting "without regard for the party" after he has abolished all parties except his own. It is telling, furthermore, that the speaker, in order to appear politically knowledgeable, uses the term "partisan pressure," but in the wrong way. Nothing is left here of the language of democracy but empty shells.

This experiment participant in particular is an example for the aftereffects of National Socialist slogans in those people who do not think of themselves as fascist in any way. When asked how one could get such an ideal dictator, this high schooler answers:

H.: It shouldn't be just one, it could be hundreds of people who are picked out, and really those who have a name, if they are famous.

Here the notion of prominence, the confusion of the familiar name with objective quality, is raised blindly as a criterion without regard to any kind of political or social content. This demonstrates the affinity of the politically neutral cult of celebrity, which the culture industry imposes on the population, with totalitarian forms of domination.

3. Nazi Reactions

A fifty-seven-year-old master metalworker delivers a kind of National Socialist convention speech:

Sch.: Gentlemen!
Let's follow the time up to 1933. I certainly was politically active at the time and I concluded that there is only one thing for the German, after the bourgeoisie had to a certain extent failed, they just stuck their heads in the sand *(sich hinter den Ofen verkrochen)* as we say in German, there were two opposed choices, on the one side Communism, that is to say Bolshevism, on the other side National Socialism. Every decent person and every decent German who still had German blood in his veins, said to himself, I'll take the lesser evil, and that is National Socialism. And we did it, me too. I did not turn to National Socialism to hear later that National Socialism committed atrocities, rather I turned to it so Germany would get under control again, so everyone could walk down the street without being attacked. And it was in fact like that afterward. Every person could move freely, he was not attacked, wasn't beaten to death, and so on. No, no.
Mod.: Except those who thought differently back then, they were, indeed, attacked on the street.

(Interruption: That's not true . . . Even if somebody was attacked, one would have to check whether he himself was not to blame.)

Sch.: I'll continue. We really learned from the First World War what Bolshevism means for a civilized nation, and for that reason we rejected Communism top to bottom [mit Strich und Faden]. When other countries today tell us, yes we wanted the war, and we have only ourselves to blame for Bolshevism, which we rejected top to bottom, then I say that the Western nations by far did not recognize the danger of Bolshevism, and it is now confirmed by certain diplomats that it was indeed that way. If they had perhaps known what a danger they were running by allying themselves with Bolshevism in order to fight National Socialism, perhaps they would not have done it. Recently I, eh [*sic*] that Hitler as such *(als solcher)* offered the Western powers peace, and was rejected. Moreover: When National Socialism collapsed, [rear admiral] Dönitz was still the executor in the German state, he offered the Western powers peace and said: Give us a free hand, give us our weapons, set our troops free. Now we will fight Bolshevism. We'll give them hell.

(Interruption: Quite right.)

And what did the gentlemen say? No, that's out of the question. You are supposed to be the vanquished. Gentlemen! Had they had a bit more brains back then, we would be faring better today, the next war, the Third World War wouldn't be just around the corner. The world would finally be free from Bolshevism. And this was rejected. As a result, today: When in Korea the Americans are having to in a certain sense retreat there, that is to say the U.N. troops, and they are cut down today, mowed down, gentlemen, what did our generals do in a fight with bandits? I myself took part in fighting bandits when I was fifty. I know what it means to fight against the enemy, to fight someone I can't see, who only reveals himself as a bandit in the last moment, as a partisan. I believe America to a certain extent changed the views they used to have against us, against our generals. And I hope . . . that our generals, who today are still locked up and condemned to death, will be free one day, and that it will be said: You have fulfilled your duty as a soldier.

It seems worthwhile to examine this speech a bit more closely. Formal and substantive elements can hardly be separated from one another. Immediately telling is the formulation: "I did not turn to National Socialism to hear later that National Socialism committed atrocities." Perhaps the speaker wants to say he joined the party in good faith and not with cruel intentions, but the linguistic slip, if it is a matter of one, indicates his state of mind today: The indignation is not directed against the deeds, but against their being mentioned. The terms "decent man," "decent German," "German blood" are associated in a row as if they were synonyms, and the vague memory of idioms of outrage, such as that a decent man's blood boils, are brought in smooth connection to National Socialist racial theory. The phrase "top to bottom" *(mit Strich und Faden)* appears repeatedly: often the aggressively minded experiment participants grab hold of some expression that seems especially powerful to them, most often an ordinary yet simultaneously strange formula, which they exploit for the purpose of agitation, and from which they derive a kind of claim to authority. They are the voice of the people. "Top to bottom" says the same thing as completely and thoroughly *(ganz und gar)*; the emphasis is on the totality of the attitude; a phenomenon is not weighed, but exaggerated without qualification to the furthest extreme. The phrase "by certain diplomats" is intended to prove the speaker's political expertise, but is at the same time so vague that it is exempt from any concrete predicate, which is a technique of the semieducated. At the same time, one can see with the word "certain" the wagging finger of Hitler, who, while pretending to know about unspeakable world conspiracies, cleverly declines to let the miserable plebes *(misera plebs)*, whom he impresses with his knowledge, partake of his secrets.—If Hitler "as such" *(als solcher)* supposedly offered the Western Allies peace, then the expression "as such" makes no sense whatsoever; it merely serves to lend this whole speech the appearance of precision and of erudition at the same time.—The absurd idea that the Dönitz government could have entered an alliance with the West and defeated Russia is far from rare in the discussions. Similarly, the speaker rehashes the old alternative between National Socialism and Bolshevism and defends National Socialism as the lesser evil, without engaging the counterargument that the Russians most likely never would have become the threat they are today if Hitler had not provoked the war against the Soviet Union.—The phrase that in May 1945 the victor should have shown "more brains" is particularly characteristic. This expression, which is used frequently in this session, stems from the sphere of the cabaret and the garment industry, from a linguistic layer in which one talks, for example, about "Jewish brains"; it belongs to the gray area of imitating Jewish phrases and gestures in which the mockery of the victims mixes with the hidden desire to be like them.—Partisans are equated with bandits and are contrasted with "our generals": an echo of National Socialist technique of identifying political criminals with ordinary criminals. As concerns the generals, the pathos knows no measure. The speaker strings together one bombastic term after the other, regardless of the logic: they are "today still locked up and condemned to death." In the end the "duty as a soldier" is conjured up, with the hidden thought that the "soldierly" is a special area with its own ethical norms and the character of absolute obligation. Especially in such a speech, in which a weak intellect puffs himself up with the aid of all imaginable randomly collected themes, the essence of the new nationalist ideology comes into especially clear relief. For this man, nothing has changed: he experiences no conflict between National Socialism and the current situation, but drifts along in the sluggish current of slovenly language. Even the fact that the National Socialists lost the war is viewed only as a kind of interlude in the great crusade, for which he is still hoping. His fanaticism blocks any kind of intervening experience. The manner of speech, which is at the same time derivatively confused and rigid, demonstrates the ideology itself.

An openly Nazi reaction to the bombings of the cities occurs in a speech by a nineteen-year-old mechanic:

> *Pf.:* It is true, I know a case, it was in the newspapers often enough, a plane was shot down. The crew bailed out and was somehow mistreated by the population. The people who mistreated the crew of this plane were in part condemned to heavy prison sentences. Can you blame them? If now . . . they bombarded . . . the city, my parents died . . . if I had gotten my hands on such a guy, I would have ripped him to shreds, and today I would have to sit out my ten-year sentence because I killed him?—First of all, they acted without premeditation, secondly, I find it a cruelty to convict such a person after that.

The speaker knows how to depict the situation in such a way that the gruesome excesses against the downed pilots appear humanly understandable, even as a natural expression of piety for the dead parents, and in doing so conveys a high measure of plausibility to the defense. The participant forgets that in truth defenseless people were murdered by the kind of people who exercise their aggressions when there is no danger. It is part of the psychology of defensiveness that, depending on the situation, arguments are proffered that contradict each other in terms of their content: symptoms of the fact that objectivity is replaced by apologetic or psychological purposes. It thus appears as natural in contexts like this one that downed pilots, that is to say functionaries of the military apparatus, fall prey to personal revenge, whereas, inversely, it is argued in the case of the murder of the Jews that it is here a matter of anonymous administrative measures, which cannot be blamed on individual people. The pilots are blamed personally, as it were, for the bomb damage, while the executors of the extermination measures are exonerated with the argument that they were supposedly obeying orders.

4. Master Race

Aggressive nationalism, blind overvaluation of everything German in the nationalistic sense, is common.[1] At times, a shadow of critical self-reflection accompanies it, but mostly only in order to bring the self-praise into even sharper relief.

Watered-down Nietzsche is used for nationalistic purposes in a session of unemployed women:

> R.: Yes, I believe, a German can then only say: Of course only equal rights, because on any other basis we cannot recover at all, we cannot live at all, let's say. Because a German is not a herd animal, which can be pressed into service by others, is certainly not a slave or a servant; because a German, each German, is in fact a master human *(Herrenmensch)*.

Karl Mannheim pointed out that among the ideological functions of race theory, giving the majority the consciousness of being elite was not the least important. The absurd nationalization of the term "master human" shows the lasting success of this propaganda trick.

Often, the "German people" are presented to a certain extent as the sole proprietors of introspection *(Innerlichkeit)* and similar precious goods. The Germans are still depicted by many as a community of a special kind, as more human than other humans, a kind of order of the holy grail. In a group of orphans and refugees, a seventeen-year-old girl, who fled from Hungary, says:

> R.: The American claims the Germans always wanted to seize power—but he doesn't say—and I'd like to hear that from somebody—how the German actually is taking advantage of power. Until now, he actually hasn't taken advantage of it. The German people is highly suspicious, justifiably so. In my opinion, the German people is namely the purest people there can be, at least the purest in spiritual life. And the foreigners set a very bad example. The German namely is not as liberal in his views on society as are the foreigners. And he can't bear it; he probably has a very strong prejudice, but also in my opinion he's the purest human who can exist. I'd like to hear in what way the German actually took advantage of this and why he strives for power. I can't believe it. I also can't see how he took advantage. In the first place, he wanted to try to get all the Jews out of Germany, justifiably so, so the races don't get mixed up together.

A great deal of murkiness is mixed up in the word "pure": the racial ideology, the sentimental belief in the pure heart, the regressive urge for endogamy, the obsessive neurotic drive for order ("so the races don't get mixed up together"). Politically these statements are an example for the extremist sentiment, which is particularly widespread among foreign Germans *(Auslandsdeutsche)*, who, since they experience their national identity as in danger, overplay the aspect of ethnic belonging. The role of foreign Germans in National Socialism is well known.

5. Residues of Racial Theory

Individual Nazi theories appear qualified to a certain extent. However, when the experiment participants really get going, this is quickly forgotten. Once they insist on the idea of the natural distinctness of the races, it helps little if equal rights are initially afforded to the races each in their own way: in the end, the Jew is burned anyway, and the Nazis supposedly were in the right:

> N.: The one thing is right, that through all the racial doctrine, one can almost say, during National Socialism most of the people who didn't concern themselves with this problem at all before are only today starting to regard (interruption: "Exactly") the issue from this standpoint. Earlier, someone who hadn't especially concerned himself with these themes, didn't care at all about racial matters, didn't assign any value to them, and maybe they were wrong not to assign any value to them in certain respects. Because a race problem, in some form or other, certainly exists. It really is not the case that one race is exactly like the other. This is not a value judgment, but this, what we experience with the others as a difference, that is not—that we say, he is worse than us, but he is different from us. And it is, in my opinion, quite a normal reaction that one views this other critically, and it is— I think—this is also a positive effect of this naturally hugely exaggerated race theory of the Third Reich, but in some ways it was certainly necessary that the people thought about it a bit. Because certainly some fundamental mistakes were made back then, in that one paid too little attention to these problems, and the Americans also have the same thoughts about these problems.

The extermination policy is neutralized here: one was just giving some thought to the racial problem.

In the BDJ session, all sorts of stereotypes proved themselves highly tenacious alongside the racial theory. In place of the Aryan and the master race, here it is a matter of the white race, which is supposed to defend occidental culture:

> E.: It is not a matter of Americans or of Englishmen or of Russians, but it is a matter of us wanting to defend the white race, in this case occidental culture. And we as . . . just members of the white race are obliged to work together with the Americans here. Because it would be crazy if we ourselves sawed off the branch—to speak figuratively—on which we sit together with the Americans and Englishmen, if we say: We won't cooperate.

The passage permits insight into the subtle mechanisms of the adaptation of the racial theory to the changed political situation. Instead of the "white race" the speaker "in this case" substitutes "occidental civilization"—probably thinking about the contemporary conflict between West and East. It is not rare that fascist nationalism transforms into pan-European chauvinism, as, for example, the title of Hans Grimm's journal *Nation Europa* indicates.* The noble word "culture" replaces the proscribed term "race," though it remains a mere disguise for the brutal claim to domination.

The centrality of race is dogmatically fixed in the following statement of a schoolteacher:

> A.: That it's a different race is in fact completely clear. That by this we don't mean to persecute this race and that we want to let this other race exist and want to accept it as well, that's just as clear. But let's say we had a parliament, and this parliament were comprised solely of Jews—let's assume for the sake of argument—then I would also be against this.

No doubt this participant consciously distances himself from anti-Semitism, but the racial theory seduces him into constructing a nonsensical fiction like that of a German parliament comprised entirely of Jews and then into protesting against such a possibility with the countenance of indignant common sense.

Something similar is found in a different discussion, when a participant constructs the case of a Negro becoming German prime minister, and polemicizes against this. It is particularly possible to conclude from such examples that the National Socialist indoctrination went much deeper than the manifest political conviction of our participants and, arguably, of large sectors of the German population in general.

The conflict between fascist doctrine and what one thinks to be opportune in present circumstance also occurs with anti-Semitism. A frequent compromise between bad conscience due to the persecution of the Jews and National Socialist indoctrination is to replace the term "racial inferiority" with "racial foreignness." There one touches on a sphere of general confusion, for example in a refugee session:

> Mod.: May I still ask you to talk a little bit about what you mean by racially foreign?

---

*Grimm, a nationalist writer who had spent fourteen years in South Africa, was a supporter (though in some aspects critical) of the Nazis. After the war, in response to the archbishop of Canterbury's message to the German people, he published a notorious statement in which he portrayed Germany's aggression apologetically as an effort to defend "European culture."

G.: Racially foreign—perhaps I can say, it's a different race, not foreign, well, it is not related to us, this race.

Mod.: Do you in this circle here believe there are big differences between human races?

F.: I don't think so. Differences, I don't think so, also that one cannot regard this as a difference. This is what I think: for example, take Protestant and Catholic!

(Interruption: No.)

No, I mean, those also don't fit together, in their beliefs they don't really fit together. And that's the way it is with race, no?

(General consent)

M.: Yes, but people don't need to hate each other because of it.

These participants are in their own minds open-minded, but they cannot free themselves from the conceptual apparatus of racial theory.—The ideology of race helps to deny the hatred and to downplay it into a mere awareness of difference, which is then nevertheless employed in the service of discrimination.

The fashion school group arrives at a self-critical reflection on these remnants:

O.: Yes, I believe that it really is like that, if, today, we hear "Jew," that we do somehow pull back or at least give the man or woman a second look. We are really not . . . negatively disposed from the beginning, but we—really want to examine the thing again from the beginning. And I believe, this socialization in the Third Reich is to blame for this as well.

(Interruption: Yes!)

We would really like to do it differently today—but we still have something in us, we are still slightly handicapped by this, that this was constantly talked into us. We want to judge it objectively, but—and we will certainly get there, but as I already said, I believe that there is still a small prejudice inside of us when we hear "Jew."

The clash of racial theory and lived experience occurs in a much later passage of the discussion:

N.: I would say: . . . with a Negro, no way (that is fall in love) and with a Jew—absolutely possible.

(Agreement)

B.: Well, I don't know.

N.: I want to make another caveat—well, I believe falling in love absolutely to be possible, but, on purely rational grounds, whether I would seek a real marital relationship, I don't believe this.

Mod.: Have you . . . the difference between . . .

N.: Because purely—let's say—emotionally or instinctively, I do make a distinction, in this case I consider it absolutely possible. So, just as I consider it impossible with someone so racially other as a Negro or Chinese or such. But purely on rational considerations, I would at the least not rule it out, but I would think about how far—view it critically because it is a Jew.

Mod.: So you still see a difference in it?

R.: I would also by all means view this case critically, but if I really loved this Jew, then nothing could prevent me from it—from a marriage—, that he is a Jew.

N.: Exactly!

R.: No, not me!

N.: But insofar as you aren't only responsible for yourself and for the other person in a marriage but also for the children, and because the responsibility is not taken seriously these days, unfortunately, by a lot of people, and in my opinion one of the first problems and the first issues in a marriage is because one, let's say, makes a decision in that moment not just for oneself, but for a whole generation that comes after oneself, and has to suffer maybe because of this decision that was not made only on rational grounds.

R.: It is definitely a critical question. Maybe one judges very impulsively in the moment, but I am not moving away from my compromise.

M.: I don't want to exclude the possibility that one could fall in love with a Negro because he, first of all, is a person like us, after all, and because he can have the same spiritual and intellectual qualities as any other person. But a marriage I would completely rule out, and I actually also want to say the same about the Jews. Maybe the reason for that is that I also have religious commitments, and that of course also plays a very big role there. (Agreement)

Mod.: Let's assume for a moment that the creed were the same . . .

(Interruption: This is absolutely possible.)

M.: Yes, well, I could imagine that, if one weren't committed in terms of belief, then I could imagine a marriage with a Jew just as well as with any other Christian . . .

If the adherents of racial theory delight in appealing to a natural racial instinct, the passage seems to indicate that the factor of social control is far more decisive with the erotic taboo against Negroes, and certainly most clearly in the form of fear.

The discussion continues similarly for a long time, whereby the female participants eventually engage in all kinds of awkward but silly questions, like whether Josefine [*sic*] Baker is a racially pure Negress, among others. Finally the prejudice is rationalized with the conclusion that all half-breeds are unhappy people.

Z.: Yes, one doesn't see what kinds of problems these people have.

Such reaction-formations at times lead to absurdly apologetic theses: the racial measures were in some way or another good for the Jews or at least morally commendable for the sake of their "integrity." One can assume that the unconscious feelings of guilt are so strong here that the rationalization mechanism has to resort to the most drastic means to defend against them, even if these also give up the slightest hint of reason.

In a women's group that is in no way anti-Semitic, a participant claims:

> *Ra.*: And I would even argue that the Nuremberg Laws* were made together with the Jews for the Jews at that time. I knew Jews who were quite content with them . . . Jews told me before 1933: This Hitler is making our Israel for us. A Jew said this again to me in 1933: Now we are going to get our Israel. It was right actually, they are getting their Israel. And the Jews actually got what they wanted through the Nuremberg Laws.

In a much later passage this speaker utters the same thought again:

> *Ra.*: November 1938 actually only happened because of the murder of Herr Rath,[†] and the burning of the synagogues too. I personally thought it was a total swindle because I told myself the whole movement is actually aimed at getting the Jews to Palestine. Perhaps the Jews were in agreement that these pious synagogues all disappear so that later they could also disappear. That was my personal opinion.

The participant saw through the swindle of the supposedly spontaneous people's action, but replaces the lies of the National Socialists with her own delusional idea, perhaps in this way to weaken the thought of the horror that otherwise would be unbearable for her.

In neither case did a single one of the decidedly Jew-friendly participants, who remembered the Pogrom of November 1938 with horror, confront this nonsense. In general, it seems that precisely in naïve groups, the mere authority of the speaker, the fact that something was said, sufficed so that even obvious foolishness has a chance of being accepted or tolerated as long as it at least does not openly contradict the group opinion. Something similar is likely observed in court hearings, an issue that generally warrants attention in discussions in which putative facts are supposed to be determined.

6. The Jews Themselves Are to Blame for Everything

Yet it does not stop there, with the argument that certain anti-Jewish segregation measures supposedly took place at the Jews' behest or with their

---

*The Nuremberg Laws of 1935 established racial distinctions between Jews and Germans based on parentage, and outlawed intermixing of these putative races.

†Ernst vom Rath was a German diplomat who was assassinated in Paris in November 1938 by a Jewish youth. The Nazis used this as an excuse for *Kristallnacht*, a massive series of pogroms against German Jews.

consent. Rather, anti-Semitic participants argue openly that the Jews altogether are themselves to blame for everything that happened to them.

The legend of ritual murder, Jewish unscrupulousness, the shirking of physical work—no anti-Semitic accusation against the Jews is too absurd to not be repeated with this intention.

> *H.*: That Jews slaughter Aryan children for Easter celebrations, etc., one cannot pluck something like that out of thin air . . . because one always used to say in earlier times: The Jew, he started with a vendor's tray and ended up with a department store. This cannot be mere cleverness, because other people are after all hardworking as well and aren't dumb either. They are just more unscrupulous, the Jews. It's just like I said, they stop at nothing, they are more unscrupulous. They don't have these scruples, like the others.
>
> *Mod.*: In principle, I think, there are also Christians who have this unscrupulousness . . . You are probably familiar with the history of the Jewish people . . . and . . . that the Jews the whole world over were often not admitted to professions other than business affairs. They were only merchants and only worked in this area and, as a consequence probably became more polished at it . . . If you only always do one thing, then naturally you will always be a little better at it, right?
>
> *H.*: And the flip side of this was also that you rarely saw a Jew who . . . manual labor . . .

That there are numerous Jewish manual laborers in America and that there were also many in eastern Europe before the extermination does not change anything about the fact that the Jews supposedly shirked honest work and lived from usury and fraud. That the same conflicts as occur in any group also occur among Jews, as far as they even constitute a somewhat coherent group, does not shake the conviction that they are as thick as thieves. And the specters of made-up Talmudic commandments to deceive the Christians, and bloody rituals—the projections of the pogrom—are still haunting imaginations.

In the Bavarian dignitaries' group the same argument occurs, now conflated with the idea that one proceeded against the Jews everywhere and at all times, and still does:

> *J.*: No Jew ever worked with pick and shovel, only swindled.
>
> *M.*: In all of the Balkan countries and everywhere else they chased out the Jews, one sees it everywhere, in the end it's always them. Where do they actually come from? Before, the gypsies were a nomadic people—right? And today it's the Jews. And why them? Because no country doesn't want them [*sic*], because every country says: We don't need the parasites *(Drohnen)*, we kick them out or we make it so unpleasant for them that they are happy to leave. And we, we of course have to take them in.

H.: Well, in the Middle Ages, Christians were not allowed . . . to charge interest, until later the canonical interest came, that is three percent, four percent . . . The Jew was allowed, he was not bound to these canonical laws,
and he exploited history where he could. Because those who came to him,
they could not get anything from anyone else anymore, they were desperate, and so now they went to the Jew, and he had a free hand in these things
and of course took rates from them that often . . . that's also why he became suddenly and quite rich, and then there was always a great restructuring *(Bereinigung)* right away, so that they had to disappear again from
these financial districts. They had to live outside, or they were even plun-
dered. Basically, this thing, which occurred around 1900—shortly before
the war—, a pattern, as it already says in the Bible, that from time to time
the Jews got their comeuppance . . .

What was done to the Jews, for example, that one denied them residence,
is turned into an argument against them—the mere fact of the old anti-
Semitism features as a justification of the new. The pogrom is thereby softened
to a kind of restoration of reasonable relations, restructuring *(Bereinigung)*,
in the sense that one speaks of a land restructuring *(Flurbereinigung)* when
the dispersion of agricultural property is too fragmented [and thus must be
redistributed so that a single farmer does not have too many small pieces
of land dispersed too widely]. Historical reflection on the significance that
the prohibition on charging interest had for the fact that the Jews entered
the moneylending profession has no power over the verdict.

The group of women refugees in a barracks, which ranks among the
poorest covered by the study, is anything but anti-Semitic in its overall
mood. However, this does not change at all the fact that the stereotype of
Jewish dishonesty is brought up and that the experiment participants complain that the Jews do not work and support themselves like everyone
else—only that here the theme does not remain unchallenged and that it
does not lead to a verdict:

X.: The Jew is in principle, he . . . recovers faster than a German who has to
work with his hands. The other, he does it somehow with a bag of money
and with cheating . . .

R.: One also has to say here that the Jew also simply really immigrated to
Germany only with—I mean, he really did well here . . . But they should
not have . . . mistreated them in the way they did. They could have . . .
properly expelled them, and give them the opportunity to support themselves further and work like everybody else on their own soil.

Just as widespread as the accusation of dishonesty is the one that Jews
come quickly into money. In contrast, Jewish doctors are praised, as by the

way was the case during the rise of National Socialism as well—presumably because their profession is a sphere in which immediate positive experiences can be had, while in business affairs no experience whatsoever contradicts the idea that the Jews do everything for their own good: if they take low prices, it is just to undercut competition, if they take high ones, it is to get the better of their customers. A passage from the BDJ group sheds light on this entire complex just as on the current notion of Jewish "clannishness" and, finally, on the tendency to justify anti-Semitism by the fact that everybody is against the Jews:

I.: Then there was a Jew in . . . [refers to an organization of British occupation troops] who had recently come from the East; he was simply not taken seriously, he was, moreover, labeled a Russian and was avoided by almost everybody, and they said: Yes, he does not have good character; you can't work with him. Moreover, he is a Jew. Well, that is not based on some kind of talk or something . . .

Th.: The Jewish people is, because of its kind of business, also perhaps itself to blame for being hated by particular peoples. Among us in Silesia, for example, when the Poles invaded, the Jews followed quickly after. The Polish militia brought the Jews under guard in a closed transport from the train into the city. And after eight days these Jews, who arrived in caftans and dirty and ragged, had stolen so much property from the Germans that they could open businesses, that they had a four-room apartment with all the furniture, and then went about buying up German businesses on the cheap. And particularly here the Jews have themselves to blame, because the individual always sees that and is bothered by the Jews and says to himself: Oh God, but why? And extends this to the others of the kind. And perhaps that is where all the hatred comes from.

Sch.: We were of the opinion that the Jews had always been pretty big racketeers and ripped off others. And that's also why they probably weren't very well liked among other peoples.

K.: But I think the Jews stick together well, no matter what, one can be doing badly, the other is rich; he does not look down on the other, as is particularly common in Germany right now, but sees him as equal. He helps him. And that's really quite a good trait . . . of the Jews.

E.: One really can't blame the Jew terribly for his characteristics because it is not only the Jews who have this business sense, but it is also people from the Balkans, the Hebrews in general, for instance the Greeks too. So he is ultimately not to blame; and then something else comes into play. I know a great many Jews who are highly intelligent. And the way they support themselves and how they behave here in our environment, all that is mostly due to the fact that . . . at the core of it they are an intelligent race. This again is in my opinion due to the fact that they have kept themselves relatively pure in general, so that there is a certain good breeding—it sounds a little strange—but that it is a race of pure culture, and that then an intelligence in this form appears and that they afterward—I mean to say—then afterward it is already a manifestation of decadence, in that sense an overbreeding.

K.: Herr E. also attacked the Greeks. And as concerns Greece, I worked at the German-Greek trade association for a while, and I can say with certainty: the Greek is in fact basically much more genuine than the Jew. I also have to agree with Herr E., when he said, the Jew is basically not bad. Especially the Jewish doctors treated the Germans very well too, and especially the older generation had more confidence and more trust in the Jewish doctors than in the German doctors. And after 1935/36, Jewish doctors . . . still treated Germans, even though it was basically forbidden for them; but they then thought again about the people in general.

Th.: The individual man will certainly never identify an entire people with the actions of an individual. To a large extent I only got to know bad Jews—with the exception of two, and those were my bosses. One really has to start from the standpoint: good, the Jew trades in a certain coin, and you have to trade back in it. That's the only way to get anywhere with Jews. And there are no Jews who carry out any kind of manual labor; they are all business people.

Even though especially in this group it is actually discussed and considered that the Jews were historically forced into professions such as the money changer, it is then argued that it was commanded of them in "age-old Jewish writings" "to injure the non-Jewish parts of the population in all countries." It is highly characteristic for the complexion of the new anti-Semitism that mythological fantasies about the Talmud appear in administrative language. The tendency to extend anti-Semitic reactions to all the peoples of the eastern Mediterranean is quite widespread. In turn, this speaker tries to forge a kind of common front with the occupation power, in this case the British, under the sign of anti-Semitism: he refers to the British as "comrades," very similar to the way in which the Nazis after the first war tried to construct a fascistic union of combat soldiers. With the phrase "to a large extent I only got to know bad Jews," the experiment participant wants to appear judicious and at the same time to come to a summary judgment, and this contradiction is manifest in the illogical language. He allows two exceptions in his two "bosses"—whether from a general attachment to any kind of authority, or because he really had good experiences with the Jews whom he knew. Nevertheless, he does not let go of the anti-Semitic stereotype, and for that reason categorizes the good experiences as exceptions.

7. Defense of the "Honest Nazis"

Finally, we found that the fascist ideology survives at times in the form of distinguishing between good and bad Nazis—analogous to the stereotypes of the good and bad Jews—and that in these cases a special spotlight falls on the "honest" ones, as if the distinction between those who were National Socialists out of conviction and those who were National Socialists out of interest already constituted a moral criterion.

As an example, a quote from a session with refugee women:

> Gö.: I believe one cannot talk about Nazis at all anymore today in Germany. Anyway: this word Nazi causes all of us discomfort, right? It has become a kind of swear word. And how many decent, fine, honest men were in the party and really worked with good conscience for the fatherland; they take this as an insult, always to be labeled with the word Nazi.
> (Interruption: . . . to be insulted!)
> Yes, there are still a few old Nazis; yes, one will probably never be able to change them, but they are dying out. But our young generation went through such an ordeal that they will never, not even remotely, be able to become Nazis again. This is completely impossible.

Two themes are muddled: the first is that one does not want to hear about National Socialism anymore, and the second is that one does not want to be reminded of having been a Nazi oneself. The indignation nevertheless seems more directed against the use of the word Nazi than against what it stands for.

The group of Bavarian dignitaries tries to distinguish between the bad Nazis, "the ne'er-do-wells," and the good ones, i.e. oneself:

> V.: But until '35 there were only ne'er-do-wells, who were not up to standard. We only joined in then after '37. Why did we join in? Our mayor said that at that time . . . well, don't you see where this is leading? We had one whose name was . . . who ran around singing and yelling: "Put the blacks [referring to politically active Catholics] against the wall! So we actually said to ourselves, if it is like this and it has to be like this, then we also have to do something, otherwise they will take over everything, and we're going to get caught up in it.

Here the chronology is treated in exactly the opposite way as usual in defensiveness. First, there were supposedly only ne'er-do-wells involved, then one joined as a decent person in order to prevent worse, a rationalization that mostly covers the opportunists.

The material presented allows the conclusion that the National Socialist ideology did not in fact exist anymore as an internally coherent organized structure of thinking, since its strongest integrating power had disappeared through its failure; that, however, numerous individual elements of fascist thinking, now removed from their context and thereby doubly irrational, are still present and could be manipulated again in a changed political situation. The modifications these elements underwent all stemmed from the adaptation to the political constellations and power relations that dominated in the winter of 1950/51. It is the tendency of fascism not somehow to arise again in the old form but to hibernate by ingratiating itself to whoever is currently strongest, especially by exploiting the conflict between West and East, and to await the hour for which the exponents of dictatorship are hoping.

VII. The Ambivalent Ones

If we have occasionally indicated that opinion formation in Germany today depends to a large extent on power arrangements, the same content applied psychologically shows that people are ambivalent in their opinions and that, depending on the objective arrangements, one or the other of the effective intellectual and psychological forces wins the upper hand.

Thus, in order to safeguard our interpretation from the danger of insignificance no less than from naïve exaggeration, it is advisable to look more closely at the phenomenon of ambivalence, insofar as it appears in the material, without in the process somehow distinguishing ambivalent from unequivocal experiment participants a priori. Ambivalence is a general designation of the ideological and social-psychological complexes that concern us. We restrict ourselves to one sore spot where the ambivalence is most palpable: the relationship to the Jews.

1. Ambivalence in Individuals

We begin with a statement from a session of the unemployed:

> *H.:* It is obvious that the Jew has a certain measure of common experience with us and can co-exist on a friendly basis because of questions of geographical dependence and co-existance. But I was of the opinion, and I want to emphasize this, that one should deal with the Jew in good will . . .

The relation to the Jews is, according to this statement, supposedly possible on a friendly basis; the speaker, a fifty-four-year-old unskilled worker, would unquestionably deny the charge of anti-Semitism. But the "friendly basis" is full of holes. By limiting the common element of German and Jews to the vague and unhistorical term "geographical dependence" and the hardly less vague social term "co-existence," room is left for the supposition of an unresolvable qualitative difference, as is argued immediately beforehand by the same experiment participant, namely with reference to a rabbi's son who supposedly confirmed this:

> H.: So the way it turned out, I regret it enormously (namely the persecution of the Jews). At that time I was still in office in . . . I said without hesitation, what happened on *Kristallnacht*,[1] that is a disgrace, with that I cannot identify. That I want to say clearly. At the time, I talked about this with a gentleman, a rabbi's son from Leipzig. We argued vigorously that the Jew does not really belong to the body of the German people and also for this reason can never be German, and that's certainly because of existential reasons, for instance like a German.

This qualification, though, has such a lasting effect that whatever happens on a "friendly basis" is presented from the beginning as an "argument"— and not as, for example, a human relation—only that this argument is meant to occur in "good will." This speaker would probably prefer it if the Jews themselves, as it appeared in a Nazi-era joke about the Naumann group,* were to say: "Out with us." In the light of the last sentence, the friendship consists of nothing but "not to lie to each other"—thus, in telling each other that you do not want to have anything to do with the each other. Here the tolerance and willingness for understanding are thwarted by the power of the Nazi stereotype of "foreign races." One may assume that the aggressive current is stronger than the censorship by conscience and that such a participant would easily defect to anti-Semitism under changed social conditions, without being able to speak of him here today as anti-Semitic.

A general index for the ambivalent attitude toward the Jews in general is the tendency to qualified disapproval of the Nazis' anti-Semitic measures. A very typical passage from a group of unemployed women is quoted below:

> A.: I think so, too, and this also applies in the same way to the Jewish question. The Jews were in the government. Now, the Jews are eminently qualified, on average are very bright . . . and they also understood how to reach the highest positions and they did not represent the interest of the German people there, but their own interest. And that's why Hitler was right in my opinion to remove them from these leading positions; but, he should not have . . . well he should not have let it come down to a matter of life and death. He isn't allowed to do that, but he had the right to remove them

---

*The *Verband Nationaldeutscher Juden* (Association of National German Jews), led by Max Naumann, a splinter group formed in 1920 from the *Central Verein deutscher Staatsbürger jüdischen Glaubens* (Central Association of German Citizens of Jewish Faith), opposed emigration of Jews into Germany from the East.

from the leading positions, because they are not Germans, after all, and they did not conduct their business in the spirit of the German people.

Mod.: So, in your opinion, Fräulein A., Hitler and his regime were entitled to banish the Jews from Germany?

A.: No, to remove them from the leading positions; he could . . . was entitled to remove them from the . . . leading positions. But I already said, the persecution of the Jews should not have gone so far that the Jews had to die; this should not have happened, because, as Fräulein W. said just now: "Every person has the right to work"; yes . . . that I would not deny any person.

Another participant addresses the same topic:

D.: Yes, I want to say—as long as they don't harm the general interest, as long as they don't act with bias, so that maybe a certain class is harmed by it,— the workers—that he would only look after the fancy gentlemen among the people, who . . . then of course the workers would be bitter. This leading Jew would have to have understanding for all the social strata in Germany. Then, I want to say, one would have to leave him in his high position.

The passage presents not only democratic and socialist themes like that of the "general right to work," but also, toward the beginning, the claim about the extraordinary intelligence of the Jews—a generalization that often serves as a segue to anti-Semitic statements, and that stands ready to switch into a thesis of Jewish slyness and the simple honesty of one's own group. This statement is often followed by the unsubstantiated claim that Jews "understood how to reach the highest positions," and did not attend there to "the interest of the German people," but to their own. Hitler is defended because he removed them from these top positions.

It is also advisable to search for a basis in reality in reference to the phenomenon of ambivalence. One comes across, for example, the long known fact that the Jews were often the bankers for the little man, helped him with loans, but then presented the bill and incurred his wrath.

O.: These were small farmers, they had no money, and if they needed something, such as some cattle, they went to the Jew, because without money they couldn't get anything from the Christians, and when the time was due and they couldn't pay, then he took the best piece and left the bad behind.

Mod.: I understood you to say that the Jews cheated the Rhön farmers.

O.: Yes, I was a child back then, but I only heard this from hearsay because my father was a blacksmith. So, I don't know it. The farmers told my father again and again that the Jew didn't pressure them, but if they couldn't pay it, then he took a cow from their stable and gave them the bad one.

Mod.: Well, doesn't the Christian do that as well?

O.: That too, but there was a lot of cheating going on.

Mod.: The farmers were intelligent enough not to—to distinguish whether it was a good or a bad cow.

O.: Well, I just don't know that. I don't have a good opinion of the cattle Jew (*Viehjud*).

The economic function of the Jewish cattle merchants is acknowledged here along with their good side: They are said not to have "pressured them." If, however, the cattle merchant finally wanted his money, then he turns into the greedy beast that, the saying goes, takes the good cow from the stable and leaves the bad cow in it.

2. Ambivalence in the Group

The phenomenon of ambivalence cannot always be grasped clearly by individual statements. Often it appears in a certain fluctuation in the course of the discussion, in a vacillation between positive and negative propositions, without this vacillation actually being grounded, in the logical course of the discussion, in factual argument. One has the impression that the participants, when they come to a critical point, would prefer to take back everything that has just been said. A passage from the session with high school seniors is cited below in which the denial of anti-Semitism and the almost obsessive inclination to operate with expressions like "Jewish puppet master" and profiteer alternate with each other. By the way, it is precisely this group in which a participant for once becomes aware of his own ambivalence:

D.: I want to point to the following: Here in . . . we have about five hundred thousand inhabitants and German citizens. But we have here perhaps twelve to fifteen hundred Jews. I can't refer to any precise data. Now, if you can name five or six of those twelve hundred to fifteen hundred Jews and ten or fifteen of those five hundred thousand . . . I believe that the percentage of profiteers is proportionally larger, is in fact higher in the one population than the other. And moreover—if as was just claimed that there was profiteering by the Germans as well—the actual puppet masters were Jews. (Interruption: Dear fellow! Nonsense!)

P.: I wanted to respond to what Herr R. said. It was said that the Jews were profiteers, at the time when almost all Germans were profiteers. I regret to say from my own experience—because I live in the Jewish district—that today Jews are also still the ones profiteering, even though there is not much left to sell on the black market. Nevertheless—some items are scarce still today—and they are sold on the black market by Jews. And, apart from that, a big crackdown was made just recently, that could prove it . . . When the job market for Jews—one also isn't exactly looking for work here—is difficult, they move to their new country Israel and help to build up their new state there, which should be easy. But they feel very good here and are not really inclined to take on a hard life. So they would rather pursue their profiteering business here, where they earn relatively more and can lead a better life.

Mod.: So you think that a certain degree of anti-Semitism is not totally unjustified.

P.: That also means that it isn't necessarily wrong and there is probably anti-Semitism present in the German people.

Here, as so often, the phenomenon of unmentionability surfaces with experiment participant P. He correctly recognizes that after the abolition of rationing in Germany there was "really not much left to sell on the black market"; nevertheless, though, "today Jews are also the ones profiteering." The ambivalence is due to the clash of living and rational experiences with frozen stereotypes.

3. Specific Ambivalent Attitude

There is an ambivalent attitude of individual experiment participants that has a completely unique structure compared to the clearly anti-Semitic participants as well as to the unbiased ones. The ideology underlying this is in no way to be understood only as a median between the extremes, but requires a qualitative assessment of its essence. It appears to be characteristic that certain traditional democratic impulses, such as that of equal rights for all and the hatred of privilege, underlie it, but that these impulses turn themselves specifically against the Jews, who appear here as "protected Jews," as exactly those who enjoy privileges, who fare better than is warranted by their statistical proportion in the population, and who supposedly generally violate the democratic rules in some way. In other words, the ambivalent participants do not link anti-Semitism with antidemocratic sentiments, but argue against the Jews precisely from democratic principles, without thereby asking the question whether their principle of excluding Jews from the universe of citizens does not basically offend the democratic principle they invoke. The mode of reaction is: we have nothing against the Jews, we do not want to persecute them, but they should not do anything that contradicts an interest of the people, which is wholly unspecified and declared arbitrarily. In particular, they are not supposed to have a disproportionate share of highly paid and influential positions. This kind of thinking, which, by the way, has a considerable tradition, opens a back door for those who have a conflict between bad conscience and defensiveness. They can maintain for the themselves that they are human, open-minded, and unprejudiced, and at the same time in practice reconcile with their conviction any kind of anti-Semitic measure as an act of compensatory justice, as long as some measure of legality is maintained. Part of the pseudorationality of this behavior is the balancing gesture that both parties must be to blame, even where monstrous deeds are concerned, and that the Jews are the ones who need to make up for it. Even the segregation of the Jews is at times blamed on them here.

The following example shows how lines of thinking of this type proceed. The investigator asks in a group of elementary-school teachers whether the position of the Jews in German life is to be determined according to a quota:

A.: A proportion of the population went into a certain number of professions. It was probably mostly based on their characteristics. That's justified as far as that goes. But it's not only like that with the Jews, but also with the Germans from Latvia. Who was sitting in the highest positions in Latvia? Only the Germans. And as soon as the Latvian-Germans came to Poland, if one of them was already in it, then it didn't take very long for so and so many from just that circle to end up in their position.

Mod.: This is applicable for every sphere of life. Every minority closes ranks more easily, represents its own interests more strongly . . .

A.: That's where the danger lies, then, in my opinion. Either they are not a minority and they are Germans just like us, or we create a demarcation, and then there is a danger in this demarcation, and this demarcation did after all exist.

Mod.: This demarcation, was it wanted by the Jews or by the Germans?

A.: I'm not entirely clear on that myself . . . I don't know how it came about, only how it was there.

O.: You say, the Jews themselves are to blame. They were an extreme minority in this court. That's not the fault of the Jews.

A.: No, that's not their fault, that is a fact.

O.: Why should the Jews behave just like the Germans? They should also remain Jews, even if we do not want to give them the same recognition we give ourselves. Shouldn't they also be in a court?

A.: But in a certain proportion, if they place themselves outside. If they don't place themselves outside, this question wouldn't arise.

It may be mentioned that perhaps the whole group, socially lower middle class, but at the same time relatively educated and inclined toward reflection, can be considered ambivalent.

MORE frequent, however, than the formal argument against the disproportional share of the Jews is the fluctuation among the ambivalents between the rejection of the National Socialist misdeeds and the reference to putative Jewish failings later on. This is the sense of a statement from the labor youth session:

> K.: Yes, well, I'm of the opinion that what Herr B. just said, that this is basically correct, especially for the youth. Because it is obviously clear that at least the largest proportion, or the proportion that I am for instance familiar with, that everybody understood that, that in the beginning, so what was done to the Jews during the whole Nazi period, that it was truly unjust, that there is no doubt about it, that somehow this could be defended or somehow be denied. I have to agree with that. But what he then said after that, that the Jews did not exactly behave properly, especially at that time, this is really a fact.

A bleak connection is constructed here between the extermination of the Jews and what is ascribed to the DPs after the war. At first, the wrong done to the Jews is begrudgingly acknowledged, even if still in the convoluted and qualified manner that occurs so often among our participants. Then it is said that the Jews "did not exactly behave properly" afterward—in the process, the question of the proportion and causal nexus between Auschwitz and the behavior of the DPs is disregarded. When the investigator tries to sum up and then offers an easy way out to the participant by asking him whether he really wants to infer from this the right of the National Socialists to their behavior, the speaker replies: "No, absolutely not!" He thus takes back the acknowledgment of wrong halfway—a textbook case of ambivalence.

4. Reasons for Ambivalence

If the ambivalents accept humanitarian ideas in principle, but with the help of all sorts of rationalizations distort them with regard to the Jews to such an extent that the Jews are excluded from them, it cannot be surprising that the ambivalents particularly like to rely on authentic or bogus observations that are meant to show that the Jews themselves, or at least the orthodox or eastern Jews, onto whom contemporary anti-Semitism has largely shifted, had erred against humanity. It is very difficult in such cases to decide how far the Sadism of the experiment participants is being projected onto the Jews, to whom one ascribes atrocities, and how far practices such as kosher butchery really do contain elements that repel humanely-minded experiment participants. The following passage about kosher butchery at any rate appears in a context that as such is in no way anti-Semitic, and the report is supposed to account for the feeling of the "foreignness" of the Jews cultivated by the Nazis rather than to damn the Jews in general. Much more, the participants in a group of neighbors distance themselves energetically from what was done to the Jews. The passage reads in context:

> F.: I can say from my practice that a Jewish banker with whom I interacted, that we also talked about this issue. It was in the years 1934–35. And that he himself was of the opinion that it was mostly through the influx of East Galician and Polish Jews after the First World War that the tension against the Jews in Germany first grew at all. Because many of the old families had been here for hundreds of years, they were basically integrated . . . No one thought anything of it. But at that time, this Barmat and Kutsiker* and similar associates came from the East, and it [the tension against the Jews] was later generalized. And then it was said: The Jews again! But it was actually: The people who lived among us, they weren't really Jews anymore. They had really become basically Germans because of the centuries-long cohabitation with the German tribe *(Volksstamm)*. Musicians, poets, etc., if we look at them, they don't look any different from our own. But the people from the East, naturally they stood out.
>
> B.: We also treated a lot of Jews in the practice . . . and then a certain Mr. Jew [*sic*] said: The eastern Jews are the ones who kill us local Jews. Just look in . . . then you'll find all of them . . . Look at them. And that's our downfall. And this Mr. . . . . already left for Australia before Hitler's era. He had a linens store here.
>
> G.: Back then propaganda was . . . when it was said: Those are German Jews, it was said at once: There's no such thing, German Jews. It's always the race.
>
> Mod.: Frau B. was talking about the time after the First World War. And this is nevertheless from the time after 1933?
>
> B.: Yes, the people . . . they were really riled up by the propaganda. Whenever someone wanted to object to something, they got the same answer: Those aren't Germans, that's a foreign race.
>
> Mod.: Even though the Jews had lived in Germany for centuries, they were nevertheless still regarded as a foreign race?
>
> B.: I also saw that often in the market hall. Those were Polish Jews; this was clear by their language and all and by their wigs. They weren't elegant at all. The way they pushed themselves forward there, treated people like nothing. They bought everything live, slaughtered everything live. Nobody

---

*Julius Barmat and Ivan Kutsiker were Jewish businessmen reputed to be from East Galicia (though at least Barmat came to Germany from Holland) and who were associated with the Social Democrats, particularly with party leader Gustav Bauer. During the Weimar Republic they were accused of manipulating markets and of exploiting the inflation for their own financial benefit. The scandals surrounding their trials were marked by virulent anti-Semitism, and their names were used by the Nazis to discredit the Social Democrats, namely by implying that the Social Democrats were serving the financial interests of wealthy Jewish families.

could say anything. Even if you whacked a fish, they already got frantic. They took everything with them alive, in nets. And then it was wiggling. And there were the chickens. They went straight to the butcher downstairs. I watched the whole thing very closely. I also felt that it was cruelty to animals. There stood the Jewish butcher. He slaughtered the poultry according to kosher . . . I didn't think this was right.

(Interruption: How did they do that?)

Well, he went straight into the chamber; it had to be bled properly. There was real torture there. The beast didn't just get one on the head like usual. It was stabbed and had to be bled out properly. Where I was evacuated to the Rhön, a butcher also told me all about it, they really praised the Jews. Those were merchants. They had their kosher pans there and everything. They wrote something onto them, because they always roasted their meat there. They always said: when they slaughtered a piece of cattle, it was quite a cruelty. The head butcher was also against kosher slaughter.

Mod.: Do you believe that things like, for example, kosher butchering also somehow stirred anti-Semitism a little bit?

F.: Certainly, I do believe that.

B.: I mean, the animal feels it as well. It was always said: Never hurt an animal for fun, just think if it were done to you. When I saw that—the Jewish women, they just reached into the baskets, I saw it all, when they pawed the chickens and the stuff . . . I certainly didn't have anything against the Jews, because we had many Jewish patients.

U.: I treated quite a lot of Jews in the practice, even in 1938, right?

Mod.: What did you want to say about your practice?

U.: That I treated many Jews. The whole time and even secretly, even in evenings or mornings, let people in the back way and treated them, as long as it was possible. I also just walked with my wife across the train square. A horde *(Korona)* sat there on their suitcases, etc. This disturbed me a lot. Then I said to my wife, that isn't right, what's being done there. I thus condemned this, I have to say right off. I said, that might be in store for us too one day, that we have to sit waiting for transport in the train station, like these people here, who didn't actually do anything wrong.

That the woman watched the kosher butchering "very closely" certainly raises doubt about the indignation. When there's talk about "a Mr. Jew . . . ," it is an expression of the fact that the people widely identified the Jews with the bourgeois upper class. They qualified as Mr. X. At the same time, however, the humiliating collective "Jew" is used, and the grotesque-ambivalent form "Mr. Jew" arises from it.—And again in the expression of sympathy with the victims who were sitting on their suitcases, at the end of the passage the stereotype prevails—they are called "horde," in much the way an anti-Semite speaks of Jews as of a "clan" *(Kille)*. Once again, in the process, outrage renders the speaker speechless: one has to look at the ending very closely to realize it is the story of a deportation scene.

5. The Unconsciously Ambivalent

In a similarly ambivalent context a participant in the group of high school seniors ends up speaking about kosher butchery. This group might be typical for young intellectuals who seriously want to shake off the fascist ideology but were so saturated with National Socialist material in their early childhood that they react unconsciously and just as much against their own intention in the way that has been beaten into their heads—a special sort of ambivalence, which must be rather widespread. Once again, in order to judge the weight of the conflicting elements correctly, one must read the larger context:

> U.: I would like for a moment to turn to another theme Mr. Colburn mentions in his letter, and it is to be sure a fairly delicate one, it concerns the Jewish question. There he criticizes us that lately, at least in the last two years, a general, one can say baiting, one can say antipathy against the Jews has arisen in Germany, and he mentions, moreover, if I recall correctly, among other things, that in Germany there is a general opinion that the profiteers—as he likes to put it—are the DPs. We are supposed to have claimed this, and I could infer from his words that he himself is not quite sure about these words. Right off the bat, something very general about that. I believe I can say that the Jew-baiting, as took place in . . . on the anniversary of the affair in the year 1938, is spreading not only in Germany. If one looks at the world today in general, one will see that the Jews, I don't want to say hated, but are at least not very popular, not only in Germany but in other countries. I would like to think of Russia as an example. Furthermore, it can be said that we are reproached for having been opposed to the Jews in the past. It is not correct, insofar as at least a large part of the population was not in agreement with the measures that the dictatorship brought about. I do not want to go into everything that was and is written in the newspapers, but instead briefly mention something personal, that I experienced personally. I was living at that time in Ostend, it was a mixed area with a lot of Jews, rich Jews. I believe that, when these actions suddenly began in 1938, at least my acquaintances were very much opposed to it, and, I want to express myself strongly, looked away in disgust. How do you explain that? We live again today as well . . . in an area where a lot of Jews live. I can say that after 1945–46, most people had nothing against the Jews. If one now observes how the whole thing has developed, we come again to the DPs and there it is also not to be disputed that a large percentage of the DPs are Jews or from Poland and other states and have been very actively involved in smuggling and black marketeering, and then before 1947–48, before the currency reform, when we still had a pretty low standard of living, low in regard to food and everything that belongs to it, at least an aversion had to spread against the Jews back then, who lived in abundance. I would like to recall that many Jews arrived someplace with a

cart and, after hardly having been there for four weeks, they had a
Mercedes or even a American limousine. That this is not the way things
should happen is clear. I want to say something else: across from us live
many Jews who are very religious. Now, we have to watch all the time how
during the holidays a gentleman made himself at home downstairs and
started to slaughter animals in a not very pleasant way. That not everyone
was exactly delighted about this is perfectly clear. That it doesn't exactly
contribute to generating a big sympathy for our Jewish fellow citizens is
just as clear. Additionally, the Klibansky affair* is generally known here.
That's all I want to say to the Jewish question.

R.: I believe this thing with the Jewish question is not as urgent as Herr U. emphasized here. The time, back then when the Jews attracted attention as
black marketers was a time in which there was a lot of black marketeering
in general. And I believe that here people profiteered even in the highest
governmental circles, and the biggest business people profiteered more than
any small DP, etc. I believe it is very difficult for the Jews, who often speak
another language than we do, and for the DPs who were Poles, to find em-
ployment either in a technical or business enterprise in Germany today.
Who wants to hire a Jew or a DP? It is very difficult. They would at least
have to be skilled workers. And I think Klibansky and Morgenbesser† were
mentioned—those are two names on which the entire mass, which is maybe
still a little bit anti-Semitic, throws itself. I want to ask, which other names
are well known here?

Here too, just as in the passage cited immediately before, one has the
feeling that anti-Semitic emotions are certainly still allowed through, but
no longer have their full force. Even kosher butchery is qualified with the
careful epithet "not very pleasant"; very similar to the way in which, conversely, unrepentant fascists are in the habit of speaking about the Nazi
atrocities in grotesquely reserved ways. Perhaps it is in accordance with
this attitude, which separates itself from the inculcated prejudice, to rely,
insofar as antipathy still rings true, on more concrete and less projective
factors than is usual where the unreconstructed fascist legacy is present. In

---

*Josef Klibanksy, an attorney, was one the founders of the Central Council of Jews in
Germany. During the trial of Philipp Auerbach, Klibansky was held in contempt of court for
his aggressive accusations against the court and the press. In addition, his legal and business
ethics, especially through his involvement with the Jewish Bank for Industry and Trade, were
widely questioned, and several founding fathers of the Central Council were concerned that
this reputation would extend to the entire council. See especially Jay Howard Geller, *Jews in
Post-Holocaust Germany, 1945–1953* (Cambridge: Cambridge University Press, 2005).

†In 1949, the stamp dealer Siegmund Morgenbesser brought a libel suit against the newspaper *Die Zeit*, which had written that his dealership had put up stolen stamps for auction.
He was represented in the case by Josef Klibansky. The following year, Morgenbesser was accused, as a member of the board of the Jewish Reparations Bank, of embezzlement.

particular, it may be pointed out that the speaker calls the "theme of the Jewish question" "fairly delicate"—an expression that indicates the strong affective charge, as well as fear, of saying anything about it at all. It is remarkable as well that the speaker U. claims that "many rich Jews" lived in Ostend, which is not the case. A projective factor is in effect here that emerges even more forcefully later, when the experiment participant speaks of Jews who "came with a cart" after the war and are said to have had a Mercedes or an American limousine after four weeks. Highly prejudiced people are governed by a peculiar inclination to ascribe special luxury precisely to downtrodden groups; thus, in an interview analyzed in *The Authoritarian Personality*, there is talk about the "provocatively luxurious cars" possessed by Negroes in America.[2] In general, mechanisms like those touched on in our study are prevalent internationally and can be applied to any experiential material without changing substantially in the process.

VIII. Open-minded Participants

If mainly subjective phenomena like repression of guilt and defensiveness and objective ones like nationalist and fascist ideology appear in the study, the reasons for this lie in the topic of the study as much as in the material. In the material, statements that express a defensive posture in regard to opponents predominate; they make up an overwhelmingly large portion of the relevant contents of our discussion transcripts. As we have seen, this can be traced to the fact, among other things, that whoever finds himself on the defensive is continuously inclined to extensive argumentative speeches. In contrast, people who do not feel essentially guilty or those who look guilt in the eye—and this group seems to a great extent to coincide with the open-minded group—tend to speak much less about what for them is not in fact an unmastered trauma. The basic stimulus was already conceived in such a way—particularly the first version—that the defense mechanisms would become operative. The nature of these mechanisms, the concrete form they assumed precisely in those who were once Nazis or for some other reasons identify with this and for that reason have to fend off the memory of what happened, required investigation. For that reason, the analysis was mainly applied to the critical zone and not to the opposing potential. It was supplemented through observations about ambivalent statements and ambivalent characters. The remarks about open-minded modes of behavior that now follow are meant merely to correct somewhat the unavoidable one-sidedness and to broaden the overview. For the reasons discussed, it cannot be our goal to give a sufficient idea of the position of the open-minded in regard to the guilt complex on the basis of this material. Much more, that must be reserved for a future investigation directed specifically at such a task.

To begin, some notes on the general position of the open-minded experiment participants in regard to Jews are in order. In the process, what is not said by them is just as important as what is said. For example, the so-called Jewish intellect, which the prejudiced so often acknowledge equivocally, apparently does not play an essential role with the unprejudiced. The latter reject racial theory, as expected; what is remarkable, however, is that they are not concerned much at all with characterizing the Jews as a group; their thinking renounces the construction of rigid group images. Differences are not denied but instead are traced back to social factors rather than to natural ones. Throughout this attitude, social thinking in the sense of a more or less explicit solidarity with oppressed strata prevails. At times, the Jews themselves are differentiated as well in this sense, the rich, capitalist ones contrasted to the poor. The open-minded generally like to distinguish individual Jewish groups as especially positive, perhaps in connection with their insistence on their own experience and their basic aversion to stereotypes.

1. Against Stereotypes

In the BDJ group, the existence of Jewish manual laborers is pointed out against one of the most widespread stereotypes:

> E.: Fräulein K. said that the Jews do not appear at all as manual workers. And I can only respond that in America, for example, the Jews have a completely different position than they had in Germany and in Europe in general, and that there are also manual laborers among the Jews in America, and even a rather large number. In my opinion the Jews can't trade among themselves, because without work there is no capital, and without capital one can't engage in trade. As a result of this, the Jews do have to—be manual workers in Israel, too, have to accept other professions than just that of wheeler-dealer whether they want to or not.

Later on in the same session it is said:

> A.: I actually didn't raise my hand, but I do want to say that this problem has to be traced back deep into history. In the Middle Ages the Jew was not allowed to practice a craft, as Herr G. said earlier, because the guilds wouldn't allow it. Furthermore, he wasn't allowed to practice the art of war, which was very lucrative back then. As a result of this, they were naturally com-

pelled to make their money by trade, and this increased from generation to generation, so that today they probably have more or less at least a certain skill in trade, in making money . . . And I don't know whether it is now . . . the fault of the Jew that many reproach him with that, or the fault of those who, back then, started to lock the Jew in the ghetto and said: "You mustn't practice a craft and so on."

Such statements derive from the simplest common sense. This common sense appears to be much more assailed by rationalizations, half-baked theories, and delusional speculations among the open-minded than among the others.

Jewish traits are in no way denied, but there is an attempt to deduce them rather than to incriminate them; as in the last example, this appears as well in a group of parentless girls who were expelled from the East, in a context in which all sorts of anti-Semitism appears:

E.: With one hand they borrowed money from the Abraham but with the other they drove him into the ghetto. And when was that? The Jewish quarter . . . was only opened in 1800. I mean, that's two generations, those are things that we really shouldn't forget. I mean, we do want to be reasonable and want to see how such a situation comes about at all. And these people who come out of the Ghetto over there in Warsaw and Galicia, and yes, that's its own story . . . if . . . over there, the Russian or Galician farmer talks about the pig and in doing so is referring to the Jew, then that is a situation that necessarily has to lead to a defensive stance . . . If the child grows up from the very beginning in the cellar and lives like an animal, it is completely clear that it will be difficult for this individual to find his place in humanity again.

However clumsily this is expressed, the insight is nevertheless clear, in conjunction with the intention to be reasonable, that the Jews do not on their own tend to everything that is attributed to them, but that they were forced into this kind of existence by the Ghetto.

In the session of high school seniors, there are also strong arguments against anti-Semitic generalizations:

R.: Because everyone knows three or four names, there is the danger of generalization. We could name many more German names. We could also give hundreds of names, both in the East and in the West, where the biggest government people, business people, etc. are up to their necks in the black market. Furthermore, we greatly wronged the Jews, so much that we cannot restore anti-Semitic sentiments on the basis of such trivialities. Just today, the vandalism of cemeteries. I believe those are more serious occurrences than the profiteering of the Jews . . . in public.

(Interruption: Careful! Careful!)
    I'm sorry that here again sentiments in this direction were voiced.

This theme is taken up again in the course of the session:

W.: I wanted to say, when on . . . street, the Jews stand on the street, then it is
    kept quiet that on other corners . . . other people who are not Jews are
    standing as well.
(Interruption: Very true!)
    And then I want to say, the Jews aren't profiteering because they're Jews,
    but, that's what I want to say, because they are enterprising. We have to re-
    ject this enterprise, but I have the impression that some people only turn
    against the Jews due to a certain jealousy. Subjectively, this may all be jus-
    tified, also emotionally. But I don't believe that one can discriminate
    against a whole race of millions of people only . . . because here . . . a few
    dozen . . . And then I want to say the following: people say: Send the Jews
    to Israel! By this, one wants to expel the Jews from countries here in order
    to send them to their own state. This method, in my opinion, should be
    outdated. Whoever wants to emigrate can do that. Whoever wants to stay
    can do that as well. He just has to make sure he obeys the laws. But it is not
    right that one discriminates against an entire human race. If there is a cer-
    tain anti-Semitic attitude here, the reason for that is, in my opinion, to be
    found less in an objective than in a subjective attitude, that there is a cer-
    tain antipathy against the Jews on the basis of the influence of National
    Socialism, and I want to turn resolutely against attacking the Jews as such,
    but one should attack the people who profiteer, without emphasizing: this
    is a Jew, this is a Catholic or atheist, or whatever.

After this, the critique of generalization is extended to the anti-German
stereotypes as well, whereby by the way the rather insightful remark is
made that the speaker who most energetically opposes generalizing also
speaks in generalities about "the Jew."

2. Rejection of the Racial Principle

The arguments leading to a substantive rejection of the racial principle are
even more precise and clearer than those concerning the formal principle
of generalization. If the National Socialists take racial theory time and
again since H. Stewart Chamberlain as the centerpiece of their doctrine, it
is this doctrine that is in fact the element on which opinions part ways. We
must conclude, however, that unequivocal rejections of racial theory are
rare and hesitant, and that formulations such as that of the "somewhat
misguided racial theory" predominate. The expression "fully exaggerated
things like race and Jewry" belongs here as well.

A seventy-year-old woman speaks unambiguously, even though she has not yet freed herself from the Nazi stereotype "Negro and Jew":

> *H.*: I never had anything against the Jews. I had friends in Jewish families from childhood and interacted with Jewish families as a school girl . . . These were the finest people I can think of. I was never harmed by a Jew; I absolutely condemn all this racial conflict. Nobody can help being black or white. I am much more generous in my thinking in this respect.

Also in the BDJ session there is an unequivocal statement, according to which one should approach every human as human.

> *Z.*: I think one should also in general—to get back to the racial problem—approach every person as a person and disregard not only races but also nationalities. And if we now say: The British also did this and also did that . . . We should not take that as an excuse for what Nazi Germany did with the Jews, but we should actually try to approach it without prejudice and see what happens, and not condemn the Jew but the person who was dealing in shady businesses or showed character weaknesses. Because I ask you—I want to recall the era of the profiteering. And the black market . . . I believe people behind the scenes who were making money, about whom we know very little, the Jew . . . could not have been worse. I mean, for this I finally came to the realization that one should not condemn the Jew over-all in any way, but, as has been said, always approach the Jew as human to human . . . We have so many Germans among us who are unappealing to us insofar as we believe that we have a better character and he has the worse character and so on and so forth. Especially the German—if the others don't do it yet, oh well—then we should start with directing all our thinking, all our actions from human to human.

A high school senior says something similar:

> *B.*: May I say something about that? I also have an aversion to the Jews. I don't want to discuss where it comes from. But I want to say one thing, how this could be met. If I try to be objective toward the Jew and to treat him the same way I would treat any other person, I cannot accept in myself the anti-Semitism that I feel, wherever it comes from. I believe I am not the only one like that, but many Germans and many other people feel this way.

This high school senior discovered for himself the cathartic method of psychoanalysis, based on the simple duty of objectivity and self-reflection.

3. Propaganda Is to Blame for Anti-Semitism

The open-minded experiment participants, who either reject the usual jus-tifications for anti-Semitism entirely through a critique of racial theory or allow them only limitedly with social arguments, raise the question of where anti-Semitism comes from. In the process, the terms propaganda and agitation appear regularly. This shows the correct consciousness of the non-spontaneous, manipulative character of anti-Semitism; at the same time, however, the terms employed act a bit like magical formulas that take the place of more difficult and less accessible reflections on the social, political and economic mechanisms that produce anti-Semitism.

In a session with urban women, the remarkably rare but entirely appropriate statement that before Hitler one hardly knew whether one was with a Jew or a Christian appears in connection with the propaganda thesis:

> K: I even know that before, one hardly knew whether one was sitting together with a Jew or with a Christian, and it was just as good with the Jew as with the Christian, one did not make any distinction there. I can remember that I was together with people, with truly pleasant people, and only found out that they were Jews when they emigrated. So it seems to me that the antipathy didn't really emerge at all until 1933.

It is claimed in a group of women that something of the propaganda always sticks—a theme that is closely related to that of defensiveness, asserting that resistance was not possible:

> D.: And if it was instilled in the people over and over again for years, even if he struggles against it in the beginning, something of it will always stick and will perhaps even become his own opinion over time. So . . . that is the way it is with all questions and problems that were taken up by the National Socialist state.
>
> E.: May I refer to a concrete example, that was the sign "German Store." No merchant could evade this sign. If he evaded it, I know this from acquaintances and from many others, his store was targeted if he didn't do it. And if he took it off, other reprisals were taken against him. I mean, these are facts; I mean, one can't say it was up to him that it was done. But that pretty sign, the yellow with the Black German, it was just hung up at certain times. Naturally, it was different in different cities and regions, could be. But where it was there because of the workers' front or some other institution, he just thought the more signs he hangs, the . . . better place he'll get in heaven.

Explaining the pogrom, it was said in another session:

> R.: We awoke in the morning, and then it was said, the synagogue is burning. Who was that? It was only the Nazi boys. Someone must have done it; and then there was a leader there, but this actually was not a leader, this was an agitator! This, in my opinion, is not a leader, no, when boys as young as

thirteen to fourteen years old—they didn't have any control over that, they were allowed to . . .

The same woman says later on:

R.: . . . through their associations, what they got drummed into them there.

One can see the lack of independence. The participation of children in the riots compels the insight that at the same time it must have been a case of manipulation. The distinction between "leader" and "agitator" indicates that the speaker must have been aware of something of the anarchical element of the authoritarian state. Even so, the passage sounds as if the Hitler propaganda succeeded in imbuing the term leader with such a halo that when something disgraceful occurs and the woman looks for the manipulators she has to reach for a different word than leader. In such minimal traits as these, the thought patterns of the Third Reich are still alive in the well-disposed too.

4. Positive Relationships

There are numerous statements of unprejudiced participants referring explicitly to positive relationships with Jews within their own closer circle of experience. The tenor of such statements is: "We didn't have anything against the Jews." This is often documented with the fact that one shopped in Jewish stores; in contrast, personal interactions fade noticeably away. A group of women from a Hessian village, for instance, is rich in such statements. The Colburn letter is rejected, not out of anti-Semitism but because one disputes being anti-Semitic:

K.: I also don't think it is right when it is written in the letter here that we are still ill-disposed toward the Jews today. A large proportion of people didn't even do it back then. And I myself went to the Jews back then even when it was truly dangerous.
W.: Me, too, I was still with the Jews in 1936 (affirmation). I also still visited them.
Th.: We still bought there on the second to last evening . . . but only on the sly . . . I couldn't really . . .
K.: I certainly didn't have anything against Jews back then and nothing today either. (General agreement.)

In a refugee group that shows a certain thoughtfulness, it is generally assured that one did not have anything against the Jews, and this assurance is given once again in opposition to the passage from the Colburn letter about the reemergence of anti-Semitism:

> M.: And the letter also in fact said that we probably still hate the Jews today. Didn't it?
> Mod.: Yes, he writes this, that there are still people today who hate the Jews.
> M.: Yes, I have to say about this, that I actually haven't observed this anywhere in Germany and here among us. I think we also did not hate them personally earlier either. We lived in a small city. The Jews lived among us there. Our neighbors were Jews or half-Jews; our children played with each other, right up to the last moment. My daughter went to school with a girl who was half-Jewish right up to the end. We socialized with each other, we wrote to each other after they fled, he contacted us himself. So a personal hatred of the Jews, I must say, that was never the case with us.

Especially those who do not have to repress a guilty conscience and do not have to take on a cramped defensive posture have the freedom to express the truth that not all Germans are anti-Semites. A passage that is in no way political but borne from experience in the group of girls whom we have already cited multiple times in this section says:

> I.: I only wanted to say that not everybody was unfriendly toward the Jews, and that there were very many people, whole families, who were friendly toward the Jews, and who sometimes also helped some Jewish family, and who then, when the Jews came to America or anywhere else at all, they wrote to each other, and the connection between these families continued until after 1945. So not all Germans were 100 percent against the Jews.

Finally, the unemployed women came to the following overall assessment:

> X.: Pretty much all of us, the overwhelming majority of the German people, condemned these persecutions of the Jews.

The tendency recognizable here to distance large groups from anti-Semitism probably stems from completely different motives from those discussed previously, which were to vindicate one's own group. Rather, at the base of this lies much more the impulse to speak for the entire people *(das Volk)* and the closely connected tendency to separate the people from those who from the beginning connected anti-Semitism with hostility toward the workers. These experiment participants do not want to praise themselves and their own group; it is unbearable to them that people in the same social situation as themselves do not share their disgust with the diversionary tactics of the dictatorship.

5. The Ordinary Person Not Anti-Semitic

Just as the class aspect, the distinction between little and big Jews, plays into the evaluation of the Jews by many of the non-anti-Semitic experiment participants, the social theme also makes itself felt in the subjective delimitation of anti-Semitism in the thesis that "the ordinary person is no anti-Semite." In this matter, what is at stake is not so much the truth or untruth of the sentence, but much more an indication that in it there is a more or less clear recognition that anti-Semitism serves the interests of certain influential groups.

A passage from the discussion of a group of rural women was already cited in which "a large proportion of people even back then" were not hostile toward the Jews. A little later it is said in the same session:

A.: Well, they were stirred up by the upper echelons, that was only an incitement. Because I think the ordinary man, he never had anything against the Jew.

This is substantiated in the further course of the session:

K.: Yes, as far as the ordinary people were concerned, they certainly showed consideration for the people.
Sch.: Sometimes we . . . gave them a piece of bread, you know, and they were so grateful for it.

A similarly concrete example about a group of allegedly non-anti-Semitic craftsmen who were drinking buddies is reported:

Th.: Once I was in a neighborhood pub on . . . street. By chance I happened to sit at the table of regulars—this table was almost all German master craftsmen. The political conversation also got onto the subject of the Jews. They only praised those . . . Jews. They were said to be decent in every way, always paid decently, and also gave their employees a vacation bonus. That was said to be quite common. And when there were family celebrations, baptisms or death in the family and so forth, they supposedly always found support from the Jews.

The same theme appears in the session of the trade unions and workers' councils, with respect to the workers:

U.: I would just mention the magazine *Der Stürmer.** *Der Stürmer* as such was certainly a magazine that one in general rejected here in the circles in

---

*A vehemently anti-Semitic weekly newspaper published by the Nazis from 1923 to 1945.

which I moved as a worker. It was supported mightily with the power instruments of the state, and the people in the end really just had to take it.

However, the discussion does not stop with the thesis that the organized
workforce was traditionally immune to anti-Semitism. It goes on to assert,
furthermore—and probably rightfully so—that the specific climate was overall anti-Nazi:

> F.: I know that here in . . . where I lived at that time, whole piles of ballots
> were falsified; they were simply rejected by the brown bandits at the time,
> and were declared invalid. I am convinced that, especially here in . . . the
> majority was against the Nazi regime, and I cannot share the point of view
> that the German people is fifty-fifty guilty for the things that happened
> there, and as far as that is concerned . . . this mass lynching of the Jews,
> that the German people actually knew about it.

This speaker rejects the difference between lynching and the Nazi measures: he calls the latter "mass lynching"!

6. Admission and Condemnation
of Anti-Semitic Measures

It stands to reason that unprejudiced experiment participants would deny
anti-Semitism in general or minimize its significance, and the material just
presented gives weight to this assumption. But the truth is more complicated. Assuming that, among the participants who more or less generally
deny anti-Semitism, the wish is father to the thought, there are, on the
other hand, also those unprejudiced participants who recognize the seriousness of the persistence of Nazi ideology and develop their own conviction in opposition to precisely what they have recognized. The division
between "in-" and "out-group" [English] is in no way limited as a psychological constituent to those among whom it forms an element of ideology.
Those participants who deny anti-Semitism are in general rather harmless,
credulous, and slightly naïve people who are not overly burdened with
reflection, whereas those who see the reality of anti-Semitism and take
it seriously are to be found rather among the aware and critical people.
Especially in these people, the tendency not to wallow in generalized de-
liberations but to rely on their own experiences is pronounced. The main
role in this is played by *"Kristallnacht,"* which was the source of these experiences; the administratively coordinated extermination took a back seat
to it. The indignation is not measured by the extent and the size of the
deeds, but by the closeness of the speaker to the events. A negative conse-

quence of this attitude in some situations is that especially those people who were warmer and capable of immediate feeling are reached only to a small degree by what happened beyond their proximity, beyond their living presence.

How deeply the shocking experience of injustice can nevertheless sometimes penetrate becomes apparent in the group of fashion school students:

> M.: This made a huge impression on me. I was twelve years old back then and since that time I was crazy about politics, if one can talk about a twelve-year-old girl being concerned with politics. But since that time, I have been thinking about it. This was somehow such an experience, and since then I haven't just accepted everything, as I did up to then, and it definitely made an impression on me.

Once again, the story sparks reactions from other participants. A twenty-one-year old colleague continues:

> R.: Yes, well, I also experienced in . . . all these events with the Jews and I said to myself back then as a ten-year-old child: This is crazy, or, if I think about this now later, this furniture and these valuables, for instance, were seized from the houses and carried away by the SS people, and one didn't know where to. As a child, one said then: Oh well, he is taking it with him now. And this whole thing was also a very impressive experience, that all this stuff was lit on fire in the streets, and one said to oneself: for God's sake, why is everything being destroyed? Well, it was an experience for all of us, and led more and more to the clear conviction: this is nonsense, what is being done. What did those people do to us? Because no Jew ever did the slightest thing to us.

The most important thing, that millions of victims were innocent of what was done to them, is stated plainly and without caveats:

> G.: These were people who had basically done nothing, who were hauled off. If someone else was hauled off, if he was politically active, if he ended up in a concentration camp, but the Jew really couldn't help it.

This speaker is struck by the arbitrary and at the same time blindly fatal quality in the identification of an objective enemy, which is so characteristic of totalitarian regimes; more than anything, the complete separation between what a person does and what happens to him spreads terror of randomly executed violence.

In the barracks for refugees, special tensions with the locals were prevalent and that may contribute to the sympathy of these women for others who were persecuted. The following discussion arises:

Z.: In our area, it was the middle of the night, they threw the Jews out of their apartments, the furniture out, set the Jew churches on fire and everything. The Jew, he was sixty-three years old or sixty-eight, he talked with us and brought us the laundry and everything, he cried bitterly all the way into our apartment.

Sch.: Yes, we also had a very good man in . . . At his place we bought everything, he always served us well. And the man, he cried like a small child when he was supposed to leave. They took his store from him, someone from the party took it over, and he simply had to get out with his family. And these were really elegant people. They didn't get any bread at the bakery any more, they weren't allowed to get anything. Naturally, we just slipped them the bread in secret, because the people also shouldn't starve. A baker wanted to get me onto the black list. There was a blackboard, right? If my mother hadn't gotten along so well with the baker, I would have been put on it, simply because I thanked the Jew. (Slaps the table.) And I can't pass a man and not thank him, when he greets me friendly, right, and he hasn't done anything to me. I don't accept that at all.

I.: With us it was such that the Jews were driven out, were put into prison, and the account books and everything were burnt and ripped apart. They were allowed to take with them, and then they were . . . naturally, they were allowed to take only so much, so much money and were later on to Argentina, etc. . . . Were allowed to continue to travel from . . . in . . .

(Interruption: The poor people, they never came back.)

I don't know. Well, they actually still had it pretty good, they also got food from the population and such things.

Mod.: When did that happen?

I.: Yes, when all the Jews had to get out, right? They were taken out to the prisons and came . . .

Mod.: Pardon?

(Interruption: Many refugees were still able to take things with them.)

H.: They were actually chased away. We lived in the Jewish street, it was really an outrage, I can tell you! I then said to my husband: The same thing is going to happen to us, but with even less! They still had a small wagon . . . and I stood there behind the curtain, and I said to my husband: We're next!

Mod.: Where did you experience that, Frau H.?

H.: In . . . I lived in the Jewish street, where the synagogue, they have a, what do you call it, a children's home, very little children, they threw them out onto the street, I saw it.

(General indignation)

U.: And the synagogue, which they burned, these were churches just like our churches.

(Interruption: That was an outrage! They're still people!)

H.: And what does a small child have to do with it? That they throw him on the street, really!

B.: They can't do anything about being Jews, just as we are Christians.

(Agreement)

Here, as often, the theme of deservedness follows on the detailed account. Even sympathy is not able to detach itself from self-interest: injustice is condemned because it can fall back onto one's own group. It is as if one were gaining insight into primitive phases of identification, almost into the prehistory of humanity.

7. Acknowledgment of German Guilt

In the analyses of the defense against guilt for what happened, we pointed out the role played by the balancing out of suffering and the thought that everything has been settled. The most important argument of the open-minded against this is that total war and the persecution of civilians were indisputably started by Hitler.

The following statement is made in the often-cited session of urban women:

> *B*.: But Hitler started it. He actually said, he'll wipe out all cities. He actually did destroy so and so many children's homes and so and so many children in England, so they returned it in kind. And it is absolutely clear, if I'm beaten today, I don't stand up and say: "Thanks!" but I give it back to him double.

A trade unionist, who is apparently politically trained, asserts German war guilt fundamentally:

> *H*.: When talking about guilt, then, I believe, one can fully affirm that Germany is to blame for the war. The aggressive foreign policy that Germany pursued in the years of his regime proves it.

In rare cases, this attitude leads to identification with the former enemy, and the bombings are accepted as deserved.

Especially those who are themselves completely innocent tend toward moral identification with guilt. Accordingly, in the group of policemen:

> *H*.: There is too much talk. But we have to take our time and each for himself take a good look at the facts that are the causes of current events. Who is to blame for the current events? Who is to blame for all the misery? All of this didn't have to happen if the war hadn't come. And who started the war? The government! And the government—who is that, after all? I want to say: the people. It is us, then, isn't it? The people were complicit, of course, insofar as the foreigners found out enough through the press—the radio, about what was going on in Germany . . . And that the Americans came here and took it out on us and wanted to take it out on us, that's understandable . . . right. The atrocities had already been held up as an example back then. One has

to say over and over again: the cause of it is the war, and we have to endure the suffering, whether we want to or not.

The entire thing culminates in the thought that the German government is to blame, and that the German people are guilty because of the elections that brought Hitler to power.

The following passage stands like a motto at the beginning of the session of Catholic women, which was in no way particularly political:

> H.: I am a true German, but I have to say this, the man (Colburn) is right about many things. We are very arrogant, still, right? And we still don't want to come to terms with the fact that we are the culprits, right, and were the culprits . . . who set the whole world on fire. We actually made this mess through Hitler.

Without too much difficulty, one might draw a connection between the emphasis on the speaker being a "true German" and her identification with the guilt. She draws the conclusion from the "we," which is commonly used in the language of the discussion: if one identifies very strongly as a member of the collective and takes pride in it, then one also has to accept the negative. The same idea recurs in the statement below by the woman who says that if she is proud of Goethe she also has to feel burdened with guilt because of the crimes committed against Jews. There is, therefore, in no way a straightforward identity between national consciousness and defense against guilt. One might come closer to the truth by assuming that people who desperately tried to escape a feeling of guilt are also mostly those who feign and exaggerate their national consciousness exactly because they are incapable of substantive solidarity with any other people, whereas those who really still experience something of a concept of the people shoulder that which concerns the people as a whole for precisely this reason.

8. Willingness for Atonement

However, perhaps the decisive point for the attitude of the open-minded experiment participants is not so much the admission of guilt per se, which also plays a role in the kinds of defensiveness that operate with balance sheets, but much more the willingness to take responsibility for what happened without being obsessed with the thought of it and the resistance against it. The threshold is not found in conceding or denying objective facts, but in the tendency of the individual to include himself morally. Perhaps one can say that the only one who is free from neurotic feelings of guilt and is capable of overcoming the whole complex is the one who experiences himself as guilty, even of those things for which he is not guilty in any immediate sense.

A forty-seven-year-old housewife articulates this:

G.: If I want to be proud of the fact that Goethe is one of us—and I am—then I have to, then I feel at least personally . . . just as burdened with guilt, because it was our people who did the things to the Jews. I equate these things completely, for myself. One has to shoulder the things that happen in the family, one also has to shoulder the things that happen in the nation. And even if I am not guilty for wrongdoing of my father, it still falls back on me in some ways, just as his accomplishments do.

And a fifty-six-year-old female Catholic participant says:

L.: I can testify to it, what sins were committed against the Jews. This is naturally on us again—we ourselves have to atone. I take the fact that I got bombed out as atonement onto myself at any time for the great guilt that was committed against the innocent. There is also among us Christians, and we shouldn't fool ourselves here, just the same Pharisaism hidden and even worse than among the Jews. But the American is right when he says they murdered more Jews in one year in Germany than Negroes. This is right. I can't think about this topic, I get so upset.

This woman returns to her own experiences and insists on the thought that she interprets her own suffering as atonement:

L.: Well, I told you here freely: I was bombed out twice and burnt out completely once, and had to go through a lot because of this accursed Hitler, because we were "black" [Catholic, in politics the former Catholic Center Party]. I admit this freely, also suffered a lot of misery, but I took this to mean that this was the atonement for this great guilt, which the people *(das volk)* has to bear. And our Lord always in the end picks out those people who are less guilty for something. And an innocent always has to atone for a crime. This was my perspective on my heavy bombing losses, because I have certainly not committed so many things in my life that I should get bombed three times—I didn't accept this guy, that was the worst part. And we suffered a lot. I have—I'm a very good Catholic, I say this openly, and I mean I would never say to my Lord: What have you done to me? For this one reason, because I—I told myself: There was so much guilt to be atoned, so part of the German people themselves has to atone this guilt here on earth again. Because it has to be atoned somewhere, and our children may have to atone for it again as well. Such heavy bloodshed—also in this regard in the homeland itself—that has to be atoned. That is still going to be atoned, all the things they have done, it takes its revenge (affirmation), in the twelve years, it takes its bitter revenge.

The study contains no material that allows one to decide whether thoughts like those of this speaker are always linked to religious devotion, or even whether they require such devotion. But the rarity of religiously tinged statements is striking, even though there is no lack of ecclesiastically defined groups among the transcripts analyzed here, and would have to be followed up further.

One feels compelled to hypothesize that even where the population is still ecclesiastically oriented there is no connection between the theological teachings and ethical, social, and political opinions, apart from a small circle of committed Christians. Much more, the different spheres seem to exist unconnected in the ideology, in isolation side by side. This insight has much to contribute to the explanation of the power National Socialist ideology still carries even after the collapse of the National Socialist regime.

Notes

Guilt & Defense

1. This point is discussed in Chapter 1 of *Gruppenexperiment,* and is included in our companion volume, *Group Experiment, The Frankfurt School on Public Opinion in Postwar Germany* (Harvard University Press, forthcoming).

2. Adorno, T. W., Frenkel-Brunswik, E., Lewinson, D. J., and Sanford, R. N. *The Authoritarian Personality.* (New York: Harper and Row, 1950), 280.

I. Knowledge of the Events

1. See *B. Bettelheim:* Individual and Mass Behavior in Extreme Situations, in: *The Journal of Abnormal and Social Psychology,* October 1943, vol. 38, no. 4, p. 417ff., especially the paragraph: The Final Adjustment to the Life in the Camp.

2. *Alexander Mitscherlich* and *Fred Mielke: Wissenschaft ohne Menschlichkeit,* (Heidelberg: Schneider, 1949), p. 190ff.

II. Guilt

1. These slips are treated in our study of the language of the participants. See the unpublished manuscript of the Institute. [no further reference]

2. The discussion took place in the British zone.

3. It is worth noting that the possibility of just this development was foreseen by Hegel in his critique of Kant's ethics, which is contained in the second volume of his Philosophy of Law.

4. See *O. Kirchheimer:* Changes in the Structure of Political Compromise, in: *Studies in Philosophy and Social Science,* vol. 9, no. 2, 1941, p. 264ff.

5. See *T. Taylor: Die Nürnberger Prozess* (Zürich: Europa, 1950).

6. See *F. Neumann: Behemoth,* (New York: Oxford University Press, 1943).
7. See chapter 6, *Gruppenexperiment,* Pollock, 1955.

III. *The Self-image of the Participants*

1. The topic of this section corresponds only partially to the one in the quantitative analysis about the participants' judgment of the Germans [see Pollock 1955, chapter 6, p. 203ff.]. The majority of the speakers is more critical toward the Germans than toward themselves. This critical assessment of one's own people can contribute to the individual's exoneration in a twofold way—the speaker implies that he is not blind with respect to the failings of his own people and resists them. Moreover, it is nevertheless claimed that, as a member of a people bound to authority and politically immature, one can call on extenuating circumstances. In the case of many speakers the judgment on the Germans connects to self-image in this sense.

2. See *C. G. Jung:* Nach der Katastrophe, in: *Aufsätze zur Zeitgeschichte,* Zürich 1946, p. 75ff. [C. G. Jung, "After the Catastrophe," in *Collected Works,* vol. 10 (New York: Ballinger, 1970)].

IV. *The Reality behind Defensiveness*

1. *Friedrich Nietzsche: Werke,* vol. 2, *Menschliches Allzumenschliches,* vol. 1, Leipzig 1917, aphorism 101, p. 103 [*Human, All Too Human,* sec. 2.]

2. See *E. v. Salomon: Der Fragebogen,* Hamburg 1952, p. 560 and others.

V. *Defense*

1. See: *R. M. Brickner: Is Germany Incurable?* Philadelphia, New York 1943, p. 30ff.

2. See: *T. W. Adorno et al: The Authoritarian Personality,* 1950.

VI. *Elements of National Socialist Ideology*

1. See, however: Pollock 1955, *Gruppenexperiment,* chapter 4; p. 203ff.

VII. *The Ambivalent Ones*

1. The common name for the night of November 7th [*sic*], 1938, due to the systematic destruction of Jewish stores and of Jewish property on this night. It is noteworthy that, through the ironic emphasis on smashed shop windows, the burning down of the synagogues and countless most severe abuses, which were less easily borne by the individual's sense of justice, in short the pogrom character of that night, is minimized into a relatively harmless material loss.

2. See: *T. W. Adorno [et al.]: The Authoritarian Personality,* p. 616 [p. 279].

Part Three

THE DEBATE WITH
HOFSTÄTTER

On *Group Experiment*
by F. Pollock:
A Critical Appraisal

BY PETER R. HOFSTÄTTER

F RANZ BÖHM'S preface sees the merit of the investigation at hand as making visible "nonpublic opinion," the content of which "can depart considerably from the content of the apparent public opinion, and the values of which circulate beside those of public opinion like the notes of a second currency; in fact, they may even be more durable and stable . . ." (xi).* "Here we have a master mentality, a master mentality of the crudest and most heartless sort, that has spread to every Tom, Dick and Harry over the course of centuries" (xvi). "The poorly washed and noxious perspectives of nonpublic opinion" (xvii) show "how little effect the actual public opinion has had on the minds and hearts of so much of our population" (xvi). Böhm describes as "amazing" "what a marvelous apparatus has to be constructed for this gnome [i.e. nonpublic opinion] to be comfortable enough to appear at all and to register its tidings." Of course, the observation that what the gnome says is pretty much what "every visitor traveling to Germany, every tourist or journalist can hear shouted from every rooftop if he only pays a little attention" (xiii) might raise doubts for the reader about this "marvelous apparatus."

The "marvelous apparatus" consists of 121 groups of between six and twenty-six participants each (fourteen on average; with a total of 1,635

---

*The full text of Böhm's "Preface" to *Gruppenexperiment* appears in the companion volume along with other material from the 1955 book more directly addressing methodological and theoretical issues. See our editorial preface above for further discussion of the division of material.

persons, 1,072 men and 563 women), who discussed in different places in the Federal Republic of Germany in the winter of 1950/51 a contrived letter from an American or British occupation soldier. When necessary, sociologically informed investigators interspersed further "stimulus arguments" into the discussion after the "basic stimulus" (which was a tape-recording of the soldier's letter). The tape-recorded discussions produced a transcript of 6,392 typed pages, which were evaluated on the basis of descriptive categories. Transcripts of twenty-five discussions (1,370 pages of text = 21 percent of the entire material) were then subjected to a qualitative analysis of "ideological syndromes." In this respect, the work at hand carries forward the tradition of *The Authoritarian Personality* (1950), though without addressing the discussions of the problem of the "authoritarian syndrome" that have in the meantime been published in the collection of essays edited by R. Christie and M. Jahoda (1954).

While questionnaires (e.g. the "F-scale") played a significant, though not always felicitous, role in *The Authoritarian Personality,* the organizers of *Group Experiment* distanced themselves quite emphatically from that method: "The concept of opinion in conventional opinion research, which fancies itself scientifically presuppositionless, in truth presupposes a nominalist epistemology. It operates with a subjective concept of truth, without any regard for the problem of objectivity" (18). "The individual opinion, which appears as fundamental to ordinary opinion research, is in truth highly derivative and mediated. What in contrast was initially introduced here as 'intellectual climate'—German classical philosophy calls it the 'objective spirit'—is essential to the individual opinion" (23). This results in the following formulation of the issue: "Public opinion is the embodiment of this objective spirit, the form of consciousness that is characteristic for the whole society, which mirrors the social conditions and power arrangements" (24). No one "can simply ignore that the positivistic-atomistic conception of public opinion does not do justice to the reality" (24).

If one were to find this last sentence in one of the discussion transcripts, one would expect the comment—and certainly not entirely without justification!—that what no one can simply ignore is merely an assertion and not a proven fact. Apart from that, one could probably also count on a comment about the "linguistic layer," a comment through which the negative evaluation "postivisitic-atomistic" would surely resound. On top of that comes the fact that even the opinion research of *Group Experiment* proceeds partly quantitatively, in the process of which the responses of individuals are "atomistically" taken as average values for entire segments of the population. Moreover, insofar as this research does not reject the requirement that its results be verifiable, which is taken for granted in the empirical sciences, it has no other option remaining than to comply with the "positivistic" procedural norms of research. I thus cannot see that conjuring up the objective spirit has any real meaning.

Indeed, this determination is also not especially important since it is precisely "positivistic-atomistic" opinion research that first came across the problem to which *Group Experiment* was supposed to be the solution. Already more than a decade ago, the concern was raised in the psychological diagnosis of individuals that even an averagely gifted experimental subject can manipulate most questionnaires to give whatever impression he wants. This is also true of the F-scale. *Mutatis mutandis,* this is always the case with those opinion polls in which one expects that the subjects will try to conceal and distort their views, that is to say when there is a possibility that the subjects might have inopportune perspectives. Since the Frankfurt study is aimed at attitudes toward political problems in Germany's most recent past, one can indeed not expect too much from an open questionnaire even today [1957], much less in the winter of 1950/51. The research problem is thus not new, and as a result we already have available a range of methods, grouped together under the rubric "indirect procedures," for solving it (see *Campbell* in Psychological Bulletin, no. 47, 1950, and *Weschler* and *Bernsberg,* in: International Journal of Opinion and Attitude Research vol. 4, 1950). *Group Experiment*'s contribution has to be measured against these methods if its significance is to be judged. This task, however, certainly lies within the purview of "positivistic-atomistic" research.

The psychologist who, for example, had to function as diagnostician within the former German *Wehrmacht* frequently came across the argument that his methods did not do justice to life and that, moreover, they could not stand up to comparison with the old "in vino veritas." *Group Experiment* represents a variation on that theme; its presupposition is: "in ira veritas." The anger was provided by the "basic stimulus," that is, the so-called "Colburn-letter," in which a fictional soldier of the occupation force reports for his hometown newspaper on "the Germans," who are "hardworking," "only rarely insubordinate," "rather good-natured," technically gifted, etc.; but among them one finds "only very few who unambiguously renounce what happened." "Despite the past calamity, many think of themselves as better and more capable than us. They do not want to hear anything about the fact that Hitler started it . . . They are still hostile toward the Jews . . . The risk is that, tomorrow, they will again follow a Hitler or Stalin, . . ." As the authors stress several times, "Colburn's remarks necessarily provoked many to resistance" (467). Yet, they argue to the effect that: "What an angry person says when he has lost rational control of his emotions is nonetheless a part of him" (279);—*in ira veritas.*

But what about this "veritas"? One can object that wine is not only capable of disclosing, but also of distorting; something similar could hold for a group discussion that is aroused by anger. To what extent does the tone, for instance the stereotyped thinking of the letter, lead the discussants onto stereotyped tracks? According to the authors, "In some cases there were indications that the participants played a certain role during the discussions that led them to say things that were not in accordance with their own attitudes, indeed that sometimes seemed to be clearly in contradiction to their usual attitudes. These sorts of contradictions between usual attitudes and the statements of opinion during the group discussion may be explained by the fact that in most people multiple tendencies struggle for dominance, of which one usually prevails while the other is visible only in exceptional cases. That such phenomena can be observed in the discussions suggests a result that is entirely positive for our experiment: namely, that the experimental design reduced the controlling function of consciousness and thereby allowed access to deeper layers of consciousness" (37);—*in ira veritas*. But what if a different truth lies in Chianti than in Riesling—that is, if a differently constructed basic stimulus (the letter) would produce a different portrait of opinion? This concern appears in the afterword: "We would mention here the possibility of improving the experimental design through the use of two contrasting basic stimuli in comparable groups" (482). But there was not yet any talk of this in the preface, where the truths unearthed by anger could be heard "shouted from every rooftop." Were this the case, however, certain doubts would emerge as to the depth of the targeted "deeper layers of consciousness.'"

One can ask in all seriousness to what degree the statements triggered by a single basic stimulus are typical of attitudes outside of the actual research situation. Since the selection of the participants was not designed to be a representative sample, the authors stress "with greatest emphasis . . . that the numerical findings, viewed in isolation, have no claim to validity beyond our circle of participants" (11). There is a wide gulf between this undoubtedly correct insight and the claim that nonpublic opinion in Germany consists of "poorly washed and noxious perspectives." It is hardly surprising that "a universal language of semi-education" is displayed, since 60 percent of the participants had only completed elementary school and 73 percent had not even finished high school (77). Nevertheless: "A diffuse and logically confused but still relatively solid structural whole, a medium through which reality is perceived and leveled out, is visible in the attitudes of the participants toward the most important themes of the study. The core of this structure could be called collective narcissism: exaggerated identification with the collectivity to which one belongs, especially the nation. Such a conviction dominates the majority of respondents and may supply one of the principal conditions for the often disconcerting lack of willingness to understand."

In vino veritas—some people, however, fall silent when they are full of wine. This holds for the group experiment as well: "On average the silent participants form a majority compared to the speakers at the rate of three to two (61 percent compared to 39 percent) . . . 23 percent of the participants did not speak out on any of the twelve initial topics" (266). In none of the twenty statistical groupings arranged by the authors (according to sex, age, profession, education, and military service) did the average participation in the discussion amount to even 50 percent (268). For the theme of "German self-assessment," 71 percent were "silent participants" (204); for "Jews and anti-Semitism," 78 percent of participants remained silent (162). And yet, the preface says: "Those who propound the nonpublic opinions are anything but shy and inhibited" (xv). If this were true, the group experiment would appear to be a method that produces far less material than everyday observation.

But who is actually the bearer of the nonpublic opinion, of collective narcissism? On average, a 39 percent minority of those studied. Even this figure is an overestimation since not all speakers within this minority held "noxious" views, or opinions that the authors declare "undemocratic," such as the rejection of German remilitarization. On the theme "Germans," for instance, 49 percent of the speakers expressed themselves "critically" (i.e. more or less disparagingly, which is judged as "positive" under the authors' concept of democracy) and 31 percent "ethnocentrically." Yet since only around 30 percent of the participants spoke out on this topic at all, the percentage of "collective narcissism" does not even amount to 10 percent of the entire group. If one looks at the numbers presented in this way, then elements of the authoritarian-antidemocratic syndrome are found in only

Topic	Speaker	Evaluation of attitude with regard to its democratic character			
		Positive	Ambivalent	Negative	
				Speaker	Population
	%	%	%	%	%
Democracy	53	10	68	22	12
Guilt (war and concentration camps)	48	5	44	51	24
Jews	22	28	35	37	8
Western powers	51	9	30	61	31
Russia and communism	31	83	12	5	2
Remilitarization	36	12	29	59	21
Germans	30	49	20	31	9

a relatively small percentage of the subjects. The following table makes this clear.

I am not sure whether, on the basis of this result, we have more reason to talk about an "inheritance of fascist ideology" or to use the expression "persisting anthropological disposition" (377 [p. 139 above]) in Germany than in any other country of the Western world. The book itself, however, gives this impression by overwhelmingly selecting antidemocratic utterances from its transcripts. It could nevertheless be that the authors carried the "critical" attitude toward their fellow Germans somewhat farther than is objectively justified. Within the frame of this report, it is not possible to examine whether to qualify as an honest democrat in the winter of 1950/51 one really had to be in favor of remilitarization and whether one had to abstain from all critical statements on the policy of the Western occupation authorities. Yet, to the authors these issues appear beyond any doubt.

For me, the justification for the talk of the "ideological syndrome" of an undemocratic disposition remains entirely incomprehensible. Are those experimental subjects who have a critical attitude toward Germanness really always or as a general rule friends of remilitarization, that is to say completely uncritical about the Western powers? Everything here depends on correlations; yet the study does not contain a single correlation coefficient. Apparently such positivistic-atomistic devices are not required for conjuring up the objective spirit. At the extreme limit, the fear even arises that the manner of thinking ascribed to the objective spirit will itself succumb to totalitarian despotism. Some of the authors' interpretations point in this direction. Thus, they offer the following contribution from a woman as an "example" for their handling of interpretative categories: "I don't believe that the Germans, or let's say even a large number of Germans, were gleeful when the Americans sustained casualties (in Korea)." To this it is said: "The statement implies that our participant identifies with the fate of the Americans in Korea" (98). This does not seem to me to be implied by the statement, but read into it.

The primary concern of the "qualitative analysis" is the problem of the German acknowledgment of guilt in regard to war and concentration camps. The authors proceed from the assumption that they are dealing with a matter of repression, which is maintained by collective defense mechanisms: denial of knowledge, the pretext of one's own helplessness, relativizing guilt against that of others, etc. The methodological apparatus comes from psychoanalysis; it mainly involves unmasking. One cannot completely resist the impression that the sociological analysts are continuing the discussion with their subjects after their discharge. But to what extent is psychoanalysis suited to such polemical use? Psychoanalysis follows the disputational art of an intensivized conversation in pursuit of therapeutic ends. Not infrequently, psychoanalytic interpretations are undertaken in a very precise manner aimed at provoking resistance in the partner. There are certainly solid grounds for doing so, but it quickly loses its appeal when it happens without the partner and without his ability to respond. Without the partner's reactions, psychoanalytic interpretations have a rather meager basis of truth; in this way, they lead easily to shrewd but unprovable conceptualizations, as shown by most psychoanalytic biographies. Given the multiplicity of possible meanings for all matters of emotional life, the specification of correct interpretations is possible only in dialogue.

The qualitative analysis, which covers 150 pages, is mostly nothing but an accusation, that is to say a summons for genuine psychic contrition. But to what extent can one expect that the majority of the members of a people can undertake collective self-recrimination over a long term? I think it is hardly possible that a single individual would be capable of carrying the horror of Auschwitz. The nation could (and perhaps should) try to exorcise this horror in a ritual of penitence; however, since this has not happened so far, it is not surprising that single individuals from all strata of the population avoid the topic of guilt or assess their own personal guilt as minimally (subjectively) as possible. There is simply no individual feeling that could satisfactorily correspond to constantly considering the annihilation of a million people. In light of this limit of the human ability for experience, the indignation of the sociological analyst seems to me to be either pointless or out of place. The often irritated tone of his comments thus comes across as mostly embarrassing. As an example for this, from the discussion group of dignitaries from a Bavarian village:

> G.: Are we dealing here with a moral guilt or a foreign policy guilt? If it's a matter of moral guilt, if the question refers to the moral aspect, then . . .
> H.: Belongs in the confession box!
> G.: . . . then this doesn't belong, I believe, in this place tonight, because the Americans are plainly just as guilty in the moral sense, in my opinion, are just as bad or good as we are. If it's a matter of foreign policy guilt, then I believe the events have already overtaken this question, because if you call on a people to join the same army to which you belong in order to fight a world-enemy, then the question of guilt is moot because in that case it can only be a matter of equal comrades in arms.

The commentary of the sociological analyst reads: "The passage is extraordinarily informative. It almost seems as if, in the haste of defensiveness, the art of conceptual distinction reverted to the old sophistic craft of making the weaker thought the stronger one. At first the distinction between moral and foreign policy guilt sounds as if it comes from the pedantic approach of an academic lecture. But it is not in the service of clarifying a complex subject but of compartmentalizing jurisdictions, in which the division of labor takes over the moral sphere and in the process dissolves it. Organized religion is supposed to be responsible for moral guilt: to the confession box, and then the dignitaries are excused from any further worry. The 'foreign policy guilt,' however, is—not entirely without justification—ascribed to the constellation of real power relations, and in this manner the thesis that this kind of guilt is moot is deduced from the fact that the policies of the Western Allies toward the Federal Republic have changed. With head held high, the subject [thus] strolls through the battleground of murdered concepts" (318–319 [p. 86 above]).

At any rate, it seems justified to ask whether the letter from a fictitious soldier of the occupation army, which is in part and intentionally vexatious, provides a suitable framework for addressing the question of guilt, which is laden with despair. Put differently, where in anger does truth begin and where does the group arrangement impede personal introspection? Would it not have been more appropriate scientifically and humanely to deal with the question of guilt in exhaustive individual interviews? The fact that one of the Bavarian dignitaries thought of the "confession box" in this context reveals an insight into the material limits of the group experiment, which its organizers obviously did not consider enough, despite the very pertinent reflections on "integration phenomena in group discussions" (429–477). The nonpublic opinion, which they think they have gotten hold of, is not necessarily equivalent to private meaning or even with confession tête-à-tête. The fact that almost two-thirds of the attendants did not state their position on the individual topics at all should already have called attention to this. Even the "marvelous apparatus" was apparently not able to break through the nonpublicness of their opinions. In light of this, this marvel appears to do much more poorly than any of the by-now well-known indirect methods of opinion research.

In the end, what kind of proof do we have for the claim that the views advocated in the group discussions reveal deeper strata of consciousness than, for example, a private conversation? Is the equation primitive = deep = real at all valid, or is its validity simply assumed axiomatically? Isn't it possible that the group discussion could even be seen as a seduction to superficiality? Unfortunately, the present book did not answer these questions. We are thus left with the prosaic conclusion of the afterword, which is really quite disappointing after the grand proclamation of the preface: "We do not know to what extent the extremely rich and, in terms of quality, exceptionally fruitful material that we were lucky enough to find can be generalized. An evaluative procedure that could do justice to such richness according to the standards of empirical research is not yet available."

Reply to Peter R. Hofstätter's Critique of *Group Experiment*

BY THEODOR W. ADORNO

HOFSTÄTTER'S efforts take as their refrain the generous preface that Franz Böhm wrote to *Group Experiment,* as if it were an integral part of the work and made demands that were not satisfied in the text. There is no other way to understand Hofstätter's provoking thesis—that "the prosaic conclusion" is "quite disappointing after the grand proclamation of the preface"—even though qualifications like those invoked by Hofstätter already appear in the introduction and in many other places. In truth, the preface reflects the impression that the book made on a particular scholar and politician, one who is quite alert and experienced in German affairs; this preface far exceeded what the authors had hoped for from their experiment. The book did not carry that title [*Experiment*] for nothing. Even so, Hofstätter treats the book as if the study claims it captured nonpublic opinion. This is a distortion.

It amuses him that Franz Böhm praises the study as having caused the unofficial, though still potentially quite effective, "nonpublic opinion" "to appear" and "to register its tidings," at the same time that Böhm maintains that "every visitor traveling to Germany, every tourist or journalist can hear it shouted from every rooftop if he only pays a little attention." A scientist as rigorously empirically minded as Hofstätter is nevertheless certainly familiar with the degree to which social research has to deal scientifically with facts that are accessible to immediate prescientific experience. One would certainly like to hear from him which of the empirical studies that he considers exemplary add as much new to what is already known but unproven as *Group Experiment* does. If the study had been content with merely reporting what one can hear shouted from every rooftop, he would certainly be the first one to denounce the unscientific character of such a procedure; yet, when it is recorded on tape, he is unsatisfied, because, after all, one can hear it shouted from every rooftop. The slogan that Hofstätter invents, then attributes to the study, and finally triumphantly criticizes—"in ira veritas"—may well be entirely questionable; but *Hofstätter* himself certainly did not set to work *sine ira et studio* [without hate and zealousness]. Representative of his overall charge is that the collection by Christie and Jahoda on *The Authoritarian Personality* was not taken into account in *Group Experiment,* even though the preface makes clear that the survey and the interpretation took place from 1950 to 1954, thus before that book was available. That the study as a whole is dedicated to *The Authoritarian Personality;* that *The Authoritarian Personality* triggered an entire literature in America and substantially changed social psychology's problematic there; that countless experiments using the F-scale were conducted: this is all irrelevant to such a high-minded expert in American social science as Hofstätter.

He is mainly concerned with the methodology, not with the wealth of material the volume presents, fully conscious of all the problems of interpretation. In fact, the effort to understand individual and collective opinions *in statu nascendi* [in the state of being born], instead of producing them in an ossified form that may never have existed in the consciousness of the individuals, was more important than the substantive findings, which were never claimed to have been proven conclusively. However, the study described itself much more as an "experimental contribution" toward solving a problem that had thus far only been insufficiently posed by social research, "with all the preliminary and questionable aspects that can hardly be avoided given the paradox of the task itself, and certainly cannot be avoided during the first steps" (31). Such qualifications can be found again and again in the book—more often than would be in accordance with the literary taste of the authors, who, of course, knew ahead of time what kind of ingrained reactions from their readers they could expect. On the very first page of the text, in the authors' foreword (v), it says: "The goal is to make a contribution to penetrating the surface of public opinion as it appears and to facilitate a well-founded judgment about how groups characteristic of the population of the Federal Republic actually stand toward ideological and political questions." Hofstätter nevertheless talks about the contribution as if it was already supposed to count as that judgment.

He at least implies that this would then avoid the demand that the results be verifiable (see Hofstätter, 98 [pp. 190–191 above]). In those places where it does not meet this demand, namely in the qualitative analysis and with the question of what weight to assign to the selected utterances, the volume refers to the stenographic transcriptions of the discussions, which were accurately and repeatedly checked. The authors would have preferred to be able to reprint some of the original transcripts, yet even then they would have been subject to the zealous objection that they chose these transcripts arbitrarily. There is thus no other option than to invite scholars who are not satisfied with the description of the selection process to work through all of the transcripts on site.

As concerns the criterion of verifiability itself, the book not only confirmed its claim but also discussed its challenge. This is not only addressed in the foreword, but above all from p. 57 on, where it is argued that "the application of the categories to the material . . . necessarily has to give more latitude to the cultivation of subjective judgment than is the case in the quantitative analysis of survey results." One might add that what is conventionally called subjective judgment is not plucked out of thin air but is based on theoretical considerations that the text presents throughout. Above all, an "antinomy of empirical research" is developed from p. 30 forward:

> Empirical social research faces a kind of antinomy. The more exact its methods are, the more these methods are in danger of replacing the actual object of study with one defined in "operational terms" [English], in other words, narrowing the object of inquiry to that which can be ascertained with the survey instrument and thus neglecting what is socially relevant.

This critique, subsequently elaborated more precisely, in no way disqualifies orthodox research methods; indeed the volume also contains quantitative analyses according to the limits dictated by the group method. Hofstätter believes he has to remind the initiators of the group experiment of "indirect techniques," to which they supposedly did not dedicate enough attention. But he forgets that materials are presented on pp. 496 to 500 that come from the discussions, and with the help of which "the formulation of numerous indirect questions" could be enabled, and through which quantifiable information about taboo or emotionally laden attitudes can be gained "without the interviewee realizing it." Hofstätter ignores what the Institute for Social Research has contributed to the development of the indirect method, particularly in *The Authoritarian Personality.*

But at the foundation of *Group Experiment* lie considerations that question the monopoly of quantification and quasi-natural-scientific verification.

If science dispenses with such self-reflection, it would degenerate into a mindless technique. Obviously, Hofstätter is entitled to criticize them in turn. Yet, instead, he ignores these considerations and tacitly assumes that what is called into question at the beginning of the study is in fact obligatory. He thus achieves the impression that generally accepted procedural rules were violated, whereas exactly these themselves constitute the methodological challenge.

The group experiment method arose within the problematic of survey methodology. It did not in any way, as one might think from a comment of Hofstätter, draw on the conventional organicist and irrationalist cliché that surveys would be too mechanistic for talking about the ostensible totality of the person or of the community; Hofstätter can have no doubt that the Institute is no less skeptical in this area of thought than he is. Yet, in the practice of opinion research, very often the participants' statements produced in the interview are taken, without any further specification by their origin and validity, as the "solidly fixed meanings of the individual," and the statistical averages distilled from them are taken as public opinion. Parameters of this kind can yield considerable insight—for example in the comparison of groups, i.e. for the sociological analysis of the conditions for particular verbal reactions (20). But the blind reduction of the embeddedness, of the variability of reactions, and especially of the real differences of socio-political power and powerlessness to a statistical model that is at best appropriate to elections is false. In contrast to this, we tried to create in the group discussion an investigatory situation that is closer to reality. The intention was to observe and make analytically accessible a kind of public opinion that is not constructed on the chimerical assumption that everyone has a definite opinion on anything and everything. This situation was meant to call forth real social behavior that simultaneously reflects and produces "public opinion." Its medium is the conversation and the interaction between those who are talking with each other; official inhibitions *(Zensuren)* are deactivated, new controls within the group induced.

But, and this is made perfectly clear in the text, such a research situation requires that new evaluative procedures be worked out. For in contrast to the situation with interviewing, each individual is not directly commensurable with his statements in the free group discussion. Thus, a participant's silence toward a topic can mean that he does not want to repeat the views of the previous speaker because they are in accordance with his own; but it also sometimes means that he is restraining himself from voicing disagreeable views under the influence of social control in the group; according to the chapter on integration (p. 429ff.), the force of group control gradually increases in the course of the discussion until a more or less articulated "group opinion" prevails. In subsequent work on the method of group discussions, the Institute for Social Research drew consequences from this. It is not so much the isolated reactions of the individual participants in the discussion as the sum of their interplay that produces insight into either the public or nonpublic opinion being investigated. A follow-up study of the group discussion material along with a later experiment conducted on group discussion have demonstrated the extensive substantive and psycho-dynamic agreement of group opinions that precipitates out of different discussion groups when they have the same social composition.

In this respect, the Institute's research already supersedes Hofstätter's criticism. The attempt to arrive at quantitative assertions about the nature of public opinion by statistically processing the meanings expressed by each individual participant does not fully do justice to the inherent demands of the method. The technique for quantifying the discussion materials in *Group Experiment,* used despite many concerns, stems from survey methods and was a stopgap. It was supposed to enable a rough estimate of the constantly recurring clichés of opinion and of the basic attitudes that manifest themselves in them. The objections Hofstätter raises against this would be justified had the limited generalizability of the figures produced not been emphasized to excess in *Group Experiment* itself. It is thus all the more surprising that Hofstätter himself draws on those same numbers that he previously criticized as soon as—after some recalculation of percentages—they seem to support his thesis that the "authoritarian-antidemocratic syndrome" is harmless. He thus converts the percentages for positive, ambivalent, and negative attitudes, which were based on the sum total of *speakers* in *Group Experiment* into the sum total of *participants,* and thereby implicitly assumes that the silent participants had "nonnegative attitudes." This permits him his satisfied statement that, in the face of these numbers, there is no more reason to speak of an inheritance of fascist ideology in Germany than in any other country of the Western world—even though, after all, there was no fascist ideology to be inherited there.

His following complaint is no more substantial:

> Within the frame of this report, it is not possible to examine whether to qualify as an honest democrat in the winter of 1950/51 one really had to be in favor of remilitarization and whether one had to abstain from all critical statements about the politics of the Western occupation authorities. Yet, to the authors these issues appear beyond any doubt (Hofstätter, 102 [p. 194 above]).

Yet, a footnote (p. 127, note 19) reads:

> The evaluation of the approval of remilitarization as positive, the rejection of it as negative, is meant to express nothing other than that within the syn-

dromes of democratic and antidemocratic expressions of opinion the rejection of German armament can be found more often among the enemies of democracy. By no means does this classification imply a statement on the extremely intricate problems of remilitarization. Nor is it meant in any way to imply that radical rejection is to be equated with an antidemocratic conviction, which would be nonsense.

On page 488 it is noted that it is necessary to place the problem of rearmament "into a broader context." Also mentioned there is "a social-theoretical construction of the complex position toward rearmament that strives to understand the frequently clashing aspects of the articulated perspectives as parts of a historical process." The monograph that is dedicated to this could not be included in the volume; and yet Hofstätter proceeds as if a simplistic thesis and not a wide-ranging conceptual framework were being presented. The only reason the supporters of remilitarization were added to the rough category of the "positive" was that, in the context of the discussions, the slogan "leave us out of it" that was popular at the time seemed to be coupled with rejection of the post-Hitlerian political system. The authors were as aware as Hofstätter that this was neither a matter of a conclusive result nor of a fact that could be interpreted statically, and the text leaves no doubt about this. Hofstätter nevertheless paints a picture of the study as oriented toward the politics of the occupation authority and as based on prejudicial conviction.

Even taking care not to treat the summary data of the quantitative part as statistically exact, these certainly do not exaggerate the weight of the antidemocratic dispositions that are expressed. More likely they underestimate their evolution in the course of the discussions. Affirmative or partly affirmative arguments for instance on themes of democracy, guilt, Jews, and the relationship to the Western powers are found mostly at the beginning of the discussion—that is, at a point when the Colburn letter was at its freshest in the memory of the speaker; namely, as long as uncertainty about the reactions of the investigator, who at first is still regarded as a kind of official authority, encourages respect for the democratic credo. Yet the more obvious the investigator's neutrality becomes, and the more agreement the negatives find with other participants, the more the potential that Hofstätter estimates as low dares to come out. Often after a short time, above all in socially homogeneous groups, pointedly ethnocentric, authoritarian-antidemocratic group opinions emerge, against which the potentially democracy-friendly participants either protest in vain, or fall silent. According to the observations of the investigators and the assistants, those who were silent were not uninvolved—frequently they expressed their approval of the dominant opinion through mimicry, gestures, or cheering. The Institute is working on the development of observation techniques for nonverbal indices of this kind, which are to be connected to the description of prevailing basic opinions and basic attitudes.

All this illuminates the difference between the group discussion approach and the "indirect techniques" that Hofstätter counterposes to it. Indirect survey methods investigate the psychological dimensions of a particular subject matter in single individuals with the intention of identifying its structure and correlating it with other data; the group discussion method, on the other hand, aims at dispositions or potentials, be they controlled or be they repressed, that manifest themselves in the collective. Individuals do not form the substrate of the research; they are themselves to be understood only as functional, namely in their relation to the "group opinion." Methods of group discussion and indirect surveys are thus complementary; this is discussed in the appendix to the book.

Hofstätter mistrusts the depth of the layers to which the group experiment penetrates. Yet, in the process there is an error at play. Depth means something entirely different philosophically than psychologically: the living being as opposed to the stereotyped phenomenon of the façade. In the psychological dimension—that of conscious-unconscious—precisely the depth characterized by distance from consciousness, in contrast to the ego, itself appears as in many ways stereotyped, namely as primitive and undifferentiated, as described by Le Bon phenotypically and worked out by Freud genotypically. Hofstätter takes advantage of a quid pro quo insofar as he extends the idea of depth as something won in profound thoughts or profound works of art onto the amorphous unconscious.

Moreover, one should not go overboard, our own study no less than Hofstätter. It is entirely possible that the so-called deeper motivations, the unofficial meaning that we hit upon, are not really all that deep; that psychoanalytically speaking it could be more a matter of the preconscious, and often even of fully articulated meanings than of the unconscious. In this regard, we would agree with Hofstätter's critique, but he should be the last to be pleased by this; if he is right, the nonpublic opinion is not a kind of ghost in the closet, no sleeping giant that should be left alone, but a quite present threat, one a lot less trivial than what Hofstätter feels compelled to trivialize.

Granted, he doubts that the experiment reveals anything at all, latent or not. The basic stimulus supposedly "overstimulates" the test subjects; it causes them to react in a way that does not correspond to their true being, regardless of whether the opinion is manifest or latent: this is what "in ira veritas" is trying to do. Hofstätter carefully conceals the fact that the question of "overstimulation" is thematized in the book: the basic stimulus should "not overstimulate the participants, push them into a defensive posture, or provoke them to react unnaturally" (42). Furthermore, page 50 describes how the basic stimulus was repeatedly modified in the course of the experiment, in order to recenter so to speak the stimulating effect of the letter from the psychological to the objective." The full context for the passage Hofstätter quotes on p. 99 (p. 191 above) reads as follows:

> In response to the criticism that we provoked our participants with the basic stimulus, we would like to say that it would fly in the face of all psychological theory and experience to assume that all utterances made in irritation are random and irrelevant. What an angry person says when he has lost rational control of his emotions is nonetheless a part of him. It is just as good an expression of his unconscious, latent and self-betraying [*ich-fremd*] psychological potentialities as is, on a less deep level, the supply of preconscious, current perspectives that he carries along and that he can assert or reject as a fully conscious being through his own autonomous judgment. (p. 279 [p. 52 above]).

In response to this, Hofstätter refers to the familiar assertion that one is certainly not responsible for what comes out in anger after the loss of self-control. This lack of responsibility, measured by the criteria of self-awareness, is supposed to devalue findings that refer to whatever does not obey those criteria. Yet nowhere do Hofstätter's objections prove themselves to be less convincing than on this central point. Even in its crassest form, the basic stimulus offered only the mildest criticism. It is certainly advanced in a somewhat undifferentiated and pedantic manner in order to maintain the pretense that a soldier from the occupation army is speaking, to remain accessible to all groups, and not least to spare the feelings of the groups; but it does not contain anything that, for example, a foreign visitor at the time could not have formulated on the basis of his own observations. Moreover, the critical points were carefully balanced out with approving statements. In the attempt to defend themselves against the sergeant's alleged criticisms, speakers' statements time and again confirmed exactly what the sergeant had maintained. In light of this, the accusation, formally so enlightening, that the research method caused in people something that was not to be found in them at all loses much of its weight. In the process, it also came out substantively that the same clichés Hofstätter tried to ascribe to the basic stimulus appeared *without* the basic stimulus, thanks to the social-psychological cover that the discussion groups provided for their participants. Finally, the basic stimulus was not conceived in a vacuum. The concrete experiences that the organizers of the study had with the unofficial opinion that dominated in Germany at that time also entered into its formulation. The organizers do not want to equate the fascistic potential the study revealed with the *behavior* of the German population, either at the time of the discussions or now, as could be inferred from Hofstätter's criticism. Already in 1950, when the economic miracle was just beginning, political interests took second place to economic ones. The experiment nonetheless unveils socio-psychological dispositions for a political ideology "that certainly is not fully in effect in present circumstances, whose current significance one also must not overestimate, but that could again gain unimagined power if it were once again connected to strong objective forces" (280 [p. 52 above]). In order to work out this ideological potential, no less than because sufficient quantitative techniques for the analysis of the discussions were not yet available, the evaluation privileges the qualitative analysis. The correlation coefficients that Hofstätter found missing were not calculated because they would have amounted to a statistical fiction unjustified by the material. Anything beyond a drastically rough calculation of group attitudes would have been problematic from the outset.

Hofstätter's critique tries to steer the study into a predicament that has in the meantime become quite popular. Against the background of the German tradition, quantification is accused of superficiality; one has to expect "efforts to distort and to conceal" (Hofstätter, 99 [p. 192 above]),—by the way, this is even after Hofstätter's own book was referenced (*Gruppenexperiment*, 29) on the problem of interview situations. By the same token, the qualitative analysis is confronted with demands, such as for evidence and random replicability, that come from the quantitative area; apparently Hofstätter regards scientific results as "mere assertions" until they are substantiated through quantitative methods or "intensivized conversation" (Hofstätter, 103 [p. 194 above])—[the latter being] certainly only one among several possibilities of qualitative knowledge. The handling of "interpretive categories" is said to be in danger of "totalitarian despotism" (Hofstätter, 102 [p. 194 above]). The following passage from *Group Experiment* would oppose this:

> . . . only scientific moderation *(Takt)* can ensure that the irreducibly subjective element, on which spontaneity and productivity of science depends, does not proliferate into the delusional. It would be a bad science that seals itself off from what emerges out of the material for the sake of a chimera of absolute provability. We are by no means blind to the fact that a shadow of relativity clings just as much to quantitative as to qualitative interpretations: there the inevitable remains of rigid computational methods that do not entirely do justice to the life of the discussions and the meaning of the individual statements; here the danger that the idea overshoots what the facts support according to the relevant interpretive norms, which demand the verifiability of every intellectual operation through every other researcher in the same discipline . . . The more qualitative material and qualitative interpreta-

tion based on the particular question comes to the forefront . . . , the more urgent it becomes, if at all possible, to examine the qualitative findings in a
quantitative way; or, in the face of the limits we faced statistically in this regard, to at least point out the possibilities for such an examination." (9f.; see
also 265f.)

In the meantime, even orthodox social research ["social research" in Eng-
lish] has recognized that the subjective element cannot be eliminated in
qualitative analyses and that precisely the engagement of the psychologist's
experience and ability to respond are the condition for the fruitfulness of
its discoveries (see *Barton* and *Lazarsfeld:* Some Functions of Qualitative
Analysis in Social Research, in: *Sociologica*, Frankfurt 1955, 321ff.). This
"subjective moment" in no way confines itself to intuition, which is most
often referred to by opponents in a trivializing fashion, but depends "on a
basic inventory of theory and on experiences from daily praxis, as well as
on the results of previous research" (58). Hofstätter takes no notice of any
of this.

Instead, he equates the subjective moment with malicious intent: according
to him, the study is concerned "mainly with an unmasking" (Hofstätter, 103
[p. 194 above]). This is how one imagines psychoanalysis in those areas of
"totalitarian despotism," where one prefers to bridle the intellect for fear
of its deleterious effect; one hardly expects something like this from the author of a book on depth psychology. He defines psychoanalysis overall as
"the disputational art of an intensivized conversation in pursuit of therapeutic ends" (Hofstätter, 103 [p. 194 above]). If one were to hold with this
definition drawn straight from therapy for the entire domain of psychoanalysis, all analytical characterology and social psychology—that is, a
decisive part of the literature on depth psychology—would be excluded *ab
ovo;* one can hardly imagine that Hofstätter seriously demands this. He
will hardly want to prevent social psychology from drawing from the insights registered in that literature; hardly demand that one assume the posture of *tabula rasa* and expect that each investigation would begin as if one
did not know anything about the meaning of the recorded phenomena beforehand. Such scientific asceticism would lead to unbearable impoverish-
ment. In the individual therapeutic case, it is necessary to lead those kinds
of discussions to which Hofstätter wants to limit the use of psychoanalytic concepts; but any analytic therapist would be able to inform him that
the same typical issues emerge again and again in analytical discussions, to
the point of agonizing monotony. Stated modestly, it would not be in the
interest of the economy of scientific labor not to evaluate typical findings,
without which social psychology runs the danger of bypassing essential associations.

Above all, however, Hofstätter misses that precisely this emphasis that is placed on these typical circumstances and at the same time on the objective facts that come to light in them—the inheritance of totalitarian despotism and of the manipulation of consciousness—exonerates, if one already thinks in such terms, the single individuals. He operates as if the proof of the effectiveness of those mechanisms long familiar to the analysis and the violence that fascist ideology still exercises after the collapse *(Katastrophe)* of the system would humiliate those into whom the ideology was beaten. He thus appeals to nothing other than to that collective narcissism that the study itself considers the most powerful of all those disastrous mechanisms.

The statement that "the qualitative analysis, which covers 150 pages . . . is nothing but an accusation" (Hofstätter, 103 [p. 195 above]) is a false accusation, and not only in its rudiments. If the evidence, carefully chosen from an overwhelming abundance of material, affects *Hofstätter* this way, this is not because of the study but because of the material. Furthermore, "the primary concern of the 'qualitative analysis'" is by no means "the problem of the German acknowledgment of guilt" (Hofstätter, 102 [p. 194 above]). Instead, we conducted a whole series of qualitative investigations, from which, with regard to the available space, two texts had to be selected and shortened:

> The selection caused problems. We could proceed neither systematically nor according to the significance of the investigated topics. The investigation of integration phenomena had to be limited, not simply because it refers to the total structure of the discussions but also because in the same way it provides the formal framework for the problem of conformism and of identification with the collectivity, which substantively were among the most important results.
>
> We decided on the treatise "Guilt and Defense" because it allows us to make tangible that the group method triggers affect-laden utterances stemming from deeper layers of the respondents that the traditional interview method does not reach. In addition, this study offers a kind of phenomenology of what the discussants themselves like so much to call the "German neurosis," and will be cured only when, recognized by its structure, it has been raised to consciousness. This finding seems to us to be much more important than the often odd perspective that our participants expressed concerning the most delicate subjects and that would be misjudged in isolation and separated from their psychic dynamic. (276f [p. 49f above]).

The intention is thus the exact opposite of an accusation. To notice and state a negative so that it may be changed, and: accusing the individuals who stand under the spell of this negativity—this can certainly only be confused by one who himself is reacting to the study exactly as he unjustly assumes the discussion participants do in face of the basic stimulus. For nowhere does the book promulgate, directly or indirectly, a "summons for genuine psychic contrition" (Hofstätter, 103 [p. 195 above]); this is to be reserved for the kind of counter-enlightenment best translated as black and white (*Clair-Obskurantismus* [i.e., Chiaroscuro in painting]).

Hofstätter considers "it is hardly possible that a single individual could take upon himself the horrors of Auschwitz." It is [however] the victims of Auschwitz who had to take its horrors upon themselves, not those who, to their own disgrace and that of their nation, prefer not to admit it. The "question of guilt" was "laden with despair" for the *victims,* not for the *survivors,* and it takes some doing to have blurred this distinction with the existential category of despair, which is not without reason a popular one. But in the house of the hangman, one should not mention the noose; otherwise one might be suspected of harboring resentment. Hofstätter is of the opinion that one "could (and perhaps should) try to exorcise this horror in a ritual of repentance" (103 [p. 195 above]). The psychologist would have to know that rituals of repentance do not change the minds of people who no longer live in an obligatory theological order; yet the *homo religiousus* Hofstätter sounds like in such phrases as this would necessarily be outraged about such a penitence, undertaken for practical-psychological considerations, that is, therapeutically and not for the sake of its sacred content. However, if the supposedly "irritated tone" of the commentary on particular utterances "embarrasses" him, then he need only carefully read the passage he quotes from the Bavarian discussion group in order to assure himself that the participants do not demonstrate "insight into the material limits of the group experiment" (Hofstätter, 104 [p. 196 above]), but ward off the thought of guilt with surprising subtlety. They try to use terminological pseudodistinctions to get rid of the things that are designated by those terms.

Hofstätter's intention is *apologetic*—this blinds him to the phenomenon the outlines of which become visible in the study. The method is declared to be useless so that the existence of the phenomenon that emerges can be denied. This intention violates Hofstätter's own positivism: he does not report the position of the work accurately. But even if there were more to his collected reproaches than there is, the concept of science he champions, without himself meeting its standard as a critic, is extremely questionable. The function of social-scientific positivism has thoroughly changed. At one time, the insistence on watertight facts was meant to break free of dogma and patrimonialism *(Bevormundung).* Today, it all too willingly gives itself over to the suspicion that approaches that penetrate and transcend the mindless result *(sturen Befund)* are unscientific and possibly ideological. Insofar as interpretation, which is more than a mere repetition of the facts, is tendentiously cut off, the facts are secured in their status in a double sense: they are present and have to be accepted, without any inquiry into the essence that hides behind them, and, in light of this treatment, are at the same time legitimated as respectable. But social science that allows itself to be robbed of the right to critique for fear of organized thought control does not just become stunted, does not simply fall prey to the overblown penchant for the material of research ["research" in English] that is solely tailored to administrative goals. It is also made stupid and misses precisely that reality it takes as its own highest, if obviously not that high, ambition to reflect. In the case of *Group Experiment,* the reality is exactly the non-public opinion that Hofstätter disputes. A thought experiment, which of course is not empirically verifiable, may suffice to make the point: imagine that group discussions and interpretations of the kind we have published had been available in 1932. One certainly could have learned something from them, and been able to draw conclusions. Hofstätter-style science could certainly have intervened and cast aspersions on the findings due to lack of generalizability, insufficient exactness, and arbitrariness of interpretation. But it would thereby have helped not the truth, but the calamity.

Part Four

WORKING THROUGH
THE PAST

The Meaning of
Working Through the Past

BY THEODOR W. ADORNO

TRANSLATED BY HENRY W. PICKFORD

THE QUESTION "What does working through the past mean?" requires explication. It follows from a formulation, a modish slogan that has become highly suspect during the last years. In this usage "working through the past" does not mean seriously working upon the past, that is, through a lucid consciousness breaking its power to fascinate. On the contrary, its intention is to close the books on the past and, if possible, even remove it from memory. The attitude that everything should be forgotten and forgiven, which would be proper for those who suffered injustice, is practiced by those party supporters who committed the injustice. I wrote once in a scholarly dispute: in the house of the hangman one should not speak of the noose, otherwise one might seem to harbor resentment. However, the tendency toward the unconscious and not so unconscious defensiveness against guilt is so absurdly associated with the thought of working through the past that there is sufficient reason to reflect upon a domain from which even now there emanates such a horror that one hesitates to call it by name.

One wants to break free of the past: rightly, because nothing at all can live in its shadow, and because there will be no end to the terror as long as guilt and violence are repaid with guilt and violence; wrongly, because the past that one would like to evade is still very much alive. National Socialism lives on, and even today we still do not know whether it is merely the ghost of what was so monstrous that it lingers on after its own death, or whether it has not yet died at all, whether the willingness to commit the unspeakable survives in people as well as in the conditions that enclose them.

I do not wish to go into the question of neo-Nazi organizations. I consider the survival of National Socialism *within* democracy to be potentially more menacing that the survival of fascist tendencies *against* democracy. Infiltration indicates something objective; ambiguous figures make their *comeback* and occupy positions of power for the sole reason that conditions favor them.

Nobody disputes the fact that in Germany it is not merely among the so-called incorrigibles, if that term must be used, that the past has not yet been mastered. Again and again one hears of the so-called guilt complex, often with the association that it was actually first created by the construction of a German collective guilt. Undoubtedly there is much that is neurotic in the relation to the past: defensive postures where one is not attacked, intense affects where they are hardly warranted by the situation, an absence of affect in the face of the gravest matters, not seldom simply a repression of what is known or half-known. Thus we often found in group experiments in the Institute for Social Research that mitigating expressions and euphemistic circumlocutions were chosen in the reminiscences of deportation and mass murder, or that a hollow space formed in the discourse; the universally adopted, almost good-natured expression Kristallnacht, designated the pogrom of November 1938, attests to this inclination. A very great number claim not to have known of the events at that time, although Jews disappeared everywhere and although it is hardly believable that those who experienced what happened in the East constantly kept silent about what must have been for them an unbearable burden; surely one may assume that there is a relation between the attitude of "not having known anything about it" and an impassive and apprehensive indifference. In any case the determined enemies of National Socialism knew quite early exactly what was going on.

We all are also familiar with the readiness today to deny or minimize what happened—no matter how difficult it is to comprehend that people feel no shame in arguing that it was at most only five and not six million Jews who were gassed. Furthermore, the quite common move of drawing up a balance sheet of guilt is irrational, as though Dresden compensated for Auschwitz. Drawing up such calculations, the haste to produce counterarguments in order to exempt oneself from self-reflection, already contain something inhuman, and military actions in the war, the examples of which, moreover, are called "Coventry" and "Rotterdam," are scarcely comparable to the administrative murder of millions of innocent people.

Even their innocence, which cannot be more simple and plausible, is contested. The enormity of what was perpetrated works to justify this: a lax consciousness consoles itself with the thought that such a thing surely could not have happened unless the victims had in some way or another furnished some kind of instigation, and this "some kind of" may then be multiplied at will. The blindness disregards the flagrant disproportion between an extremely fictitious guilt and an extremely real punishment. At times the victors are made responsible for what the vanquished did when they themselves were still beyond reach, and responsibility for the atrocities of Hitler is shifted onto those who tolerated his seizure of power and not to the ones who cheered him on. The idiocy of all this is truly a sign of something that psychologically has not been mastered, a wound, although the idea of wounds would be rather more appropriate for the victims.

Despite all this, however, talk of a guilt complex has something untruthful to it. Psychiatry, from which the concept is borrowed with all its attendant associations, maintains that the feeling of guilt is pathological, unsuited to reality, psychogenic, as the analysts call it. The word "complex" is used to give the impression that the guilt, which so many ward off, abreact, and distort through the silliest of rationalizations, is actually no guilt at all but rather exists in them, in their psychological disposition: the terribly real past is trivialized into merely a figment of the imagination of those who are affected by it. Or is guilt itself perhaps merely a complex, and bearing the burden of the past pathological, whereas the healthy and realistic person is fully absorbed in the present and its practical goals? Such a view would draw the moral from the saying: "And it's as good as if it never happened," which comes from Goethe but, at a crucial passage in Faust, is uttered by the devil in order to reveal his innermost principle, the destruction of memory. The murdered are to be cheated out of the single remaining thing that our powerlessness can offer them: remembrance. The obstinate conviction of those who do not want to hear anything of it does indeed coincide with a powerful historical tendency. Hermann Heimpel on several occasions has spoken of how the consciousness of historical continuity is atrophying in Germany, a symptom of that societal weakening of the ego Horkheimer and I had already attempted to derive in the *Dialectic of Enlightenment*. Empirical findings, for example, that the younger generation often does not know who Bismarck and Kaiser Wilhelm I were, have confirmed this suspicion of the loss of history.

Thus the forgetting of National Socialism surely should be understood far more in terms of the general situation of society than in terms of psychopathology. Even the psychological mechanisms used to defend against painful and unpleasant memories serve highly realistic ends. These ends are revealed by the very people maintaining the defense, for instance when in a practical frame of mind they point out that an all too vivid and persistent recollection of what happened can harm the German image abroad. Such zeal does not accord well with the declaration of Richard Wagner, who was nationalistic enough, to the effect that being German means doing something for its own sake—provided that it is not defined a priori as business. The effacement of memory is more the achievement of an all too alert consciousness than its weakness when confronted with the superior strength of unconscious processes. In the forgetting of what has scarcely transpired there resonates the fury of one who must first talk himself out of what everyone knows, before he can then talk others out of it as well.

Surely the impulses and modes of behavior involved here are not immediately rational in so far as they distort the facts they refer to. However, they are rational in the sense that they rely on societal tendencies and that anyone who so reacts knows he is in accord with the spirit of the times. Such a reaction immediately fits in well with the desire to get on with things. Whoever doesn't entertain any idle thoughts doesn't throw any wrenches into the machinery. It is advisable to speak along the lines of what Franz Böhm so aptly called "nonpublic opinion." Those who conform to a general mood, which to be sure is kept in check by official taboos but which for that reason possesses all the more virulence, simultaneously qualify both as party to it and as independent agents. The German resistance movement after all remained without a popular base and it's not as if such a base was magically conjured up out of Germany's defeat just like that. One can surely surmise that democracy is more deeply rooted now than it was after the First World War: in a certain sense National Socialism—antifeudal and thoroughly bourgeois—by politicizing the masses even prepared, against its will, the ground for democratization. The Junker caste as well as the worker's movement have disappeared. For the first time something like a relatively homogeneous bourgeois milieu has developed. But the belated arrival of democracy in Germany which did not coincide with the peak of economic liberalism and which was introduced by the Allied victors cannot but have had an effect on the relationship of Germans to democracy. That relationship is only rarely expressed directly, because for the time being things are going so well under democracy and also because it would go against the community of interests institutionalized by political alliances with the West, especially with America. However, the resentment against *reeducation* is sufficiently explicit. What can be said is that the system of political democracy certainly is accepted in Germany in the form of what in America is called a *working proposition*, something that has functioned well up until now and has permitted and even promoted prosperity. But democracy has not become naturalized to the point where people truly experience it as their own and see themselves as subjects of the political process. Democracy is perceived as one system among others, as though one could choose from a menu between communism, democracy, fascism, and monarchy: but democracy is not identified with the people themselves as the expression of their political maturity. It is appraised according to its success or setbacks, whereby special interests also play a role, rather than as a union of the individual and the collective interests, and the parliamentary representation of the popular will in modern mass democracies already makes that difficult enough. In Germany one often hears Germans among themselves making the peculiar remark that they are not yet mature enough for democracy. They make an ideology out of their own immaturity, not unlike those adolescents who, when caught committing some violent act, talk their way out of it with the excuse that they are just teenagers. The grotesque character of this mode of argumentation reveals a flagrant contradiction within consciousness. The people who play up their own naïveté and political immaturity in such a disingenuous manner on the one hand already feel themselves to be political subjects who should set about determining their own destiny and establishing a free society. On the other hand, they come up against the limits strictly imposed upon them by the existing circumstances. Because they are incapable of penetrating these limits with their own thought, they attribute this impossibility, which in truth is inflicted upon them, either to themselves, to the great figures of the world, or to others. It is as though they divide themselves yet once more into subject and object. Moreover, the dominant ideology today dictates that the more individuals are delivered over to objective constellations, over which they have, or believe they have, no power, the more they subjectivize this powerlessness. Starting from the phrase that everything depends on the person, they attribute to people everything that is in fact due to the external conditions, so that in turn the conditions remain undisturbed. Using the language of philosophy, one indeed could say that the people's alienation from democracy reflects the self-alienation of society.

Among these objective constellations, the development of international politics is perhaps the most salient. It appears to justify retrospectively Hitler's attack against the Soviet Union. Since the Western world essentially defines itself as a unity in its defense against the Russian threat, it looks as though the victors in 1945 had foolishly destroyed the tried and tested bulwark against Bolshevism, only to rebuild it a few years later. It is a quick jump from the obvious statement "Hitler always said so" to the extrapolation that he was also right about other things. Only edifying armchair orators could quickly ease themselves over the historical fatality that in a certain sense this same conception that once motivated the Chamberlains and their followers to tolerate Hitler as a watchdog against the East has survived Hitler's downfall. Truly a fatality. For the threat that the East will engulf the foothills of Western Europe is obvious, and whoever fails to resist it is literally guilty of repeating Chamberlain's *appeasement* [English]. What is forgotten is merely—merely!—the fact that precisely this threat was first produced by Hitler's campaign, who brought upon Europe exactly what his expansionist war was meant to prevent, or so thought the *appeasers* [English]. Even more than the destiny of single individuals, it is the destiny of political entanglements that constitutes the nexus of guilt. The resistance to the East contains its own dynamic that reawakens the German past. Not merely in terms of ideology, because the slogans of struggle against Bolshevism have always served to mask those who harbor no better intentions toward freedom than do the Bolsheviks themselves. But also in terms of reality. According to an observation that had already been made during the era of Hitler, the organizational power of totalitarian systems imposes some of its own nature on its adversaries. As long as the economic disparity persists between East and West, the fascist variety has better chances of success with the masses than the East's propaganda has, whereas admittedly, on the other hand, one is not yet pushed to the fascist ultima ratio. However, the same character types are susceptible to both forms of totalitarianism. Authoritarian personalities are altogether misunderstood when they are construed from the vantage point of a particular political-economic ideology; the well-known oscillations of millions of voters before 1933 between the National Socialist and Communist is no accident from the social-psychological perspective either. American studies have shown that this personality structure does not correlate so easily with political-economic criteria. It must be defined in terms of character traits such as a thinking oriented along the dimensions of power and powerlessness, a rigidity and an inability to react, conventionality, the lack of self-reflection, and ultimately an overall inability to experience. Authoritarian personalities identify themselves with real-existing power per se, prior to any particular contents. Basically, they possess weak egos and therefore require the compensation of identifying themselves with, and finding security in, great collectives. The fact that one meets figures everywhere who resemble those in the film *Wir Wunderkinder* is neither due to the depravity of the world as such nor to the supposedly peculiar traits of the German national character. It is due rather to the identity of those conformists—who before the fact already have a connection to the levers of the whole apparatus of political power—as potential followers of totalitarianism. Furthermore, it is an illusion to believe that the National Socialist regime meant nothing but fear and suffering, although it certainly was that even for many of its own supporters. For countless people life was not at all bad under fascism. Terror's sharp edge was aimed only at a few and relatively well-defined groups. After the crises of the era preceding Hitler the predominant feeling was that "everything is being taken care of," and that did not just mean an ideology of KDF trips and flower boxes in the factories. Compared to the laissez-faire of the past, to a certain degree Hitler's world actually protected its own people from the natural catastrophes of society to which they had been abandoned. A barbaric experiment of state control of industrial society, it violently anticipated the crisis-management policies of today. The often cited "integration," the organizational tightening of the weave in the societal net that encompassed everything, also afforded protection from the universal fear of falling through the mesh and disappearing. For countless people it seemed that the coldness of social alienation had been done away with thanks to the warmth of togetherness, no matter how manipulated and contrived; the *völkish* community of the unfree and the unequal was a lie and at the same time also the fulfillment of an old, indeed long familiar, evil bourgeois dream. The system that offered such gratification certainly concealed within itself the potential for its own downfall. The economic efflorescence of the Third Reich in large measure was due to its rearmament for the war that brought about the catastrophe. But the weakened memory I mentioned earlier resists accepting these arguments. It tenaciously persists in glorifying the National Socialist era, which fulfilled the collective fantasies of power harbored by those people who, individually, had no power and who indeed could feel any self-worth at all only by virtue of such collective power. No analysis, however illuminating, can afterward remove the reality of this fulfillment or the instinctual energies invested in it. Even Hitler's *va banque* gamble was not as irrational as it seemed to average liberal thought at the time or as its failure seems to historical hindsight today. Hitler's calculation, to exploit the temporary advantage gained over the other nations thanks to a massively accelerated armaments program, was by no means foolish in consideration of what he wanted to achieve. Whoever delves into the history of the Third Reich and especially of the war will feel again and again that the particular moments in which Hitler suffered defeat seemed to be accidental and that only the course of the whole appears necessary, the ultimate victory of the superior technical-economic potential of the rest of the world that did not want to be swallowed up: so to speak a statistical necessity, but by no means a discernible step-by-step logic. The surviving sympathy for National Socialism has no need for laborious sophistry in order to convince itself and others that things could just as well have gone differently, that in fact only some mistakes were made and that Hitler's downfall was a world-historical accident the world spirit may perhaps yet rectify.

On the subjective side, in the psyche of people, National Socialism increased beyond measure the collective narcissism, simply put: national vanity. The individual's narcissistic instinctual drives which are promised less and less satisfaction by a callous world and which nonetheless persist undiminished as long as civilization denies them so much, find substitute satisfaction in the identification with the whole. This collective narcissism was severely damaged by the collapse of Hitler's regime, but the damage occurred at the level of mere factuality, without individuals making themselves conscious of it and thereby coping with it. This is the social-psychological relevance of talk about an unmastered past. Also absent is the panic that, according to Freud's theory in *Group Psychology and the Analysis of the Ego,* sets in whenever collective identifications break apart. If the lessons of the great psychologist are not to be cast to the wind, then there remains only one conclusion: that secretly, smoldering unconsciously and therefore all the more powerfully, these identifications and the collective narcissism were not destroyed at all, but continue to exist. Inwardly the defeat has been as little ratified as after 1918. Even in the face of the obvious catastrophe the collective Hitler integrated has held together and clung to chimerical hopes like those secret weapons that in truth the other side possessed. Furthermore, social psychology adds the expectation that the damaged collective narcissism lies in wait of being repaired and seizes upon anything that brings the past into agreement with the narcissistic desires, first in consciousness, but that it also, whenever possible, construes reality itself as though the damage never occurred. To a certain degree this has been achieved by the economic boom, the feeling of "how industrious we are." But I doubt whether the so-called economic miracle—in which, to be sure, everyone participates even while speaking of it with some disdain— social-psychologically really reaches as deeply as one might suppose in times of relative stability. Precisely because famine continues to reign across entire continents when technically it could be eliminated, no one can really be so delighted as his prosperity. Just as individually, for instance in films, there is resentful laughter when a character sits down to a very good meal and tucks the napkin under his chin, so too humanity begrudges itself the comfort it all too well knows is still paid for by want and hardship; resentment strikes every happiness, even one's own. Satiety has become an insult a priori, whereas the sole point of reproach about it would be that there are people who have nothing to eat; the alleged idealism that especially in today's Germany so pharisaically sinks its teeth into an alleged materialism frequently owes its self-proclaimed profundity merely to repressed instincts. Hatred of comfort engenders in Germany discomfort at prosperity, and it transfigures the past into a tragedy. However, this malaise does not at all issue solely from dark and troubled waters but rather once again from far more rational ones. The prosperity is due to an economic upswing and no one trusts its unlimited duration. If one seeks consolation in the view that events like Black Friday of 1929 and the resultant economic crisis could hardly repeat themselves, then this already implicitly contains the reliance on a strong state power that, one then expects, will offer protection if economic and political freedom no longer work. Even in the midst of prosperity, even during the temporary labor shortage, the majority of people probably feel secretly that they are potentially unemployed, recipients of charity, and hence really objects, no subjects, of society: this is the fully legitimate and reasonable cause of their discomfort. It is obvious that at any given moment this discomfort can be dammed up, channeled toward the past, and manipulated in order to provoke a renewal of the disaster.

Today the fascist wish-image unquestionably blends with the nationalism of the so-called underdeveloped countries, which now, however, are instead called "developing countries." Already during the war the *slogans* about Western plutocracies and proletarian nations expressed sympathy with those who felt shortchanged in the imperialist competition and also wanted a place at the table. It is difficult to discern whether and to what extent this tendency has already joined the anticivilization, anti-Western undercurrent of the German tradition and whether in Germany itself there exits a convergence of fascist and communist nationalism. Nationalism today is at once both obsolete and up-to-date. Obsolete, because in the face of the compulsory coalition of nations into great blocs under the supremacy of the most powerful country, which is already dictated by the development in weapons technology alone, the individual sovereign nations, at least in advanced continental Europe, have forfeited their historical substance. The idea of the nation, in which the common economic interests of free and independent citizens once united against the territorial barriers of feudalism, has itself become a barrier to the obvious potential of society as a totality. But nationalism is up-to-date in so far as the traditional and psychologically supremely invested idea of nation, which still expresses the community of interests within the international economy, alone has sufficient force to mobilize hundreds of millions of people for goals they cannot immediately identify as their own. Nationalism does not completely believe in itself anymore, and yet it is a political necessity because it is the most effective means of motivating people to insist on conditions that are, viewed objectively, obsolete. This is why, as something ill at ease with itself, intentionally self-deluded, it has taken on grotesque features nowadays. Admittedly nationalism, the heritage of barbarically primitive tribal attitudes, never lacked such traits altogether, but they were reined in as long as liberalism guaranteed the right of the individual—also concretely as the condition of collective prosperity. Only in an age in which it was already toppling has nationalism become completely sadistic and destructive. The rage of Hitler's world against everything that was different—nationalism as a paranoid delusional system—was already of this caliber. The appeal of precisely these features is hardly any less today. Paranoia, the persecution mania that persecutes those upon whom it projects what it itself desires, is contagious. Collective delusions, like anti-Semitism, confirm the pathology of the individual, who shows that psychologically he is no longer a match for the world and is thrown back upon an illusory inner realm. According to the thesis of the psychoanalyst Ernst Simmel, they may well spare a half-mad person from being completely so. To the extent that the delusional mania of nationalism openly manifests itself in the reasonable fear of renewed catastrophes so, too, does it promote its own diffusion. Delusional mania is the substitute for the dream that humanity would organize the world humanely, a dream the actual world of humanity is resolutely eradicating. Everything that took place between 1933 and 1945 goes together with pathological nationalism.

That fascism lives on, that the oft-invoked working through of the past has to this day been unsuccessful and has degenerated into its own caricature, an empty and cold forgetting, is due to the fact that the objective conditions of society that engendered fascism continue to exist. Fascism essentially cannot be derived from subjective dispositions. The economic order, and to a great extent also the economic organization modeled upon it, now as then renders the majority of people dependent upon conditions beyond their control and thus maintains them in a state of political immaturity. If they want to live, then no other avenue remains but to adapt, submit themselves to the given conditions; they must negate precisely that autonomous subjectivity to which the idea of democracy appeals; they can preserve themselves only if they renounce their self. To see through the nexus of deception, they would need to make precisely that painful intellectual effort that the organization of everyday life, and not least of all a culture industry inflated to the point of totality, prevents. The necessity of such adaptation, of identification with the given, the status quo, with power as such, creates the potential for totalitarianism. This potential is reinforced by the dissatisfaction and the rage that very constraint to adapt produces and reproduces. Because reality does not deliver the autonomy or, ultimately, the potential happiness that the concept of democracy actually promises, people remain indifferent to democracy, if they do not in fact secretly detest it. This form of political organization is experienced as inadequate to the societal and economic reality; just as one must adapt, so would one like the forms of collective life also to adapt, all the more so since one expects from such adaptation the *streamlining* [English] of the state as a gigantic business enterprise within a certainly less than friendly competition of all against all. Those whose real powerlessness shows no sign of ceasing cannot tolerate even the semblance of what would be better; they would prefer to get rid of the obligations of autonomy, which they suspect cannot be a model for their lives, and prefer to throw themselves into the melting pot of the collective ego.

I have exaggerated the somber side, following the maxim that only exaggeration per se today can be the medium of truth. Do not mistake my fragmentary and often rhapsodic remarks for Spenglerism; Spenglerism itself makes common cause with the catastrophe. My intention was to delineate a tendency concealed behind the smooth façade of everyday life before it overflows the institutional dams that, for the time being, are erected against it. The danger is objective, not primarily located in human beings. As I said, there is much that indicates that democracy with all it implies has a more profound hold on people than it did during the Weimar period. By failing to emphasize what is so obvious, I have neglected what circumspect consideration must not ignore: that within the German democracy from 1945 to today the material life of society has reproduced itself more richly than during any other time in living memory, and this is also relevant from a social-psychological perspective. It certainly would not be all too optimistic to affirm that the German democracy is not doing badly these days and that therefore the real reappraisal of the past is also doing fine, provided that it is given enough time and much else besides. Except that the concept of having enough time contains something naïve and at the same time contemplative in the bad sense. We are neither simply spectators of world history, free to frolic more or less at will within its grand chambers, nor does world history, whose rhythm increasingly approaches that of the catastrophe, appear to allow its subjects the time in which everything would improve on its own. This bears directly on democratic pedagogy. Above all enlightenment about what has happened must work against a forgetfulness that all too easily turns up together with the justification of what has been forgotten—for instance, parents who must endure embarrassing questions from children about Hitler and in response, indeed to whitewash their own guilt, speak of the good aspects and say that in fact it was not so awful. In Germany it is fashionable to complain about civic education, and certainly it could be better, but sociology already has data indicating that civic education, when it is practiced earnestly and not as a burdensome duty, does more good than is generally believed. However, if one takes the objective potential for the survival of National Socialism as seriously as I believe it must be taken, then this sets limits even for a pedagogy that promotes enlightenment. Whether it be sociological or psychological, such a pedagogy in practice will probably reach in general only those people who are open to it anyway and who therefore are hardly susceptible to fascism. On the other hand, it is certainly not at all superfluous to fortify this group with enlightened instruction against nonpublic opinion. On the contrary, one could easily imagine that from this group something like cadres could develop, whose influence in the most diverse contexts would then finally reach the whole of society, and the chances for this are all the more favorable, the more conscious the cadres become. Obviously, the work of the enlightenment will not be limited to these groups. Here I will refrain from a question that is very difficult and laden with the greatest responsibility: namely of how far it is advisable to go into the past when attempting to raise public awareness, and whether precisely the insistence on it does not provoke a defiant resistance and produce the opposite of what it intends. It seems to me rather that what is conscious could never prove so fateful as what remains unconscious, half-conscious, or preconscious. Essentially, it is a matter of the way in which the past is made present; whether one remains at the level of reproach or whether one withstands the horror by having the strength to comprehend even the incomprehensible. For this, however, it would be necessary to educate the educators themselves. But such education is gravely impaired by the fact that what in America are called the *behavioral sciences* [English] are either not represented at all or are woefully underrepresented in Germany at present. It is absolutely imperative that universities strengthen a sociology that would work together with the historical research about our own era. Instead of holding forth with secondhand profundities about the Being of man, pedagogy should set itself the task *reeducation* it is so vehemently accused of having superficially handled. Criminology in Germany is not yet up to modern standards at all. But above all one should think of psychoanalysis, which is still being repressed today as much as ever. Either it is altogether absent or it is replaced by tendencies that while boasting of overcoming the much-maligned nineteenth century, in truth fall back behind Freudian theory, even turning it into its very opposite. A precise and undiluted knowledge of Freudian theory is more necessary and relevant today more than ever. The hatred of it is directly of a piece with anti-Semitism, by no means simply because Freud was a Jew but rather because psychoanalysis consists precisely of that critical self-reflection that makes anti-Semites livid with rage. Although it is so difficult to carry out something like a mass analysis because of the time factor alone, nonetheless if rigorous psychoanalysis found its institutional place, its influence upon the intellectual climate in Germany would be a salutary one, even if that meant nothing more than taking it for granted that one should not lash outward but should reflect about oneself and one's relation to whatever obdurate consciousness habitually rages against. In any case, however, attempts to work subjectively against the objective potential for disaster should not content themselves with corrections that would hardly approach the severity of what must be confronted. Likewise, attention to the great achievements of Jews in the past, however true they may be, are hardly of use and smack of propaganda. And propaganda, the rational manipulation of what it irrational, is the prerogative of the totalitarians. Those who resist totalitarians should not imitate them in a way that would only do themselves a disservice. Panegyrics to the Jews that isolate them as a group already give anti-Semitism a running start. Anti-Semitism is so difficult to refute because the psychic economy of innumerable people needed it and, in an attenuated form, presumably still needs it today. Whatever happens by way of propaganda remains ambiguous. I was told the story of a woman who, upset after seeing the dramatization of *The Diary of Anne Frank,* said: "Yes, but that girl at least should have been allowed to live." To be sure even that was good as a first step toward understanding. But the individual case, which should stand for, and raise awareness about the terrifying totality, by its very individuation became an alibi for the totality the woman forgot. The perplexing thing about such observations remains that even on their account one cannot advise against productions of the Anne Frank play and the like, because their effect nonetheless feeds into the potential for improvement, however repugnant they also are and however much they seem to be a profanation of the dignity of the dead. I also do not believe that too much will be accomplished by community meetings, encounters between young Germans and young Israelis, and other organized promotions of friendship. All too often the presupposition is that anti-Semitism in some essential way involves the Jews and could be countered through concrete experiences with Jews, whereas the genuine anti-Semite is defined far more by his incapacity for any experience whatsoever, by his unresponsiveness. If anti-Semitism primarily has its foundation in objective society, and only derivatively in anti-Semites, then—as the National Socialist joke has it—if the Jews had not already existed, the anti-Semites would have had to in-

vent them. As far as wanting to combat anti-Semitism in individual subjects is concerned, one should not expect too much from the recourse to
facts, which anti-Semites most often will either not admit or will neutral-
ize by treating them as exceptions. Instead one should apply the argumentation directly to the subjects whom one is addressing. They should be
made aware of the mechanisms that cause racial prejudice within them. A
working through the past understood as enlightenment is essentially such a
turn toward the subject, the reinforcement of a person's self-consciousness
and hence also of his self. This should be combined with the knowledge of
the few durable propaganda tricks that are attuned exactly to those psychological dispositions we must assume are present in human beings. Since
these tricks are fixed and limited in number, there is no overwhelming dif-
ficultly in isolating them, making them known, and using them as a kind
of vaccine. The problem of how to carry out practically such a subjective
enlightenment probably could only be resolved by the collective effort of
teachers and psychologists, who would not use the pretext of scholarly objectivity to shy away from the most urgent task confronting their disciplines today. Yet in view of the objective power behind the continuing
potential of anti-Semitism, subjective enlightenment will not suffice, even
if it is undertaken with a radically different energy and in radically deeper
psychological dimensions than it has been up to now. If one wishes to oppose the objective danger objectively, then no mere idea will do, not even the
idea of freedom and humanitarianism, which indeed—as we have learned
in the meantime—in its abstract form does not mean very much to people.
If the fascist potential links up with their interests, however limited those
interests may be, then the most effective antidote is still a persuasive, because true, demonstration of their own interests and, moreover, their most
immediate ones. One would really be guilty of speculative psychologizing
in these matters if one disregarded the fact that the war and the suffering it
brought upon the German population, although indeed being insufficient
to remove the fascist potential, nonetheless offers some counterweight
against it. If people are reminded of the simplest things: that open or disguised fascist revivals will cause war, suffering, and privation under a co-
ercive system, and in the end probably the Russian domination of Europe,
in short, that they lead to a politics of catastrophe, then this will impress
people more deeply than invoking ideals or even the suffering of others,
which is always relatively easy to get over, as La Rochefoucauld already
knew. Compared with this prospect, the present *malaise* signifies little
more than the luxury of a certain mood. Despite all the psychological repression, Stalingrad and the night bombings are not so forgotten that
everyone cannot be made to understand the connection between the re-

vival of a politics that led to them and the prospect of a third Punic war. Even if this succeeds, the danger will still exist. The past will have been worked through only when the causes of what happened then have been eliminated. Only because the causes continue to exist does the captivating spell of the past remain to this day unbroken.

Index